PRAISE FOR "THE PI

With persuasive logic anu vivid detail, ... ey toward liberalism provides us with a powerful argument for re-dedicating ourselves to our nation's fundamental political values and the principles on which they are based. His balanced, thoughtful, and compelling analysis of how we have been misled and poorly served by our leaders is a wake-up call for those who will heed it and an ominous warning for those who won't." –

Douglas R. Skopp
Distinguished Teaching Professor of History Emeritus
SUNY Plattsburgh
Author of "Shadows Walking," A Novel.

David L. Smith explains how the United States has bequeathed an economic, financial and political quagmire to the Millennial Generation. The book is addressed to these younger Americans so that they will better understand how the military-industrial-technological-political complex has served the interests of the rich at the expense of the 99 Percent, and especially the younger generations, resulting in a plethora of undesirable consequences.

The Predicament offers a compelling vision of a new political process, bypassing Big Money and television, as the means of reclaiming a government now held captive by and serving the interests of the moneyed elite, and restoring government to the service of the electorate.

Peter T. Knight, Ph.D.
Former World Bank Economist and Division Chief

Navy veteran, economist and financial expert David L. Smith narrates his personal Odyssey of economic and political re-orientation, shaped by awakenings that began in Vietnam, from youthful Buckley conservative into a critic of economic inequality and counterproductive military adventures. In the book, Smith the spectator gradually transforms into Smith the agent, working without a net, shaping his own important judgments on the relationship between government, business, and national wellbeing. Because David Smith's narrative is rich in character and detail, readers are able to participate in the experience and understand his conclusions.

Daniel Tompkins, Ph.D.
Associate Professor Emeritus
Temple University

THE PREDICAMENT

How did it happen? How bad is it?
The case for radical change now!

David L. Smith

★★★★★

SIC ITUR AD ASTRA PUBLISHERS
SAN FRANCISCO
2013

★★★★★

Second Edition

Visit our book web site www.the-predicament.com

Twitter: @AmLibRevolution

Facebook: American Liberal Revolution

Cover by Joan Stepp-Smith and David L. Smith

Sic Itur Ad Astra Publishers

ISBN: 978-0-9888728-0-6

For Vicky, With appreciation.

Dedication

★★★★★

To the Millennial Generation

Courage

★★★★★

★★★★★ *E Pluribus Unum* ★★★★★

Table of Contents

ACNOWLEDGMENTS

Personal

My first thanks go out to my immediate family for their love, support and encouragement: my wife, Elizabeth Fagan; my sister, Judith "Missy" Taylor; my father, Harry L. Smith, and mother, Patricia O'Rourke Smith, both now resting with due honors at Arlington National Cemetery.

Special thanks to my Dartmouth '62 classmates, for their longstanding friendship and intellectual companionship along the way -- in particular, Dan Tompkins, Doug Skopp, Peter Knight, Ted Beal, Tom Hector, Mike Schaefer, Fairleigh Lussky, John Clark, Ed Hirsch, Frank Kehl, Irwin Kramer, Jim Blair, Henry Clarke, Alan Rapoport, John Thees, Dick Maynard, Max Roberts and my Stanford sidekick, Dave Carlson.

I am indebted to Werner Erhard and his fellow trainers and staff at *est,* Stewart Emery and Randy McNamara in particular, for their wake-up call 40 years ago.

And finally, to Virginia McIntosh, my high-school senior English teacher who kicked my butt along the path to becoming a writer.

Professional

My appreciation, to Joan Stepp-Smith, my valued friend and publicity adviser who has long encouraged me to disseminate my message to an ever-broader audience, and to Linda Cashdan, my editor, for her keen grasp of the big picture and fine detail.

Along with all liberals, I salute the truth-tellers out there carrying the load for us, national treasures all -- Aaron Sorkin, Rachel Maddow, Jon Stewart, Paul Krugman, Joseph Stiglitz, Elizabeth Warren, Oliver Stone, Oprah Winfrey, Bill Maher, Michael Moore, Maureen Dowd, Gail Collins, Frank Rich, Robert Reich, Chris Hayes, Chris Hedges, Ezra Klein, Ed Schultz, Lawrence O'Donnell, Martin Bashir, Amy Goodman, Melissa Harris-Perry, Keith Olbermann, Bill Moyers, Charlie Rose, Arianna Huffington, Julian Assange, Matt Taibbi, the folks at Truthout, Alternet, Huffington Post, The Rolling Stone, Mother Jones, MoveOn.org, The Center on Budget and Policy Priorities, Hollywood/Broadway liberals too numerous to mention, and all those in the public eye who understand America's Predicament and want us to do better.

PREFACE

Every author begins writing after answering two questions: Why am I writing this book? Why should you read it?

There are several answers to the first question. After 25 years of chronicling, analyzing, commenting and forecasting economic, financial and political events with remarkable accuracy, I felt I had achieved a sound understanding of 'how the world works' within the confines of these disciplines. Notably, in the late 1990s I warned my audiences and newsletter subscribers of an impending financial meltdown and economic crisis coming in the 2000s. Presently, I see the U.S. and, more broadly, the world heading toward further economic/financial instability, crisis and conflict. As a writer and student of history mindful of its lessons, I feel compelled to broadcast a warning and propose alternative courses of action to ameliorate those dangers.

Political pendulums:

I began this task by writing an essay for my classmates attending our 50th reunion at Dartmouth College in June 2012. The essay, from which this book emerged, explained how politics, economics and finance interacted to swing the political pendulum through various displacements between left and right in my lifetime, beginning with the Eisenhower 1950s.

Actually, there are two political pendulums: one for domestic policy and another for foreign policy; sometimes they swing together, sometimes not. From Eisenhower to Carter, the two were out of sync.

Domestically the pendulum swung from relatively balanced, prosperous, fiscally sane Eisenhower 1950s strongly leftward toward active-state liberalism in the Johnson Great Society, the Civil Rights, Women's Liberation, Gay Rights and Anti-War movements in the 1960s and 1970s. Domestic policy remained lodged to the left through Nixon (price controls, the Environmental Protection Agency and OSHA, going off the gold standard), Ford and Carter (Department of Education and Energy).

The political equivalent of Newton's Third Law of Motion ("For every action, there is an equal and opposite reaction."), coupled with popular discontent over the inflationary "malaise" of the Oil Shocks in the 1970s, prompted a sharp and enduring rightward reversal for domestic policy in the Reagan 1980s.

The pendulum for foreign policy, however, remained steadfastly displaced to the militaristic right after World War II, held there by Cold War fears prompting a superpower arms race, wars in Korea and Vietnam and a host of other lesser U.S. interventions abroad in the name of opposing communism.

With the election of Ronald Reagan, however, the two pendulums became synchronized, with right-dominated fiscal and economic policies under the rubric of Reaganomics (low tax rates, mainly for the rich, and lax regulation, large DoD budgets) merging with the right-dominated militarism calculated to drive the Soviets to economic exhaustion, successfully ending the Cold War in 1991 by which time the military's focus shifted to the Middle East in the First Gulf War under the first President Bush.

To be sure, Bill Clinton achieved a mild leftward readjustment in the 1990s with higher taxes and the "peace dividend" trimming military spending, so as to produce fiscal surpluses in his last four years. However, Clinton's leftward leanings became compromised by Republican control of Congress achieved in the 1994 mid-term elections.

With the elevation of George W. Bush to the presidency in the 2000s, Republicans, now in full control of Washington, then disastrously swung both domestic and foreign pendulums wildly to the Reaganomics/Neo-Con/Evangelical Christian extreme right, with deficit-swelling tax cuts, lax regulation, social puritanism, and two wars of choice in the Middle east. The synchronized pendulums reached what one hopes was their maximum rightward displacement, predictbly producing egregious inequality of wealth, the financial and economic catastrophes of 2008-2009 and dismal failures of G.W. Bush's military adventurism in the Middle East. Here we see realized the nightmares warned of by Eisenhower in his "Military-Industrial Complex" speech and George Orwell in his *1984*.

The election of Barack Obama in 2008 carried with it the hope of a reversal in the pendulums' direction, thwarted significantly by relentless, unyielding obstructionism by retrograde Republicans determined to regain power in 2012 in the service of Big Money – perhaps the last hurrah of the fading entrenched, rich, angry-white-male establishment. The re-election of Obama in 2012 appears to signal the continuation of an incipient leftward shift in both pendulums initiated in 2008, driven largely by demographic shifts in the electorate in favor of left-leaning women, youngsters, Hispanics, Blacks and Asians. Despite the Obama victories and the popular stirrings "in the street" within the left emanating from Wisconsin and the Occupy Movement, the present rightward displacement of the pendulum – especially in the domains of foreign and fiscal policies – remains the time bomb depicted on the cover: The Predicament after which this book is titled.

The Millennial generation has an inkling of The Predicament – sub-standard public-school education, expensive college tuition, crushing student loans, dismal job opportunities, low pay, unpaid apprenticeships, high youth unemployment, reluctant returns to the family nest, uncertain prospects for retirement security and health care. Rich folks within the senior generations are living large and sending the Millennials the bill. But it's much worse than just that, as I will fully reveal later on. For the present, however, let me summarize the situation by quoting the Jeff Daniels character, Will McAvoy, in the opening scene from "The Newsroom," the new HBO series by "The West Wing" creator, Aaron Sorkin, which aired on June 24, 2012. McAvoy responds to the question from a young college student, "What makes the United States the greatest country in the world?"

> "Well, our Constitution is a masterpiece, James Madison was a genius, the Declaration of Independence is, for me, the single greatest piece of American writing. . . [When pressed for a "human response" he continues:] It's *not* the greatest country in the world. . . there's some things you should know. . . there is absolutely no evidence to support the statement that we're the greatest country in the world. We're 7th in literacy, 27th in math, 22nd in science, 49th in life expectancy, 17th in infant mortality, third in median household income, number 4 in labor force, and number 4 in exports. We lead the world in only three categories, number of incarcerated citizens per capita, number of adults who believe angels are real, and number one in defense spending, where we spend more than the next twenty six countries combined, twenty five of whom are allies. Now none of this is the fault of a twenty-year-old college student, but you, nonetheless, are a member of the worst, period, generation, period, ever, period. So when you ask what makes this the greatest country in the world, I don't know what the fuck you're talking about. Yosemite?
>
> It sure used to be. We stood up for what was right. We fought for moral reasons. We passed laws, struck down laws for moral reasons. We waged wars on poverty, not poor people. We sacrificed. We cared about our neighbors. We put our money where our mouths were. We never beat our chest. We built great big things; made ungodly technological advances, explored the universe, cured disease, cultivated the world's greatest artists, and the world's greatest economy. We reached for the stars, acted like men. We aspired to intelligence; we didn't belittle it; it didn't make us feel inferior. We didn't identify ourselves by who we voted for in the last election; and we didn't scare so easy. We were able to do all these things, and be all these things, because we were informed, by great men, men who were revered. The first step in solving any problem is recognizing there is one. America is not the greatest country in the world anymore."

His executive producer later adds a hopeful, if overstated, afterthought:

> "You know what you left out of your sermon? That America is the only country on the planet that since its birth has said over and over and over that we can do better. It's part of our DNA."

The Predicament explains how we got into a fix far worse than McAvoy reveals, and foreshadows my second book, nearing completion, suggesting how we can do better. *The Egyptian Solution – And Other Lessons of History To Get Us Out Of This Mess,* (www.the-egyptian-solution.com) draws on useful lessons of history starting with ancient Egypt's Old Kingdom nearly five thousand years ago, and dips into subsequent history whenever it offers us profitable lessons about how the world works, where things are headed and how to *avoid* getting there. *The Predicament* reveals where "the bodies are buried" and draws unexpected conclusions from agreed-upon facts to provide liberals with compelling rebuttals to extremist conservative memes and strong evidence to support liberal convictions. You will learn how American democracy has been hijacked by Big Money to the detriment of the middle class and the poor and how the resulting inequality of income and wealth create financial and economic crises. You will understand why radical changes in policies and political processes are needed *now* to avoid further economic, financial and political calamity; to restore the solvency, prosperity and contentment of the middle class; and to relieve the plight of the poor. The logic is compelling once you start digging.

Beyond sounding a warning, unquestionably the most important contribution of *The Predicament* is the proposal for a new democratic political process bypassing Big Money and TV advertising to redirect government to the service of *We the People* This new political process, presented in Chapter 10, is designed to bring together reform-minded liberals in electronically networked multiplex theaters to hammer out a comprehensive platform meeting the needs of the American electorate and to elevate and elect new leaders to represent them in the corridors of power. Without such a political process, or something like it, all other efforts to achieve much-needed reforms will likely come to naught, given the stranglehold the rich and powerful elite now exercises in a system in which money buys votes within the limits of what the public will swallow.

> There is a mismatch between the seriousness of the things we need to get done as a nation and the quality of the system in Washington that is the means by which we must get those things done. . . . How do we turn down the political nonsense enough to hope that our political process can be the means by which we make these grave and serious decisions?
>
> Rachel Maddow
> The Rachel Maddow Show
> November 29, 2012

Both volumes are addressed and dedicated to the Millennial Generation, since the older generations show little inclination to acknowledge the full extent of The Predicament, let alone extricate us from it. That said, I hope conscience-driven readers from the senior generations will be inspired to pitch in.

As I recounted the events of the past sixty years I could not help but reflect on the concurrent arc of my own life as a participant, in some small ways, and close observer of the events I chronicled. Even so, my life seemed to me quite ordinary for a man of my generation, not likely to be of much interest, I thought, beyond my immediate family and circle of friends.

But the more I thought about it, I realized that to younger generations, for whom these events are history, my life's story, intertwined with the events of my time, and the accompanying evolution of my thinking about the themes of economics, finance, history and politics, could be instructive and interesting. Someone once said, "'His story' is more interesting than history." While my journey may have been quite ordinary, the times I lived through were anything but. We live, as the Chinese say, "in interesting times" – they mean it as a curse.

So for those readers curious as to how a staunch William F. Buckley, Jr. conservative Republican Dartmouth grad from Argentina should have morphed into a passionate liberal[1], I have appended an autobiographical narrative at the end, revealing how the evolution took place. Open-minded readers willing to accompany me through my intellectual journey of the last 60 years will probably reach most of the same conclusions I have, and realize just how far America has come in ways both good and bad. At least, that is my hope. Moreover, they may also understand that these are not the conclusions of some naive ideologue of the left, but rather those of rational man who journeyed from conservatism to liberalism with the extraordinary good fortune of having received an exceptional education and enlightening life experience, enjoying the rare luxury of a quarter century of unstructured time, free of organizational constraints and

---

[1] [1] I use the term "liberal" advisedly, without resorting to the currently fashionable substitute, "progressive," for good reason. Liberals adopted "progressive," some years ago after the conservative propaganda juggernaut succeeded in besmirching the term "liberal," to the point where all conservatives had to do was brand an idea as liberal and it was QED, point proven. Rather than mounting an effective defense of their worldview under the banner of "liberal," (with a long and noble tradition, including the American Revolution, grounded in liberty and Jeffersonian equality), liberals caved and became "progressives" without fully understanding its turn-of-the-century antecedents. While for clarity's sake I will occasionally use liberal/progressive, I rankle at the need to, inasmuch as it concedes to conservatives an unmerited tally in the ongoing debate between left and right. Sometimes I will use the term "American liberal," or "active-state liberal" to distinguish it from other variants, although that's what I usually mean when using "liberal."

responsibilities, providing the opportunity to closely observe, analyze, think, write and speak freely about these "interesting times."

Since we get much of our information about our times through television and movies, the same media by which we are entertained and sold things, there exists a propensity to conflate reality with the dramatic fiction we see portrayed on screens, both large and small. One cannot help but wonder what inflammatory effects are created on both sides of the divide by American movies, like "True Lies," "Delta Force," "The Sum of all Fears," "Zero Dark 30," and television shows like "Homeland," and "Last Resort," depicting Muslims as terrorist villains and Americans as good guys triumphing in the end. Inexcusably, television news is laced with commercials thereby compromising the integrity of the news in deference to advertisers, and diluting the gravity of events reported – "Baghdad bombed. And now a word about hemorrhoids." Given the fragmented, mixed messages we receive from these media, we may succumb to the temptation to assume the conflicts in these "interesting times" are not all that serious and will all work out fine in the end, as is usually the case with dramas we vicariously experience on screen. However, given the momentous dimensions of the present conflicts giving rise to The Predicament, and the unpredictability of human behavior, such assumptions are unwarranted. Humanity has never lived through the present times before. There are no experts; we are all novices when it comes to wending our way through the present. It behooves us, therefore, to grapple with The Predicament with humility, caution, conviviality, prudence, intelligence and objectivity – fully informed, adaptable and with due respect for both the gravity of the situation and the risk that everything may not turn out well in the end.

We older folks know there comes a time later in life when we say to ourselves with some regret: "How much better my life would have been if I only knew then what I know now." I realized that by sharing my own intellectual journey with receptive members of the younger generations, I might imbue them with the knowledge and experience they need to recognize the problem as the first step in avoiding such regrets. Think of it as a combination time capsule and primitive version of a "brain dump," (or "mind transfer," popularized by Ray Kurtzweil and others) enabling young minds to vicariously acquire life experience, historical memory, and, one hopes, wisdom, without actually having been there.

George Santayana once sagely observed, "Those who cannot remember the past are condemned to repeat it." In writing *The Predicament* and later *The Egyptian Solution*, my intention is to assist younger generations to remember the past, and thus commute the sentence.

David L. Smith
January 21, 2013

Chapter 1: Conservative beginnings. Growing up in Perón's Argentina during the 1950s

My father was a conservative, so I was a conservative. Dad was the genuine article: prep-school and ivy-league education, the Navy Cross as skipper of a pint-sized warship downing kamikazes off Okinawa, senior executive in the family import business established by my grandfather in Buenos Aires in 1914, commander of his Veterans of Foreign Wars chapter, Rotarian, president of the American Community School board the year I graduated, frequent contributor to *The Freeman* periodical in the days of Leonard Reed, loyal Fox News viewer until the day he died in 2007 at the age of 91.

Old-school, Bill Buckley, Jr. conservatism came easily to me then, not just because Dad waxed eloquent on the subject at the drop of a hat, but also because growing up I witnessed firsthand the enduring, destructive turmoil wrought by the extreme leftist policies of General Juan Domingo Perón's *Justicialismo*[2] in Argentina:

Perón came to power with the backing of powerful, politically active labor unions. He strategically nationalized British- and French-owned railroads, the Central Bank, the American-owned telephone company, radio stations, the docks, the national gas company. Perón's labor union power base required constant care and feeding in the form of government-mandated pay increases, bonuses, paid holidays, and a host of "workers' rights." Nationalized industries bled red ink after being featherbedded with incompetent Peronist cronies, starved for capital and required to render essential services at below-market prices to ensure workers kept voting for Perón. The purchase of nationalized industries and the subsidies required to keep them in business drained the Treasury; however, the nationalized central bank obligingly printed the money required to fund the deficits, producing the inevitable inflationary result. The Peróns became very rich while the country, once the seventh richest in the world, became very poor.

---

[2] The official name for the political doctrine of the *Peronista* party founded by Peron in 1947. The word *Justicialista* is a contraction of *justicia* (justice) and *lista* (which can mean clever and smart or, also, ready, is also the equivalent of "ist" denoting a school of thought or philosophy, thereby imbuing the term with triple meaning). In Perón's day, the term *Justicialista* intended to convey a dedication to "social justice," in which the interests of the masses receive special consideration from the government. Accordingly, the classical female figure of Justice, customarily portrayed as blindfolded (denoting impartiality) while holding the scales of justice, was depicted under Peronism without the blindfold, indicating partiality to the interests of the working classes upon which Perón's power depended. In the 1970s, when it became illegal to include the name of a person in designating a political party, the *Peronista* party was renamed *Partido Justicialista*, to which belong(ed) presidents Perón (Juan, upon returning from exile, and Isabel), Campora, Menem and the Kirchners.

A teenager at the time, I did not understand the workings of Peronist politics and economic policies, but I could see their effects in the rising price of Coca-Colas and hot dogs I purchased after school, and the fact that it would take two years to get a phone installed and even then the connections were crappy. Nothing seemed to work as it should; you got used to long lines for everything. Getting a passport could easily turn into a three-day bureaucratic ordeal, standing in lines in one government department after another. I saw the bruises on the face of a schoolmate, the son of Ed Morrow, the *Time Magazine* correspondent in Buenos Aires, beaten up by Peronist thugs as a warning after his father had written a piece critical of Perón. When speaking in English about Perón in public, we'd always refer to him as John Sunday (translating his first two names literally) lest some uncomprehending *Peronista* denounce us for speaking ill of the dictator. I'd listen to my father's circle of friends – top executives of the Argentine subsidiaries of Ford, GM, Kaiser, the Bank of Boston, Anderson Clayton, Peat Marwick, ESSO, Coca Cola, Parker Pen, Swift, and others – privately muttering their unhappiness with the intrusions of the Perón government.

At the movies, we watched the obligatory official newsreels featuring Evita's captivating speeches from the Pink House balcony overlooking a sea of *descamisados* (shirtless ones) flooding Plaza de Mayo and streets beyond, roaring "Perón! Perón! Perón!" -- passionate, massive, unwavering worker solidarity with the dictator, clear for all to see and for none to challenge.

A dazzling, eloquent, firebrand orator, unique in her day, Evita would whip the crowd into a frenzy extolling her husband's struggles on behalf of the working classes and railing against rapacious, rich *oligarcas*, rolling her "r's" like a machine gun. She would finish by exhorting the crowd to chant "*La vida por Perón*," and, with perfectly timed choreography, would fall into the arms of the great man himself as he emerged onto the balcony to the approving roar of the crowd.

Shedding his jacket in a gesture of solidarity with the workingman, Perón would begin by addressing the crowd and the nation embraced with outstretched arms: "Compañeros. . ." One memorable speech delivered in 1953 after a terrorist bombing, exhorted the masses to take harsh reprisals on his adversaries ("*We're going to have to return to the days when we carried baling wire in our pockets.*") duly carried out when the mob burned down the Socialist Party Headquarters and the Jockey Club, bastion of oligarchic wealth and privilege, consigning the beautiful *Beaux Arts* building, priceless paintings and furniture to the flames.

So as young aristocrats, my school chums and I were in high spirits on the day we were sent home early from private school during an attempted coup in June 1955. From a bend in the railway on the way home, across the River Plate we could see the smoke rising from the Capital in the aftermath of the bombing of the Presidential Palace at Plaza de Mayo by units of the Argentine Air Force, in what proved to be an unsuccessful attempt to kill Perón. However, three months later, the Armed Forces succeeded in unseating him in what became known as *La Revolución Libertadora.*

After the revolution, it was amazing to see how quickly the vestiges of Peronism disappeared. Nowhere to be seen were the once-ubiquitous *Peronista* Party lapel pins, keychain fobs, and other party paraphernalia. As in Germany after the World War II, there were suddenly no party members to be found anywhere. Black-and-white newsreels (still opening incongruously to the strains of Sousa's "Stars and Stripes") reported the success of the revolution and details of Perón's hurried escape with his mistress (a teenager named Nelly Rivas), up the river to Paraguay on a Paraguayan gunboat prudently arranged for the dictator. Before and after the newsreels depicting the revolution, newly emboldened patriots would stand up and shout, "Viva la Patria!" to which the giddy audience responded with a resounding "Viva!"

A lone, working-class *Peronista* bastion, the Boca (the port at the mouth (*boca*) of the River Plate) held true to its leader, as I recall one day attending a football match at the Boca Juniors stadium. Amid the singing of the team songs, the fans broke into the Peronist anthem of "*Los Muchachos Peronistas,*" followed by several minutes of the defiant roar: "Perón! Perón! Perón!"

For the next three years, before going away to college in 1958, I watched the country flounder through a succession of military and civilian governments seemingly unable to find solid footing or contain the rampant inflation, currency devaluations, and repeated strikes plaguing the country. The economic and political chaos unleashed by *Peronismo* in Argentina would persist for decades through periods of abortive democracy and military dictatorships, peace and civil war, prosperity and poverty.

With a clear picture in my mind of the negative consequences of left-wing excesses, I went off to college in New Hampshire in 1958 a confirmed conservative.

Chapter 2: "Silent-Generation conservative" during the cold war. Dartmouth College undergraduate: 1958-1962

Leaving behind the wacky tumult in Argentina in the fall of 1958, I felt palpable relief upon arriving on the tranquil Hanover plain tucked away in the "lovely, dark and deep" woods of Robert Frost country. Eisenhower was halfway through his second term; the political discourse between the administration and Congress was "balanced" as were the federal budget and the distribution of the fruits of prosperity. Internationally, the morality of the Cold War seemed as black and white as the hats the cowboys wore in the westerns dominating television ("Gunsmoke," "Wagon Train," "Have Gun Will Travel," "Maverick," "The Rifleman," "Tales of Wells Fargo," The Life and Legend of Wyatt Earp"). Nelson Rockefeller became Governor of New York; Ayn Rand had just published *Atlas Shrugged;* the cha-cha-cha was the new dance vogue; Elvis joined the Army; Johnny Mathis warmed us with "A Certain Smile;" and Perry Como crooned "Catch a Falling Star," as the newly created NASA launched the Explorer I satellite from Cape Canaveral as a response to the Soviet Sputnik. The mounting tension over desegregation in the South seemed far away as did Castro's assaults on Batista in Cuba.

With a modicum of culture shock, I settled into an idyllic cocoon of an all-male, Ivy League existence comprised of pep rallies on the steps of Dartmouth Hall, towering fall bonfires and gigantic Winter Carnival statues on the Green, "the crunch of feet on snow," a tug-of-war with the upper-classmen to rid ourselves of freshman beanies, road trips to neighboring girls' schools, fraternity house parties, varsity soccer, the freshman diving squad, occasional forays to the ski slopes, Navy ROTC drill and rifle teams, the thrill of learning for its own sake and of becoming an educated man.

I discovered the ancient Greeks – Socrates, Plato, Aristotle – the Bible as literature, Galileo and Holy Mother Church, St. Thomas Aquinas, Machiavelli (naughty boy), the Renaissance and Reformation, and then on up through modern times with James's pragmatism, logical positivism, existentialism and lotsa' other isms and philosophers including Berkeley, Leibnitz, Kant, Locke, Hume, Jefferson. There was the challenge of Newton's calculus, statistics, Taylor expansions, l'Hôpital's rule, and other mathematical exotica (long since forgotten), enjoyed for the sheer mental gymnastics. Physics and chemistry. Psychology: Freud, Jung, mainly. History (not nearly enough). Speech. Comp. Lit., including Dostoyevsky, Joyce, Kafka, Mann, Hemingway, Fitzgerald, and a smattering of Romantic poets: Wordsworth, Coleridge, Tennyson, the Brownings. Writing and composition. Spanish Lit. – Cervantes, Garcia Lorca, Unamuno. Art, beginning with the Impressionists on to their successors. A lot of Navy stuff and summer midshipmen cruises, since the Navy ROTC was footing the bill (again, following in Dad's footsteps). Looking back on this list today, it's clear that most of my undergraduate education consisted of a 4-year survey course of the liberal arts, providing a launching pad for deeper inquiry later in life – hence the aptness of the term "commencement" marking the end of undergraduate studies.

Sadly, the Dartmouth Economics Department in those days was intractably ensconced in its Ivory Tower, clueless about the real-world economy. We studied micro-economics with theoretical graphs designed to show how all-knowing entrepreneurs would add labor precisely until the marginal product of the last laborer added would equal his wages. Macroeconomics included the usual suspects: Malthus, Ricardo, Smith, Pareto, Marshall, Keynes, Schumpeter, Galbraith. We learned about Edgeworth boxes, Pareto efficiency, Adam Smith's pin makers, the elusive chimera of "equilibrium," and other neat theoretical concepts designed to show how free-market capitalism and the division of labor guaranteed optimal allocation of scarce resources -- all very reassuring to defenders of unfettered capitalism like me.

Oddly, though, in four years of studying economics not once did I come across a graph with real-world numbers on the axes. Not once. Realizing this, my thoughts trailed off to the panel in the "Epic of American Civilization" Orozco mural in Baker Library titled "Gods of the Modern World," depicting robed academics attending a writhing skeleton on a bed of books giving birth to a tiny skeleton to be placed alongside other such stillborns encased in glass specimen jars.[3]

Nevertheless, I came away with a profound respect for free-market mechanisms as allocators of scarce resources; the laws of supply and demand, and how monopolies affected them; the critical role of invested economic surpluses, technology, energy and population growth as the essential foundations for long-term economic growth; an appreciation for Marshall's classical economics and Keynes' modifications thereof.

The Department paid scant attention to the Austrians, perhaps because professor Harry Shaw, one of the Department's venerable institutions, had been gassed in World War I; or maybe they were just wedded to Keynes. A visiting Polish economist provided an enlightening insight into Soviet centralized planning admitting the communists had no clue as to what things cost, so they simply plugged in Western cost coefficients into their planning models to help them allocate resources. We came away feeling very smug about the superiority of Western free-market capitalism, Sputnik notwithstanding.

---

[3]http://hoodmuseum.dartmouth.edu/collections/overview/americas/mesoamerica/murals/P9341317.html

On the issues of the day, however, I considered myself a card-carrying member of the "Silent Generation." With Korea and McCarthyism over, the Cold War an accepted fact of life, Vietnam still only a gleam in the military-industrial complex's eye, and the racist South and communist Cuba far removed from Hanover, there really wasn't much for us to get riled up about. So we were generally uninvolved, detached and tame in comparison to our raucous Baby-Boom successors in the late sixties, who would become actively engaged in the serious business of stopping a war to which, in time, I would be ordered.

Instead, "conformity" was a hot topic for debate during our time on the Hanover Plain. "The Man in the Grey Flannel Suit" described the conformist tenor of the times. We felt a bit guilty about our lack of rebellion, but consoled ourselves with the thought that even as they rebelled against the bland Ozzie-and-Harriet consumerism of the day, our Beatnik contemporaries all looked, dressed and sounded pretty much alike, and so in their own way were "conforming," just like us.

And then, as if in a dream, it was suddenly over on June 10, 1962: Commencement Day. Trumpets, then bells from Baker Tower at high noon summoned 606 of us to the Green for the last time as undergraduates on a dazzling summer Sunday in 1962. Our procession up East Wheelock Street stopped on the Green, then divided to form a gauntlet for the faculty – somber in their mediaeval regalia accented by colorful hoods. We applauded as they walked by, and strained to catch the eye of a favorite professor to exchange one last, knowing smile and a nod. The Class of 1912 followed, commemorating the anniversary of the day 50 years ago when, as Grand Old Seniors, they looked forward to being "safe at last in the wide, wide world," only to find themselves mired in the trenches of the Great War in France six years later. How impossibly old they looked to us. How impossibly young we must have seemed to them. And how distant the prospect of a 50th Reunion!

We applauded them too; then waved at family and friends and took our seats for the 1962 Dartmouth Commencement ceremony.

Jim Hale's wide-ranging valedictory showed why he was the smartest guy in the room. Riffing seamlessly on themes from Herman Kahn, Jean Paul Sartre, Martin Buber and others, Jim exhorted us to master our personal Great Issue: the transition to responsible self-fulfillment in a nuclear-armed world balanced between "despairing, fatalistic" pessimism and "realistic" optimism about the prospects of avoiding a nuclear holocaust in a world dominated by the Cold War.

Our commencement speaker, Arthur H. Dean's address, titled "On Being a Full Man," dovetailed neatly with Jim's remarks. Ambassador Dean spoke optimistically of our departure into the "mainstream of life," setting a high bar with the hope that we would continue to develop "youthful qualities of an impatience and wish to investigate new lines of thought, to see greater progress in all fields of human endeavor, to wish to record positive accomplishments in the business at hand, to have an urge to understand things ever more fully, to be more concerned for our fellow man, and constantly to cultivate an instinct for creativity rather than reliance on things past. . . Our duty is. . . to think, to work, to contribute, and above all, to participate." He spoke of freedom and its attendant "responsibility to mankind, as individuals, and of historical purpose, as a people. We must prove," he continued, "that free, rational and responsible individuals in a free society – you and I – are both capable of, and worthy of, survival. . . And so my concluding words to you, as men of Dartmouth, are to think not too much of self, to avoid the life of too much ease, too much stability. Maintain an interest in all that is going on and live up to the promise inherent in your present achievement." Words to live by.

Ambassador Dean, a senior State Department negotiator, had carried out the thankless task of leading the American delegation negotiating the armistice talks with the North Koreans at Panmunjom in 1953 and would later chair the U.S. Delegation to the Nuclear Test Ban Conference at Geneva that would result in the Partial Test Ban Treaty signed in Moscow in 1963, as he predicted in his commencement address. He would then go on to become a member of the Council on Foreign Relations, the Asia Society and serve as a delegate to the United Nations. Over more than three decades, Mr. Dean would serve as a negotiator and adviser to Presidents Eisenhower, Kennedy, and Johnson. He was among those who persuaded Lyndon B. Johnson to stop bombing North Vietnam in 1968 and not to seek re-election. He also belonged to the Bilderberg group, one of those shadowy organizations of highly influential people some suspect of running the world. (http://www.bilderbergmeetings.org/index.php)

Not surprisingly, given the preoccupations of the times and his recent assignments, Ambassador Dean's 1962 speech focused on the Cold War as the dominant feature of the geopolitical landscape. Recent events had chilled the Cold War: the "Missile Race" triggered by the launching of the Soviet Sputnik satellite in 1957, the 1959 Cuban Revolution, followed by the Bay of Pigs fiasco in 1961, the downing over the Soviet Union in 1960 of a U-2 spy plane piloted by Francis Gary Powers, resulting in the failure of Ike's 4-way summit meeting in Paris shortly thereafter; Khrushchev's fist-banging incident at the United Nations.

On our side, a young President Kennedy proclaimed at his inauguration in 1961, "The torch has been passed to a new generation" – from the generals who commanded to the youngsters who fought in World War II. Kennedy "let every nation know" of America's willingness to "pay any price, bear any burden, meet any hardship, support any friend, oppose any foe in order to assure the survival and the success of liberty." Camelot exuded idealism and unflinching determination in its confrontation with the Soviet Union. If confronted, Kennedy could be counted on to take it to the brink, as we were soon to learn.

No surprise, then, Kennedy's meeting with Khrushchev in Vienna in June, 1961 did not go well, and was followed by the resumption of Soviet above-ground nuclear tests and the building of the Berlin Wall. The Cold War got even colder.

On this graduation Sunday in June, 1962, Ambassador Dean dutifully spoke of the Marxist/Leninist theory seeking to "completely liquidate the capitalist class," and of how "the existence of international tensions is a normal – indeed a desirable – state of affairs for [the communists] . . . and a precondition to change under the Marxist dialectic that will necessarily persist until they have won the class struggle. . . . Communistic agitation, revolutions, conspiracies and the serious problems posed for us by the monolithic Soviet empire or Communist bloc, and by its belief in subversion, infiltration and so-called wars of liberation, while never ceasing to proclaim that it is peace-loving, are but one facet of this more universal phenomenon."

While mindful of the Soviet threat, Mr. Dean nevertheless prudently urged "a long-range and calm perspective of the rivalry and struggle in so many fields between East and West," and the need to "learn to live with a standing threat to our culture" and to "reduce the proportions of the Communist menace, such as we are now trying our best to do, if you will pardon a personal note, in Geneva with the current Disarmament and Nuclear Test Ban conferences" as a means of making "our competition and rivalry less dangerous for the future of mankind." He concluded on a hopeful and, indeed, prescient note urging us to "persist in our own work at home and with our friends in such a way that eventually, perhaps, new generations of leaders in the Soviet bloc states will come to give up their Communist dialectics and their rather dull, tiresome and outdated Marxist-Leninist theories about the future. . ."

Astronaut Alan B. Shepard, Jr., followed Mr. Dean at the podium. Commander Shepard received an honorary Dartmouth degree that day, as did abstract expressionist painter, Hans Hofmann; Dartmouth alum and artist-in-residence, Paul Sample; and a radiant Leontyne Price, legendary Black opera singer.

We knew Commander Shepard's sub-orbital flight in space nearly a year before had been overshadowed by Soviet Cosmonaut, Yuri Gagarin's earth orbit three weeks before him, on April 12, 1961. The Space Race was in high gear and the Soviets were winning! Twenty days after Shepard's historic flight, President Kennedy, in an urgent address to a joint session of Congress, commended astronaut Shepard's feat and committed the United States "to achieving the goal, before this decade is out, of landing a man on the moon and returning him safely to the earth."

Following his praise for Shepard, President Kennedy's May 25, 1961 speech also highlighted Ambassador Dean's negotiations in Geneva. So we were privileged, indeed, to have two "men of the hour" speaking to us at commencement. Together, these two men subtly welcomed us to The Club and offered us profound insight at the highest levels into the mindset of the establishment we were heading off to join.

In his brief remarks, Shepard said something I took for granted at the time, and find disturbing now in view of our "Long Wars" in Vietnam, Afghanistan and Iraq:

> Why do I feel so strongly about national strategy? Well, Mr. Dean just spoke about our present antagonist, the Russian ideology. I am quite firmly of the belief that ***we must have an antagonist in our society***. In the theater, for example, without an antagonist the play is flimsy... I do not intend to speak specifically against the Communist challenge. Mr. Dean described that very nicely. I intend only to say that we must realize that for this society of ours to flourish – to exist—we must dovetail all these facets of our national strategy into a posture that will enable us to exist. Let me say this: That if you will promise to support our national strategy and our national posture, I will promise to continue to provide the motivation."

I accepted Shepard's assertion that "we must have an antagonist" because we were a generation raised with antagonists: the Axis Powers in World War II, the Soviet Communists from the time the Iron Curtain stretched across central Europe after the war, the North Koreans and later the Chinese in the early 1950s, then Cubans after the Castro Revolution and numerous other governments gratuitously branded as "communist" during the Eisenhower years. So, few, if any of us, reflected on the Orwellian undertones of Shepard's mention of the existentialist threat, plugs for sustained military spending and ongoing strategic confrontation with the communists.

Chapter 3: The end of the cold war (1945-1991) to war in the Middle East; Eisenhower and Orwell's nightmares realized. How did it come to this?

The Cold War (1946-1991) twisted and turned for 45 years in all – the Iron Curtain, the Berlin Airlift, the Rosenbergs, the nuclear arms race, the Berlin Wall, Korea, McCarthy, Hungary, Cuba, Vietnam, the various summit talks, *détente* with the Soviets, *rapprochement* with China, the Soviets' Long War in Afghanistan, Reagan's military buildup. Finally, after much unrest along the periphery of the Soviet Union in the late 1980s, the Cold War ended in 1991 not with a bang but a whimper.

With uncommon statesmanship, Mikhail Gorbachev presided over the dissolution of the Soviet Union after years of flagging economic output from a clunky, centrally planned economy; low oil export prices since 1986; the failed decade-long Soviet occupation of Afghanistan; and inability to meet the rising costs of countering Reagan's military buildup. In 1989 Gorbachev signaled his intention to replace the oppressive Brezhnev Doctrine with the "Sinatra Doctrine," a lighthearted, masterfully disarming reference to Sinatra's signature song, "My Way." The Sinatra Doctrine meant the Warsaw Pact nations could govern themselves "their way" without interference or support from Russia. Three years later -- after communist regimes in central Europe had been overthrown in 1989, and the fifteen constituent republics of the USSR declared their independence in 1990-1991 -- the Soviet Union dissolved and the Cold War was over.

The prudent "long-range and calm perspective" and patient negotiations for nuclear test bans, Strategic Arms Limitation Talks, Kissinger's *détente* and Nixon's *rapprochement*, advocated by Ambassador Dean and like-minded statesmen within the U.S. Government, combined with Mikhail Gorbachev's and Deng Xiaoping's enlightened pragmatism on the Soviet and Chinese sides, to avert a conflagration may observers thought was probable, if not inevitable.

Instead, fulfilling my classmate Jim Hale's "realistic optimism," China became a very successful, if anomalous, communist bastion of modern industrial capitalism and, just as Ambassador Arthur Dean predicted, the "new generations of leaders in the Soviet bloc states [gave] up their Communist dialectics and their rather dull, tiresome and outdated Marxist-Leninist theories about the future," and Russia again became a country rather than a cause.

Many years later on the lecture circuit, after a distinguished career in the U.S. Army, and as National Security Adviser, and a controversial stint as Secretary of State under George W. Bush, Colin Powell described an illuminating meeting in 1988 with Mikhail Gorbachev, then head of state of the Soviet Union. The story is significant insofar as it echoes Alan Shepard's observation.

As National Security Advisor, General Powell met with Gorbachev in Moscow, accompanying then-Secretary of State George Schultz, to set up President Reagan's subsequent meeting with Gorbachev in the Soviet capital in 1989. Gorbachev was trying to convince Powell of his intention to end the Cold War and release the Soviet grip on central Europe. Powell, suspecting trickery, wasn't buying it. Frustrated, Gorbachev pressed on, becoming increasingly agitated, and then, struck by a sudden realization, stopped and said: "Oh, I'm so sorry, general. You will have to find a new enemy."

"We must have an antagonist in our society." Alan B. Shepard, Jr.

Wars in the Middle East

Well before the old antagonist, the Soviet Union, collapsed in 1991, the military-industrial complex teed up its new antagonist: Middle Eastern Muslims. Arguably, the CIA, together with the British MI5, set up today's East-West conflict in the Middle East by overthrowing the popular, democratically elected government of Mohammad Mossadegh in Iran in 1953, courtesy of the Dulles brothers during the Eisenhower administration, as a means of regaining access to the Iranian oilfield concessions nationalized by Mossadegh. (Mossadegh was imprisoned for 3 years and then kept in house arrest until his death in 1967.) The coup paved the way for Shah Mohammad Reza Pahlavi to return from a brief exile in Rome and elevate himself from constitutional to absolute monarch, then duly grant the U.S. and U.K the oil rights they sought. Lingering resentment about the coup and the Shah's regime served as rallying points for the Iranian Revolution deposing the Shah in early 1979 followed by the storming of the U.S. embassy in Tehran later that year by an Iranian mob during the Carter administration. The embassy staff were held hostage for 444 days until minutes after President Reagan took the oath of office in 1981.

Without going into the justifications for each, a long series of military clashes have been undertaken by the U.S. and its allies in the Middle East. In conjunction with the French, the U.S. launched attacks against Druze and Syrian targets in Lebanon in 1983 during Reagan's first term, ending in an abrupt withdrawal after the truck bombing of the Marine barracks. In 1991 the elder Bush and a broad coalition of allies crushed Saddam Hussein's invading army in Kuwait. Clinton clashed with Mohammed Farrah Aidid's forces in Mogadishu, Somalia in 1993. Clinton also ordered ineffectual cruise missile attacks in Afghanistan (headquarters of al-Qaida) and Sudan (site of a pharmaceutical factory allegedly owned by al-Qaida) in 1998. Following the 9/11 attack on New York and Washington the junior Bush and the "coalition of the willing" invaded the Taliban's Afghanistan in 2001 and Saddam Hussein's Iraq in 2003. Under Obama, the U.S. military and NATO provided close air support to rebels who deposed and killed Gadafi in Libya in 2011. Seal Team 6 swooped down on Abbottabad, Pakistan to kill Osama bin Laden in 2011. U.S. drone strikes in Yemen and Pakistan are ongoing and the U.S. military is now fingering the trigger while aiming at Assad's Syria and Khameni/Ahmadinejad's Iran. In addition, a recurring cycle of provocation and retaliation has provoked endless clashes between Muslims and U.S.-backed Israelis in Lebanon, Syria, the Sinai Peninsula and within Israel itself ever since the foundation of the modern state of Israel in 1948.

Who would have imagined at the height of the Cold War in the 1960's that the U.S. would be at loggerheads with virtually the entire Middle East from the 1970s onward? We appear to have stumbled into an Islamic version of the "Domino Theory."

In every instance, the fundamental reality for Muslims is that Westerners, led by American "crusaders," have been killing and maiming their coreligionists, many of them innocent civilians, in staggering numbers for decades. One need only imagine the American reaction if the tables were turned and Muslims invaded U.S. states with comparable military destructiveness and loss of life, to understand the hatred animating growing numbers of Muslims increasingly receptive to the jihadist cause.

Muslims of various stripes, in turn, have allegedly carried out attacks on U.S. embassies, consulates and diplomatic compounds in Pakistan, Libya, Lebanon, Kuwait, Kenya, Tanzania, Indonesia, Uzbekistan, Saudi Arabia, Syria, Yemen, Turkey between 1979 and 2012; hijacked Kuwaiti and U.S. airliners and the Achille Lauro cruise ship in the 1980s; bombed airports in Rome and Vienna in 1985; bombed Pan Am flight 103 over Lockerbie, Scotland in 1988; bombed of the World Trade Center in 1993; attacked the U.S.S. Cole while in port in Yemen in 2000; attacked the World Trade Center and the Pentagon in 2001; attempted to bomb several airplanes in flight and other targets (like Times Square) in the 2000s; bombed a commuter train in Madrid in 2004; bombed the London subway in 2005; repeatedly attacked Israel since 1948.

Relentless escalating provocation, reprisal, attack, retaliation – where, when and why it began eventually becomes irrelevant; what matters is where, when and how will it end? (See footnote 5 below.)

U.S. Long Wars:

In the U.S., the end of the Cold War and the quick resolution of the first Gulf War in 1991 meant a lean decade of "peace dividends" significantly reducing the military-industrial complex's budget in the Clinton years. However, following the 9/11 attack in 2001, George W. Bush put the military-industrial complex back in business in the New Millennium with not one, but two Long Wars of choice -- Afghanistan and Iraq – both ostensibly motivated by the broader "War on Terrorism."

The War on Terrorism, like the Cold War before it, and the ongoing War on Drugs, is ideally suited to fill the military-industrial complex's need for Long Wars. The very profitable Cold War lasted 45 years because it would only end with the abandonment of a diametrically opposed ideology by a powerful, committed adversary – in this case, communism (dedicated to supplanting capitalism (i.e., "We will bury you")). The War on Drugs, similarly motivated by profits on both sides of the law, driven by insatiable American demand for narcotics and shrouded in puritanical pieties, has achieved nothing beyond empowering the underworld and fomenting civil wars in drug-producing countries like Peru, Colombia and Mexico, duly supplied by American arms manufacturers and paid for largely by American taxpayers. There's been no progress after 40 years and countless billions of taxpayer dollars funneled into law enforcement, imprisonment, education and rehabilitation, much of it payable to private contractors.[4] Likewise, the very profitable War on Terrorism is destined to last for a long time because it too can only end with the abandonment of a diametrically opposed ideology by a powerful, committed adversary – in this case, Radical Islam, interjecting resolve-stiffening religion and a long history of religious antagonism and slaughter. "Spread them out and bleed them into bankruptcy," said the 'martyred' Osama bin Laden. It seems to be working.

The Cold War ended only after the communists realized their goals were unattainable and continued adherence to their ideology in pursuit of their goals was detrimental to their interests. The War on Terrorism will end, I submit, only if and when Radical Islam comes to the same conclusion. The religious component underlying Radical Islam's commitment to its ideology renders this outcome a particularly distant prospect. Senator Richard Lugar, a longtime steadying hand in foreign policy, expresses the

---

[4] Stephen Fry on the BBC TV show "Quite Interesting":

"You're not allowed to bring into America anything that's been made by forced labor or prisoners. But in America, you can almost say, if you are so minded, that they have really reinvented the slave trade. They produce, for example, 100 percent of all military helmets, ammunition belts, bullet-proof vests, I.D. tags and other items for uniforms, 93 percent of domestically produced paints, 36 percent of home appliances, 21 percent of office furniture. As a proportion of the population, [the U.S. imprisons] more than twice as many as the South Africans, more than three times as many as the Iranians, more than six times as many as the Chinese. No society in history has imprisoned more of its citizens than the United States of America. One in thirty men aged 20 to 34 is behind bars, but for black males that's one in nine."

same conclusion: "The bottom line is this: for the foreseeable future, the United States and other nations will face an existentialist threat from the intersection of terrorism and weapons of mass destruction." Welcome to the United States of Oceania.

Eisenhower's and Orwell's nightmares realized

The first decade of the New Millennium – the G. W. Bush years – embodied in every detail Eisenhower's warning of "grave implications" associated with "lack of balance" and "unwarranted influence" and "misplaced power" not only of the often-cited "military-industrial complex," but also the less-mentioned "scientific-technological elite." Here is part of what Ike said January 17, 1961, three days before leaving office:

> Until the latest of our world conflicts, the United States had no armaments industry. American makers of plowshares could, with time and as required, make swords as well. But now we can no longer risk emergency improvisation of national defense; we have been compelled to create a permanent armaments industry of vast proportions. Added to this, three and a half million men and women are directly engaged in the defense establishment. *We annually spend on military security more than the net income of all United States corporations.* (Emphasis added.)
>
> This conjunction of an immense military establishment and a large arms industry is new in the American experience. The total influence -- economic, political, even spiritual -- is felt in every city, every statehouse, every office of the Federal government. We recognize the imperative need for this development. *Yet we must not fail to comprehend its grave implications. Our toil, resources and livelihood are all involved; so is the very structure of our society.*
>
> *In the councils of government, we must guard against the acquisition of unwarranted influence, whether sought or unsought, by the military-industrial complex. The potential for the disastrous rise of misplaced power exists and will persist.*
>
> *We must never let the weight of this combination endanger our liberties or democratic processes.* We should take nothing for granted. **Only an alert and knowledgeable citizenry** can compel the proper meshing of the huge industrial and military machinery of defense with our peaceful methods and goals, so that *security and liberty may prosper together.*

> Akin to, and largely responsible for the sweeping changes in our industrial-military posture, has been the technological revolution during recent decades.
>
> In this revolution, research has become central; it also becomes more formalized, complex, and costly. A steadily increasing share is conducted for, by, or at the direction of, the Federal government. . .
>
> *The prospect of domination of the nation's scholars by Federal employment, project allocations, and the power of money is ever present – and is gravely to be regarded.*
>
> Yet, in holding scientific research and discovery in respect, as we should, we must also be alert to the equal and opposite danger that *public policy could itself become the captive of a scientific-technological elite.*

Dwight David Eisenhower, Farewell Address
January 17, 1961 (emphasis added).

Twenty-three years later, many of us noted the year 1984 came and went with little fanfare, tempting some to ponder whether George Orwell had overstated his case in his classic book, *Nineteen Eighty Four*. Orwell derived “1984” simply by reversing the last two digits of the year the book was written, 1948, meaning, in effect, *don’t take the date literally, I mean sometime in the future.* Orwell’s “1984” future in Oceania arrived a couple of decades later, during G.W. Bush’s administration (2001-2009) characterized by:

- Widespread poverty amidst unparalleled privilege and prosperity for the ruling elite
- Fear of a constant external existentialist threat hyped by government-controlled media
- Perpetual war
- Pervasive government surveillance, interrogation and incarceration
- Loss of personal freedoms and privacy, subordinated to the imperatives of “national security”
- Incessant public mind control accomplished through media by a repressive state dominated by a privileged elite

If Orwell were writing today, Winston Smith would be working for Fox News.

Since Eisenhower's day, America has waged three foreign "Long Wars" of choice – Vietnam, Afghanistan and Iraq. As a U.S. Navy Vietnam vet, it distresses me to point out hard truths about these wars:

Each war was entered into under false pretenses, with inadequate force, nebulous and constantly changing objectives, un-analyzed risks, limited public support at home and abroad, and no exit strategy.

Each war was un-winnable because: *The enemy was intractable,* having nowhere to go, showed resolve, resourcefulness, discipline, and – dare we say it? – courage. *The terrain was cruelly inhospitable*, negating much of the American military's technological advantages, reducing combat to *mano-a-mano* at the platoon level, where it is numbers that count – and the enemy had numbers in their favor. *The situation was un-resolvable,* hopelessly mired in ancient local blood feuds, historic ideological and/or religious antagonisms and/or civil wars. Soldiers trained to fight pitched battles invariably found themselves embroiled in counterinsurgencies with standard operating procedures requiring them to live in small, vulnerable groups among the population whose language, culture, customs and longstanding social tensions and animosities they could not fathom.

Both wars in the Middle East have been funded on both sides by American taxpayers and users of oil and illegal opiates, thereby extending their duration.

These are all textbook preconditions for strategically un-winnable, policy-driven Long Wars.

Having "been compelled to create a permanent armaments industry of vast proportions," U.S. policymakers committed to sustain it with defense industry buildups and "wars of choice," providing endless streams of government contracts, swollen corporate profits and dividends, inflated C-suite salaries, and bounteous campaign contributions within what now should be called the military-industrial-technological-political complex (MITP complex).

In choosing wars in Vietnam, Afghanistan and Iraq, the MITP complex was either incredibly stupid or, more likely, crafty as hell in seeking out resolute adversaries engaged in civil war in inhospitable terrain at such a times as to assure U.S. tactical victories but strategic defeat essential to Long Wars. Having thus willingly stepped into quagmires, the MITP complex then confidently relied on Americans' pride, patriotism, unwillingness to concede defeat, and/or lack of interest to drag out long and very profitable, if strategically pointless, wars.

It strains credulity to think the frequent episodes of U.S. military crash spending are coincidental, random or entirely exogenous. With wars, long and short, and military buildups occurring during most of the past 45 years, logic would suggest these episodes are planned, in much the same way as the automobile industry plans obsolescence, and for the same reason.

Reviewing President Eisenhower's list of "grave implications" from the military-industrial complex today, we find *all* have been realized! Consider:

The U.S. military reportedly spends not only more than the net income of all U.S. corporations, but also more than the militaries of all the other nations combined. To what end? As Aaron Sorkin pointed out, 25 of the top 26 countries we outspend are allies.

The total influence of what has become the MITP Complex continues to be felt in every city, every statehouse and every office of the federal government. Military offices of procurement routinely farm out work on major projects to virtually every state in the Union, thus ensuring continuing local support.

The councils of government are awash in campaign contributions from corporations and wealthy individuals buying "unwarranted influence." With the *Citizens United vs. Federal Election Commission* Supreme Court decision the floodgates have been opened for the rich and powerful elite to continue underwriting policies favoring the military-industrial complex, commonweal be damned.

Power *has* been misplaced. For the last three decades, power has been dedicated not to the interests of "We the People," but rather to the enrichment of the political sector's wealthy "base" of contributors, both Democrat and especially Republican, to the detriment of the middle and lower classes suffering from stagnating real wages, high unemployment, plunging housing prices, foreclosures and bankruptcies.

Consider: The share of national income growth going to the top 10 percent of income earners shifted unmistakably in favor of the rich. In the postwar years before Reagan, the top 10 percent typically got to keep 35 percent of the growth in national income. During Reagan, their share jumped to 87 percent, most of that going to the top 1 percent of income earners who now take in nearly a quarter of the nation's income every year and control 40 percent of the nation's wealth. Chopping the top tax rate from 70 percent to 28 percent on Reagan's watch certainly contributed to the shift. The journeyman CEO earning $10 million a year, who had to scrape by on $3 million before Reagan, got to keep $7.2 million by the time Reagan left office in 1989. For the rich and powerful elite, the math is elementary: invest millions in campaign contributions and receive billions in tax relief. Astoundingly, during the first 7 years of George W. Bush's administration (before the wheels came off the wagon in 2008), fully 98 percent (!) of the *growth* in national income was scooped up by the top 10 percent of income earners, leaving 2 percent for the rest of us. Hello?

This lack of balance has polarized the United States economically and politically, creating the greatest domestic inequality of wealth among all major advanced nations while producing legislative gridlock between those politicians seeking to protect the interests of their wealthy benefactors and those seeking a broader distribution of the fruits of prosperity.

Power was misplaced militarily by invading Vietnam. In hindsight, the human tragedy of Vietnam added up to a U.S. strategic loss in Asia serving little purpose other than to debunk the "Domino Theory" and feed the military-industrial complex for a decade.

Power has also been misplaced militarily by invading Afghanistan and Iraq, soil regarded as holy by Islam.

The U.S. military invaded Afghanistan under the pretext of hunting down Osama bin-Laden and his al-Qaida henchmen following the 9/11 attack, and to displace the Taliban so as to deny al-Qaida a secure base from which to plot further attacks. With the help of a local militia, the Northern Alliance, the Taliban was duly displaced in fairly short order. However, after letting bin-Laden and company to get away at Tora Bora (which, had they been captured or killed, would have fulfilled the war's mission, thereby ending it) the military was instructed to shift to the now-familiar Vietnam-style counter-insurgency, nation-building mission to win "hearts and minds" with billions of dollars spent on infrastructure (while neglecting our own), and train Afghan security forces to protect and defend a supposed democratic, strong central government totally alien to traditional Afghan political organizing principles. Once again Washington imposed the tried-and-true formula ensuring Long Wars. And here we are, 11 years later with virtually nothing accomplished beyond engaging in a running battle with die-hard Taliban, suffering "green-on-blue" casualties from compromised Afghan security forces, and driving the remaining Taliban into neighboring Pakistan, a highly unstable, prickly Muslim ally possessing nuclear weapons. Meanwhile, the Afghan war flies under the radar, with hardly a mention during the 2012 elections, and no mention at all by Republican presidential candidate Romney in his acceptance speech in Tampa. When asked about the omission, Romney argued that he focused on things that were "important."

Two years after the Afghanistan war began, the Bush 43 administration launched the Iraq invasion under the pretense of dispossessing Saddam Hussein of what turned out to be nonexistent weapons of mass destruction, and punishing Iraq for an imagined participation in 9/11. The underlying objectives of preserving the world's oil lifeline and keeping the military-industrial complex in business remained unspoken. Having disbanded the Sunni-dominated army in the process of displacing the previously dominant Sunni minority, the administration then confronted a Sunni insurgency for which it was totally unprepared. After several iterations, the administration finally alighted on a Vietnam-style objective of counterinsurgency and costly nation building as a means of establishing a friendly Shia-dominated government as a "beacon of democracy" in the Middle East, as in Afghanistan, insisting on instituting a form of government totally alien to traditional organizing political principles. And once again, the Bush 43 administration instituted the tried-and-true formula ensuring Long Wars. The Iraq War ended 8 ½ years after it began when President Obama simply followed Vermont Senator George Aiken's formula for ending the Vietnam war: "Declare victory and bring the troops home" with an added push from the Iraqi government's refusal to extend the "Status of Forces Agreement" providing legal cover for the continued U.S. military presence in country. Meanwhile, to this day the insurgency continues unabated, the Malaki government remains shaky, Iraqi Vice President Tariz al-Hashemi remains in exile under a death sentence issued *in absentia*, oil contracts to develop Iraqi oil fields have been awarded to China and other non-U.S. contractors, the Green Zone costing billions of taxpayer dollars has been handed over to the Iraqi government and Washington worries about deepening ties between the Shia-dominated governments of Iraq and Iran. "Mission accomplished," indeed. I expect history will record the Afghanistan and Iraq wars as the greatest foreign policy blunders and George W. Bush as the worst president in U.S. history. (See "The G. W. Bush years (2001-2009) in Chapter 6 below.)

These un-winnable wars of choice create little beyond corporate profit, discord, death and destruction, providing Radical Islam with its most effective recruiting tool. Most importantly, such wars perpetuate the escalation of conflict between Muslims and the U.S. with potentially catastrophic consequences. The wars appear to be playing into the hands of al-Qaida whose strategy, I remind you, is to "Spread them thin and bleed them into bankruptcy." Al-Qaida's investment in 9/11, said to total $500,000, panicked the U.S. into spending at least a couple of trillion dollars in response. Today the U.S. is in difficult economic and financial straits; Standard and Poor's downgraded the government's credit rating. Incapable of acting responsibly on budgetary matters, the government continues to bleed red ink. The national debt skyrockets as the national economy sputters. The U.S. is courting bankruptcy.

The scientific-technological elite have teamed up with the military-industrial complex to produce ever-more technologically sophisticated (and expensive) weapons the political sector willingly underwrites, apparently for much the same reason as Mallory climbed Everest: "Because it's there." – and, more practically, because the weapons makers are "there" in congressional districts.

Policymakers, misled as to the accuracy and reliability of "smart" bombs and missiles, order so-called "surgical" strikes in Iraq and

Afghanistan, resulting in tragic civilian casualties dismissed as "collateral damage," a Newspeak phrase if ever there was one.

Liberties enshrined in the Constitution and Bill of Rights have been radically undermined by the Patriot Acts and, more recently, the 2012 National Defense Authorization Act (NDAA) – (America's "Enabling Acts"?), enacted as responses to the attack on 9/11, around which "false flag"[5] conspiracy theories rage. Suspects have been abducted and transferred to countries ("extraordinary rendition," more Newspeak) where "harsh interrogation" techniques, (usually "waterboarding," a technique hearkening back to the Spanish Inquisition) have been employed, as they reportedly have been in Guantanamo. Extra-constitutional wiretapping, record searches and "lone wolf" surveillance have been practiced in ways reminiscent of Orwell's "Big Brother." An "enemy combatant," for whom especially harsh treatment applies (including assassination and indefinite detention), is anyone, including American citizens, the President of the United States so designates, without explanation, charges or trial. Kafka, anyone?

According to Chris Hedges, "The NDAA implodes our most cherished constitutional protections. It permits the military to function on U.S. soil as a civilian law enforcement agency. It authorizes the executive branch to order the military to selectively suspend due process and *habeas corpus* for citizens. The law can be used to detain people deemed threats to national security, including dissidents whose rights were once protected under the First Amendment, and hold them until what is termed 'the end of the hostilities.'" (Truthdig "Totalitarian Systems Always Begin by Rewriting the Law" 26 March, 2012.) Peaceful Occupy protesters, exercising their First Amendment rights "peaceably to assemble, and to petition the government for a redress of grievances," have been roughed up and nonchalantly pepper sprayed while quietly seated in orderly rows, heads bowed.

---

[5] **False flag** (aka Black Flag) operations are covert operations designed to deceive in such a way that the operations appear as though they are being carried out by other entities. The name is derived from the military concept of flying **false colors**; that is: flying the flag of a country other than one's own. False flag operations are not limited to war and counter-insurgency operations and can be used during peacetime. (Wikepedia) False flag operations are sometimes used to gain tactical or strategic advantage through surprise and deception, or provide a pretext/incitement for war by covertly creating an incident against its own people to which the otherwise non-belligerent population responds by demanding war in retribution. Google "9/11 conspiracy theories." Numerous attacks by Muslims on Western targets, previously mentioned have been attributed by conspiracy theorists to Mossad, the Israeli Intelligence Service, presumably to incite anti-Muslim sentiment in the West. Getting to the bottom of such allegations exceeds the scope of this book. Suffice it to say, the net result of such attacks, whatever the source, is dangerous, potentially irreversible escalation of hostilities possibily leading to all-out war. Therein lies the danger we must address.

The democratic processes, while ostensibly still functioning, have been severely compromised by priorities distorted by campaign funding, irregularities in tallying votes, gerrymandering, and state-legislated impediments to voter registration by Republican-controlled state legislatures. Lest we forget, the pivotal 2000 presidential election was decided, amidst raging controversy, in a state governed by the future president's brother by a single vote in a Supreme Court stacked with justices appointed by his father.

Further instances of political cronyism abound: The impetus for the war in Iraq came largely from Vice-President Cheney, formerly the CEO of Halliburton, the company which then received a multi-billion-dollar "no-bid" contract to provide oil and infrastructure for the war. These are the same wonderful folks whose alleged negligence brought us the catastrophic Deepwater Horizon oil spill in the Gulf of Mexico, thanks in part to lax regulatory oversight by the administration run by two former oilmen. Where's the outrage?

> The war against Iraq, in the end, was nothing more or less than a massive money-laundering operation that took American taxpayer dollars, soaked them in blood, and redirected them to Certain Friends In High Places.
>
> William Rivers Pitt
>
> "The United States of Aftermath" Truthout 21 February 2013

In foreign policy, the United States seems to have adopted the very qualities Arthur Dean in his 1962 commencement address deplored about the Soviets, namely: Regarding international tensions as a normal – indeed a desirable – state of affairs and a precondition to change under an ["unfettered capitalist"] dialectic. Fomenting agitation, revolutions, conspiracies subversion, infiltration and so-called wars of liberation, while never ceasing to proclaim that it is peace-loving – think U.S. in Iran in the 1953, Guatemala in 1954, the Congo in 1960, Cuba 1961, Brazil 1964, Ghana 1966, Iraq 1968, Chile 1973, Afghanistan 1973-74 and again in 1978 and the 1980s, Nicaragua 1981-1990, Panama 1989, Haiti 2004, Somalia 2006-2007, in addition to the three aforementioned Long Wars.

Not by chance did Doonesbury creator, Gary Trudeau, choose a battered Roman legionnaire's helmet to symbolize President George W. Bush – America has morphed into the modern Roman Empire.

Bottom line: Americans today are living the worst fears of President Eisenhower and author George Orwell. The pieces are in place. America is a dictatorship waiting to happen.

How did it come to this?

Chapter 4: How the economy, finance and politics interacted in the U.S. – Part 1. The political pendulum swings to the left. Dwight Eisenhower (1953-1961), John Kennedy (1962-1963). Lyndon Johnson (1963-1969). Richard Nixon (1969-1974). Gerald Ford (1974-1977). Jimmy Carter (1977-1981)

Being something of an economic determinist, I find it helpful to track economic developments when analyzing the evolution of socio-political trends. So let's rewind to the 1950s and see how economics, finance and politics interacted to get us from there to where we are today.

The Eisenhower years (1953-1961): My Dartmouth classmates grew up in the U.S. during a Golden Age of American postwar prosperity in the 1950s. The United States, the only combatant nation to emerge relatively unscathed from World War II, possessed the world's most formidable industrial complex and enjoyed the admiration, gratitude and respect of friend and foe alike in the West for its enlightened postwar reconstruction policies embodied in the Marshall Plan for Europe and in General MacArthur's enlightened administration of Japan.

After the war, the U.S. economy expanded vigorously, as most wartime factories retooled, producing a cornucopia of consumer goods to satisfy the pent-up demand of Americans forced to save by the wartime absence of things to buy, matching supply to effective demand. A slimmed-down armaments industry kept busy as well, devising new weapons to counter the Soviet threat and to equip the military for the three-year Korean War. Recessions did occur on average every 4 years, but were manageably brief, with unemployment rarely reaching 7 percent, averaging a very respectable 4.6 percent. Recurring recessions had the salutary effect of curbing borrowing and lending, avoiding potentially destabilizing over-extension of credit, (something Alan Greenspan's Fed later failed to recognize in implementing its counter-cyclical policies to create "perpetual prosperity"). Long-term benchmark interest rates ranged between 2.5 percent and 4.5 percent. Consumer price inflation averaged about 1 percent. Stocks generally prospered, with the Dow Jones Industrial Index trebling from around 200 to just over 600 during the decade. Most agreed the fruits of prosperity were fairly distributed, with the richest 10 percent of income earners garnering 26 percent of the *growth* in national income, with the remaining 90 percent sharing 74 percent in the 1950s.

Political discourse on economic matters and fiscal policy was generally civil, responsible, cooperative, and importantly, *balanced,* as Eisenhower stated in his prescient Farewell Address:

> But each proposal must be weighed in light of a broader consideration; the need to maintain balance in and among national programs – balance between the private and the public economy, balance between the cost and hoped for advantages – balance between the clearly necessary and the comfortably desirable; balance between our essential requirements as a nation and the duties imposed by the nation upon the individual; balance between the actions of the moment and the national welfare of the future. Good judgment seeks balance and progress; lack of it eventually finds imbalance and frustration.

The first tenet of conservatism in the Eisenhower era was to balance the federal budget, with an appropriate combination of highly progressive taxes (top bracket 91%!) and judicious spending, including the job-creating Interstate Highway System. Contrast Eisenhower's constructive characterization of the relationship between the Executive and Legislative branches of government with conditions today. Ike said:

> Our people expect their President and the Congress to find essential agreement on questions of great moment, the wise resolution of which will better shape the future of the nation.
>
> My own relations with Congress, which began on a remote and tenuous basis when, long ago, a member of the Senate appointed me to West Point, have since ranged to the intimate during the war and immediate post-war period, and finally to the mutually interdependent during these past eight years.
>
> In this final relationship, the Congress and the Administration have, on most vital issues, cooperated well, to serve the nation well rather than mere partisanship, and so have assured that the business of the nation should go forward. So my official relationship with Congress ends in a feeling on my part, of gratitude that we have been able to do so much together.

The leftward swing of the political pendulum initiated fiscally during the Roosevelt administration in the Great Depression, gathered strength in the social arena during the Eisenhower years with the emergence of the Civil Rights Movement. The Supreme Court's 1954 landmark *Brown vs. Board of Education of Topeka, Kansas* ruling desegregating public schools launched the movement, followed in 1955 by the Montgomery Bus

Boycott initiated by Rosa Park's refusal to sit at the back of a bus, and in 1957 by Eisenhower's decision to send in the U.S. Army to assure the integration of public schools in Little Rock, Arkansas. If called upon to judge Eisenhower's fiscal and social policies, today's Republican Party would probably brand Eisenhower as a treasonous, flaming socialist.

Regarding domestic policies, the Eisenhower years could justifiably be said to represent a relatively sound baseline of economic prosperity fairly shared, social stability, fiscal probity, and political civility against which the fiscal craziness of subsequent decades can be measured. Regarding foreign policy, not so much.

Discourse on foreign policy reflected the profound polarization of the Cold War initiated during the Truman administration. Anti-communist paranoia fomented globally by Churchill in his 1946 "Iron Curtain" speech, and hysterically ignited in the U.S. by Wisconsin Senator Joseph McCarthy in 1950, carried over into the Eisenhower administration as McCarthy instigated what would become shameful Senate and House witch hunts against the State Department, the U.S. Army and Hollywood. While privately opposed to McCarthy's tactics, Eisenhower never publicly attacked him, and allowed the "Red Scare" to burgeon under the leadership of the hard-line Dulles brothers (at State and the CIA) and J. Edgar Hoover at the FBI. Anti-communist paranoia was rampant in the U.S., as exemplified by the enthralling television show "I Led Three Lives," and a companion radio show "I Was a Communist for the FBI" (duly approved by Hoover), loosely based on the life of a mild-mannered Boston adman named Philbrick, portrayed as covertly foiling an increasingly outlandish series of communist plots.

The right-wing demonization of "communists" soon included not just the Soviet Union and the People's Republic of China, but also as anyone or any government anywhere attempting to achieve reforms on behalf of "the people" in the name of "social or economic justice" or independence from colonial rule. The communist bogeyman would, in varying degrees, infuse the foreign policies of U.S. governments, whether left- or right-wing-oriented, for the duration of the Cold War.[6] During the Eisenhower administration, non-alignment became viewed as "immoral and

---

[6] Old habits die hard. Even today, the right wing trots out the old epithet ("communist") when demonizing President Obama's active-state initiatives on behalf of the people. However, to the old cold warriors, Richard Nixon and Ronald Reagan, and their respective Secretaries of State (Kissinger and Schultz), goes the credit for overcoming their anti-communist prejudices to achieve *rapprochement* and *détente*, respectively with the communist Chinese and Soviets.

shortsighted." Governments like Sukarno's Indonesia, Nasser's Egypt, Nehru's India and Ho chi Minh's North Vietnam, whose driving impetus had been liberation from colonialism, abruptly found themselves peremptorily branded as communist or Soviet-aligned, setting the stage for eventual confrontation with the U.S. and/or its allies – in the case of North Vietnam, with particularly tragic consequences. Eisenhower coined the term "falling domino principle," morphing eventually into the "Domino Theory."

At the same time as the Soviets exploded their first hydrogen bomb, the Cold War ratcheted up further yet as the CIA and the British military intelligence service engineered a coup to depose the democratically elected Mossadegh government in Iran on the Soviet Union's southern border, heightening Soviet fears of "encirclement" by returning the exiled, Western-friendly Shah of Iran to power.

Paradoxically, having opposed the nuclear bombing of Nagasaki and Hiroshima, Eisenhower nonetheless used the threat of tactical nuclear weapons to end the Korean War and proposed nuclear weapons to be "as available for use as other munitions," menacing the Soviet Union with a policy of "sudden atomic retaliation" without Congressional approval. After the Soviets developed nuclear capability, the Eisenhower administration shifted to a policy of "Mutually Assured Destruction" (MAD), as the means of avoiding war with a successful nuclear stalemate. Eisenhower authorized the creation of an overwhelming nuclear strike force on land, on and under the sea and in the air, as did the Soviets. Not long after the nuclear arms race began, the U.S. and Soviets reached the point where their combined nuclear arsenals could annihilate all human life on earth. Under any sane scenario, the weapons became both essential and useless, since each side knew it faced certain obliteration regardless of whether it launched a first or retaliatory strike. Delegating authority to initiate a nuclear attack to field commanders in the event the President could not be reached, risked global annihilation in the event some commander decided to take matters into his own hands, as was depicted in the dark comedy "Dr. Strangelove." Students practiced "duck and cover" in schools and doomsday preppers built bomb shelters – risibly ineffectual methods of surviving nuclear war.

Commenting on Eisenhower's Farewell Address warning about the dangers of the military-industrial complex, Oliver Stone, in his excellent "Untold History of the United States" television series observes, "Eisenhower seemed to understand the monstrosity he had created, and seemed almost to be asking for an absolution. . . . Aside from overthrowing foreign governments and intervening freely around the globe, it was Eisenhower who did more than anyone else to create the very military-industrial complex he warned of."

The Kennedy Years (1961-1963): In the 1960s, the U.S. economy grew somewhat faster than the prior decade, with only one recession, in 1960-61. In its aftermath, Kennedy responded in 1963 with proposals for personal and corporate tax cuts that would come to haunt Democrats in future years. Foreshadowing the Arthur Laffer supply-siders by two decades, Kennedy spoke of: "... the paradoxical truth that tax rates are too high and revenues too low; and the soundest way to raise revenue in the long term is to lower rates now." The top tax bracket at the time stood at a confiscatory 90 percent, a holdover from World War II, at which point one could reasonably make the supply-side argument for the inverse relationship between tax rates and revenues. (Kennedy proposed reducing the top bracket to 65 percent-70 percent depending on which deductions would be allowed. Years later Reagan supply-siders would gleefully invoke Kennedy's statement in successfully arguing for a reduction in the top bracket from 70 percent to 28 percent -- demonstrably an instance of carrying a logical argument to an absurd conclusion, producing a corresponding falloff in revenues and a widening deficit.) President Johnson eventually enacted Kennedy's tax proposals.

However, for Kennedy, the wheels came off the wagon in the geopolitical arena with the Bay of Pigs fiasco in April 1961, followed in October 1962 by the Cuban Missile Crisis, the high-water mark in the Cold War.

The Johnson Years (1963-1969): Lyndon Johnson became the 36th U.S. president in November 1963 following Kennedy's assassination, and was elected in 1964 with a whopping 61 percent majority, plus landslide Democratic majorities of 68-32 in the Senate and 295-140 in the House. In both fiscal and social policy, President Johnson, a consummate legislator, accelerated the leftward momentum of the political pendulum to a breathtaking extent, a pinnacle for active-state liberalism. Johnson's ambitious Great Society and War on Poverty programs increased federal support for:

- Education (including Head Start and other programs increasing federal funding for education)
- The arts (establishing the National Endowments for the Humanities and the Arts), public broadcasting (establishing the Corporation for Public Broadcasting)
- Attack on disease (creating Medicare, Medicaid)
- Urban renewal (Housing and Urban Development Act and The New Communities Act of 1968)
- Consumer protection (Fair Packaging and Labeling Act, Wholesome Meat Act of 1967, Flammable Fabrics Act of 1967, Child Safety Act of 1966, Truth-in-Lending Act of 1968)

- Beautification, spearheaded by Lady Bird Johnson, notably requiring tall fences around auto junkyards and other eyesores
- Conservation (Clean Air, Water Quality and Clean Water Restoration Acts, Endangered Species Preservation Act of 1966, Land and Water Conservation Act of 1965, Solid Waste Disposal Act of 1965, National Historic Preservation Act of 1966, National Environmental Policy Act of 1969 and others)
- Development of depressed regions
- A wide-scale fight against poverty (the Equal Opportunity Act of 1964, Volunteers in Service to America (VISTA), Jobs Corps, Food Stamp Act of 1964, increased Social Security benefits)
- Transportation (elevating the Department of Transportation to cabinet level, creating what is now the Federal Transit Administration, and enacting the Urban Mass Transportation Act of 1964, the National Traffic and Motor Vehicle Safety Act of 1966 and the Highway Safety Act of 1966 (largely in response to Ralph Nader's "Unsafe At Any Speed")
- Control and prevention of crime

In the social arena, Johnson advanced the cause of the Civil Rights Movement with major legislation including:

- The Civil Rights Act of 1964 forbidding job discrimination and the segregation of public accommodations.
- The Voting Rights Act of 1965 assuring minority registration and voting.
- The Immigration and Nationality Services Act of 1965 abolishing the national-origin quotas in immigration law.
- The Civil Rights Act of 1968 banning housing discrimination and extending constitutional protections to Native Americans on reservations.

Johnson's legacy contains several noteworthy ironies: First, the extraordinary magnitude of his liberal achievements energized the conservative counter-reaction – including, notably, among conservative Democrats (the original "neo-conservatives') – that would eventually reverse the direction of the political pendulum when Reagan came to power in 1981. Basically, the pendulum exhibits the political equivalent of Newton's Law of Motion: "For every action there is an equal and opposite reaction." Johnson's advancements of civil rights for Blacks initiated the swing in the Deep South from reliably Democratic to staunchly conservative Republican. His extensive liberal social agenda mobilized the corporate elite to oppose the regulations contained in and costs imposed by many of his programs. It also stirred up resentments within the upper classes who saw themselves as bearing the brunt of the costs associated with them, notwithstanding Johnson's lowering of the their tax rates. To gauge how far the pendulum has swung away from Johnson's liberal legacy today, consider how different are the conservative mindsets of two other prominent Texas politicians: George W. Bush and Governor Rick Perry.

Second, despite Johnson's monumental contributions to a liberal agenda in the fiscal and social arenas, (including reducing the number of Americans living below the poverty line from 22.2 percent to 12.6 percent), the left did him in because of his support of the right-wing agenda in foreign policy. By enmeshing the U.S. in the quagmire of Vietnam, in the late-1960s Johnson stirred up a hornet's nest of opposition primarily among students, forcibly engaged in the war issue by compulsory military service – the draft.

The anti-war movement surged at the same time as the civil rights (morphing into Black Power) and women's liberation movements hit their stride. Consequently, throughout the mid- and late-1960s and into the early 1970s, street demonstrations and riots became commonplace. Racial violence in the streets erupted with unnerving frequency, leaving iconic geographic markers in the American vocabulary: Harlem, Bedford-Stuyvesant, Philadelphia in 1964, Watts in 1965, Atlanta, San Francisco, Cleveland, Cincinnati, Columbus, Newark, Oakland, Baltimore, Seattle, and especially Detroit in 1966 and 1967. The assassination of Dr. Martin Luther King, Jr. In April 1968 in Memphis unleashed another wave of riots, mainly in Black neighborhoods, including Baltimore Detroit, Newark, Boston, San Francisco, New Orleans, Washington and Atlanta. The anti-war protests, sometimes violent, originated primarily on college campuses, and were often complemented by massive demonstrations in major cities like New York, San Francisco and Washington, DC. The women's liberation movement, while separate from the anti-war movement, nonetheless made common cause with it, adding the energy and organizational skills of liberated women to the anti-war protests.

It's hard to fathom why President Johnson engaged the U.S. in the Vietnam folly – a war he continued to pursue even after it became obvious to him, Secretary of Defense McNamara and other top advisers, that it could not be won. Johnson agonized, arguably, like no other president since Lincoln: "I can't win, and I can't get out." "I'm tired. I'm tired of feeling rejected by the American people. I'm tired of waking up in the middle of the night worrying about the war." "I knew from the start if I left a woman I really loved – the Great Society – in order to fight that bitch of a war in Vietnam then I would lose everything at home. My hopes, my dreams."

It is understandable, then, when faced with massive anti-war demonstrations, race riots and challenges from within his own party in the presidential race in 1968 from Eugene McCarthy and Bobby Kennedy – both united in their opposition to the war – President Johnson decided not to run for re-election. It was a sad finale for a proud, powerful, capable leader who, had he demonstrated the will to stand up to the military-industrial complex, arguably would have been numbered among America's greatest presidents.

The Vietnam War destabilized the country not only politically but also financially and economically. At a time when the economy reached full employment (with unemployment falling to 4 percent in 1965) President Johnson decided we could have both "guns and butter": the war in Vietnam and the War on Poverty and The Great Society. (This decision marked the beginning of the mindset finding its ultimate expression in the presidency of George W. Bush, namely that wars could be waged without financial sacrifice on the part of the electorate. While Johnson waged war in Vietnam without raising taxes, Bush waged wars in Afghanistan and Iraq while *lowering* tax rates, predictably creating huge federal budget deficits, in effect, fobbing off the cost of wars on to future generations.) Consequently, with no slack in the system in the late 1960s, the economy overheated, putting upward pressure on consumer prices (around 6 percent for the consumer price index (CPI)), which in turn pushed up benchmark interest rates to around 7.5 percent, causing the stock market to gyrate wildly in the second half of the decade, then plunge as the economy slumped into recession in 1971.

The Nixon Years (1969-1974): In 1969, President Nixon inherited Vietnam and an economy beset by incipient inflation – modest in comparison to levels reached during the 1970s oil shocks – to which the administration responded by imposing wage and price controls briefly and, in hindsight, unsuccessfully.

Politically, the leftward populist shift of the 1960s extended into the 1970s. Democratic majorities in Congress passed, and Nixon, a Republican, signed legislation creating what would in time become the *bêtes noir* of conservative Republicans: the Occupational Safety and Health Administration (OSHA), the Environmental Protection Agency (EPA) and the requirement for environmental impact statements for many Federal projects, according to the National Environmental Policy Act. Congress overrode Nixon's veto of the Clean Water Act of 1972, but Nixon impounded the funds he deemed unjustifiable.

Nixon's presidency frayed badly as the war in Vietnam dragged on. The second march on Washington in November 1969 drew a reported 500,000 demonstrators. Public outrage mounted in 1970 as news of the My Lai massacre finally became public in February. Soldiers returning from Vietnam suffered shameful verbal and sometimes physical abuse. Nixon announced the incursion of U.S. forces into Cambodia in April. National Guardsmen fired on student protesters at Kent State in May, killing four and wounding sixteen. In April 1971 another 500,000 protesters marched on

Washington. The Senate Foreign Relations Committee chaired by Senator William Fulbright, held hearings in April and May on proposals to end the war, at which future senator (and chairman of that very committee) and presidential candidate, John Kerry, a decorated Vietnam vet, testified, urging immediate, unilateral withdrawal. In June 1971 the *N.Y. Times* published the Pentagon Papers revealing the true nature of the war, and, as Daniel Ellsberg, who leaked the documents, put it, "demonstrating unconstitutional behavior by a succession of presidents. . ." Protests in the streets and on campuses across the country continued unremittingly until the clamorous left forced an end to the war in Vietnam. An angry left also forced the unprecedented resignations of both Vice-President Agnew (in 1973 for bribery and tax evasion) and President Nixon in August 1974 for the Watergate cover-up – its anger exacerbated not only by frustration with slow progress in ending the Vietnam War but also by economic discontent stemming from an unprecedented, game-changing economic event: the First Oil Shock in 1973.

The First Oil Shock (1973)

To discourage Western support of Israel in the October 1973 "Yom Kippur" Arab-Israeli War, the Muslim members of the OPEC cartel embargoed oil to the U.S., Great Britain, Canada, Japan and the Netherlands, causing the price of oil to skyrocket from its longstanding level around $2.50 a barrel, to around $12 a barrel. OPEC was eager to raise prices anyway, inasmuch as dissolution in 1971 of the Bretton Woods Accord, ending the Gold Exchange Standard, had resulted in a devaluation of the dollar in which oil purchases were denominated. Consequently, even after the end of the embargo, OPEC curtailed oil production to sustain high oil prices. From that point forward, economic, financial and even political events would be dominated, as I would state a decade later in my first *Cyclical Investing* newsletter, "by the contest between the interests of oil and industrial capital over the price and availability of oil."

The Ford Years (1974-1977): Given the pervasiveness of oil as a prime mover, lubricant, and industrial raw material, the rapid increase in oil prices spread throughout the world economy, igniting unprecedented, double-digit global inflation, far worse than anything seen in the late 1960s. President Ford attempted to ameliorate the adverse effects of dependence on high-priced foreign oil by signing the 1975 Energy Policy and Conservation Act, setting federal standards for energy efficiency in new cars for the first time. He also mounted an unsuccessful "Whip Inflation Now" (WIN) campaign, and reiterated support for Nixon's Project Independence (subsequently abandoned at the insistence of Big Oil), setting a goal of becoming independent from "any other country for the energy we need."

However, it was left to the Federal Reserve Bank (the Fed) to counter the inflation produced by higher oil prices by reducing the real money supply, thereby jacking up interest rates so as to reduce oil demand (and, therefore, force down oil prices) by crippling the economy. Prodded by a hawkish Federal Reserve Bank and other central banks, credit markets experienced a sudden surge in interest rates, producing a deep worldwide recession in 1974-1975. The world economy slumped, stock and bond markets crashed and unemployment rose sharply – economic conditions provoking massive political change around the world by both ballot and bullet.

The Carter Years (1977-1981): In the U.S., Democrat Jimmy Carter was elected President in 1976 as a protest against the dismal economic conditions prompted by the First Oil Shock, popular resentment of President Ford's pardon of Richard Nixon, and as an antidote of honesty ("I'll never lie to you.") in a political arena poisoned with deceit and distrust during the Nixon years.

The Second Oil Shock

The Second Oil Shock (1979-1984), largely the product of oil shortages caused by the Iran-Iraq war (1980-1988), rocked the world economy from 1979 to 1985. However, the Federal Reserve Bank's determination to force an oil price rollback, overcame reductions in oil supply with even greater reductions in demand through tight monetary policy, creating a reported 50 percent supply overhang in the global oil market by 1985.

However, in 1980, again reflecting the same intersection of economics, oil and politics which brought him into office, the Second Oil Shock torpedoed Carter. Oil prices surged from around $13 a barrel in early 1979 to $34 on the official market and as high as $40 a barrel on the spot market in the early 1980s – this time as a result of production curtailed by the Iran-Iraq War (in which the MITP complex backed its future enemy, Saddam Hussein.) In 1980-1982, the world experienced another oil-price-driven cycle of double-digit inflation, high interest rates (topping 20 percent in the U.S.!), economic contraction, crashing stock and bond markets and high unemployment. The double-dip recession fueled political discontent around the globe, manifested politically as anger against incumbents and votes to replace them with opposition candidates. In the U.S. and U.K., the hard-line-right, neo-conservative governments of Ronald Reagan and

Margaret Thatcher replaced the predominantly left-of-center governments of Democrat Jimmy Carter and Labour's James Callaghan.

In a stark demonstration of economic determinism, the discontent with the economic "malaise" inflicted by the inflationary tidal wave of the Second Oil Shock overwhelmed the Carter administration, already weakened by the humiliation of the Iranian Hostage Crisis. In the 1980 election, California Governor Reagan piled on, flattening Carter with his question "Are you better off than you were four years ago?" and offered an upbeat alternative ("Let's make America great again!"). *What became known as the "Reagan Revolution," marked the end of the leftward displacement of the political pendulum – characterized by anti-war/military sentiment and active-state liberal fiscal and social policies – and the beginning of a sharp and enduring reversal to the right.*

In the Reagan Revolution -- sparked by conservative reaction to perceived active-state liberal overreach and foreign policy failures during the Johnson administration, fueled additionally by the public exasperation with the "malaise" of the 1970s oil shocks – we will find our answer to the question posed earlier: "How did it come to this?"

Chapter 5: How the economy, finance and politics interacted in the U.S. – Part 2. The political pendulum swings to the right. The Reagan Revolution (1981-1989). George Herbert Walker Bush (1989-1993). Bill Clinton (1993-2001) and a Republican Congress (1995-2007).

The Reagan Years (1981-1989): Ronald Reagan's presidency was a game changer.

"The Great Communicator" tailored his platform in 1980 as a politically astute response to the hopes and fears of Americans stressed financially by the economic/financial "malaise" inflicted by the first two oil shocks, and humiliated by the defeat in Vietnam.

To understand Reaganomics you have to understand not only what it was, but also how it was sold, what its true purpose was and, finally, what results it produced. We have three decades of data to illuminate our way – a fair enough trial period by any standard.

What is Reaganomics?

The Reagan Revolution rested on three pillars:

1) Lower tax rates "across the board"
2) Less government regulation
3) Strong military "defense"

How was it sold?

1. **Lower tax rates**: Lower tax rates were proposed "across the board" in the interest of "fairness" and as a vehicle for economic stimulus. Reagan's promise of lower tax rates offered the appealing prospect of more jobs and more disposable income for a working-class electorate squeezed by prices rising faster than income and by mounting joblessness in the midst of a serious two-year, double-dip recession commencing in early 1980. Throughout most of the final year of the run-up to the election in November 1980, the talk was about the recession, the first installment in a double-dip contraction that would eventually push the unemployment rate to a peak of nearly 11 percent in late 1982, accompanied by ongoing double-digit inflation and disaster in the stock market. Reagan tapped into *fears* created by the economic turmoil in 1980 and *hopes* for recovery by promising that lower tax rates would spur economic growth and employment, even going so far as to call the enabling tax-reduction legislation "The Economic Recovery Tax Act of 1981." The benefits of economic revitalization would then "trickle down" from the rich to the rest, according to Reagan's supply-side economists. Estate and capital gains taxes were also lowered. Businesses also caught a tax break with accelerated depreciation.

2. **Less government regulation and spending**: Following the wave of deregulation by Ford (railroad reform) and Carter (airlines, railroads and trucking), Reagan continued deregulating buses, freight forwarding, shipping, telephones and to a lesser extent, finance. He overrode state regulations for motor carriers, partly rolled back environmental and worker safety regulations, and cut back on regulatory enforcement. Reagan promoted less regulation as a means of creating new jobs by "getting government out of the way" of the private sector so as to "unleash the productive potential of American business." Less government spending, although never implemented in the aggregate by Reagan, was an ideological corollary to the reduction in tax rates and Republican antipathy toward the civilian side of government.
3. **Strong defense**: As with the other two pillars, Reagan pitched a military buildup as a source of new DoD-related jobs. "Peace through strength," also meant to reassure Americans of the U.S. ability to counter the threat posed by the Soviet Union in what would prove to be the final stage of the Cold War.

What was the real purpose of Reaganomics?

The genial Gipper, proved to be a wolf in sheep's clothing. Reagan pitched each of Reaganomics' three main themes enticingly to working Americans as a source of new jobs and more disposable income at a time when the "misery index" – unemployment plus inflation – remained uncomfortably high because of the "malaise" created by the Second Oil Shock.

What Americans would discover over the course of the Reagan presidency, and again during G. W. Bush's reprise between 2001 and 2009, is that Reaganomics was and is a stalking horse for the most massive government-instigated upward redistribution of wealth since, let us say, the Spanish conquest of the Americas in the 16th century.

Lift up each plank of the flag-draped Reagan platform and underneath the populist veneer you will discover its primary purpose to serve the Republicans' wealthy "base" by a) shifting more of the tax burden from the wealthy to the middle classes while reducing their government benefits b) diminishing government power over corporations while increasing its power over the population c) maintaining high levels of Department of Defense spending on procurement to funnel public funds into the corporate treasuries of defense contractors and from there into the bank accounts of C-suite executives and shareholders.

To fully comprehend the source of our present predicament, it is necessary to understand the underlying methodology and lingering effects of Reagan's three-pronged campaign to enhance the wealth and power of the rich and powerful elite at the expense of the rest. While this statement may sound like opinion, it is amply substantiated by the facts.

1. **Lower tax rates:** Candidate Reagan's pitch for tax cuts "across the board" seemed fair enough in theory. In practice, however, President Reagan, in conjunction with a Democrat-controlled Congress passed legislation sharply reducing income, estate and capital gains taxes for the rich and to a lesser extent income taxes for the middle class while raising payroll taxes imposed mainly on working Americans. Reaganomics introduced the following tax changes:

    a. Reduced the 70 percent top income tax bracket to 28 percent – that's a 60 percent reduction in rich people's tax bills!
    b. Cut the tax rate from 50 percent to 33 percent for upper-middle-class taxpayers earning between $72,000 to $150,000 – a reduction of 34 percent, proportionately about half the tax relief provided the top-tier taxpayers.
    c. Cut the bottom rate initially from 14 percent down to 11 percent but raised it later to 15 percent, resulting in *a net tax increase for the poor* from what was supposed to be Reagan's "across-the-board" tax cuts!

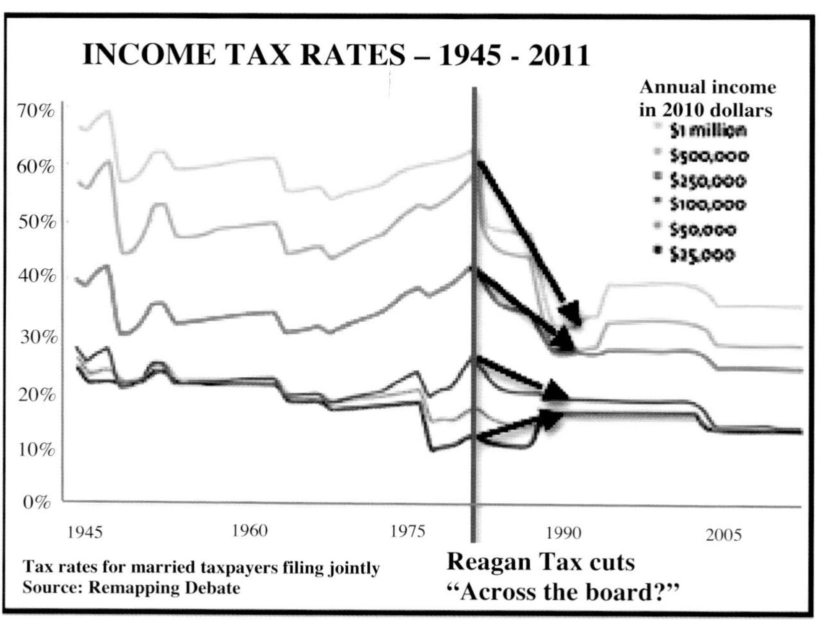

Tax rates for married taxpayers filing jointly
Source: Remapping Debate

d. Increased the tax burden on the working classes in other insidious ways, such as disallowing the interest deduction for credit card and other consumer debt -- mainly a working-class phenomenon (since at the rich tend not to borrow for consumer purchases) -- meaning the working classes pay more taxes than before.
e. Eliminated public offerings of tax shelters after the middle class had the audacity to avail themselves of tax dodges and deferrals previously available only to the very wealthy (though still leaving the wealthy the option to continue sheltering taxes with private offerings with large minimum investment requirements, open only to very affluent "qualified investors.")
f. Increased payroll taxes for Social Security (FICA) and Medicare from 9.3 percent (employer/employee contribution) to 15 percent, a 61 percent increase – another reverse-Robin Hood tax policy.
   - FICA taxes fall proportionately heaviest on working Americans who pay the tax on all their income, whereas those currently earning more than $110,100 stop paying the tax above that level (in 2012). For the generic CEO paid $10 million/year, the tax dwindles into insignificance (0.18 percent vs. 15 percent for those earning less than $110,100 in 2012).
   - The increase in payroll taxes was enacted to create surpluses in the Social Security and Medicare Trust Funds to be set aside to pay for predictable increased outlays when the large Baby-Boom generation retired, beginning in 2010. *However, in a practice dating back to the Johnson administration, rather than setting aside the surpluses, Congress routinely spent them on non-Trust-related outlays, like wars, tax cuts and routine government expenses, in effect insidiously shifting to the working-classes an ever-greater portion of the current costs of carrying government while burdening future generations with the retirement costs of their parents and grandparents.*
g. Cut long-term capital gains tax rates from 40 percent to 20 percent (later raised to 28 percent), thereby further easing the tax burden on the wealthy, who tend to realize the bulk of capital gains. Ditto estate taxes.
h. Boosted corporate profits by increasing depreciation deductions. More money for dividends and C-suite compensation.

2. **Smaller government, less regulation:** Reagan sold this idea to the electorate as a means of promoting job creation by lowering corporate

costs and giving management a freer hand in running their businesses so as to increase productivity and investment – as previously mentioned, "unleashing the productive potential of American business" was the operative phrase.

a. The connection between less regulation and more jobs is debatable. However, any creation of new jobs was incidental to the underlying motivation for less regulation, namely to boost corporate profits by reducing the costs of regulated activities, like pollution control; worker safety; responsible and fair dealings with consumers, borrowers and investors. Given the prevailing formulas for distributing corporate revenues, the main beneficiaries of demonstrably higher corporate profits from deregulation were shareholders and C-suite executives whose compensation skyrocketed in the three decades since Reaganomics was introduced. For eye-opening graphs showing how since Reagan, gains in income have been captured by the wealthy, while the middle class and the poor have essentially marked time, as shown by the following graph prepared by the Center on Budget and Policy Priorities and reproduced with the Center's permission. Imagine, no real pay increase for the middle class in more than 3 decades! http://www.cbpp.org/cms/index.cfm?fa=view&id=3629.

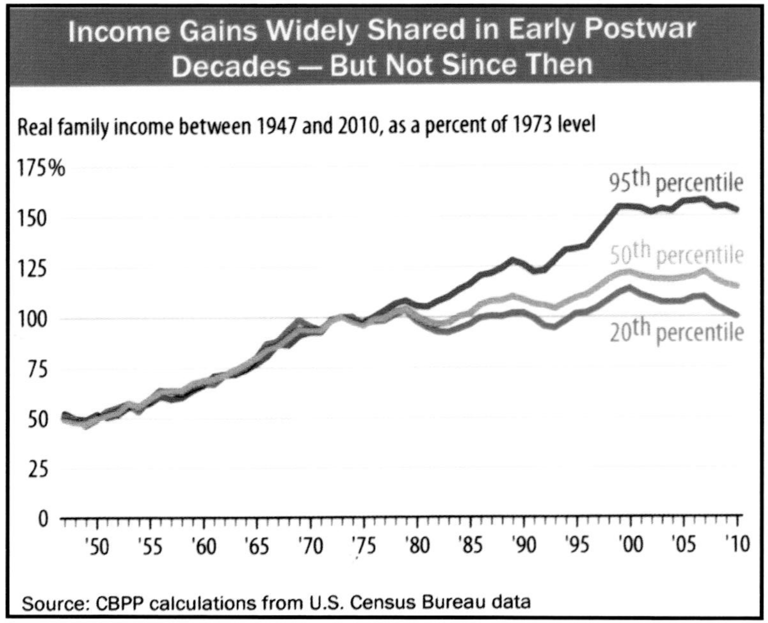

b. The various acts deregulating the savings and loan industry in the early 1980s best illustrate the downside of deregulation during the Reagan era. The acts raised Federal Deposit Insurance guarantees and allowed thrifts to offer a wider array of savings products while greatly expanding their lending authority with minimal regulatory oversight. Consequently, the resulting flood of deposits into the thrifts overwhelmed their capacity to make sound loans, prompting not only a real estate bubble, but also the eventual lowering of lending standards (shades of the 2000s). The bubble collapsed into a full-blown credit crisis when dubious loans soured, prompting a massive federal takeover of thrift institutions by the Federal Deposit Insurance Corporation and Resolution Trust Corporation, ably captained by the late Bill Seidman, one of the most competent, sensible, personable bureaucrats ever to set foot in Washington. Seidman asserted that *fraud had played a role in more than half the failed institutions* taken over by the government, prompting the question: How do you eliminate fraud in financial institutions? Those on the right say, rather unconvincingly, given the evidence, "let the free market handle it" (with a big assist from the judiciary). The left says, fraud flourishes in free markets; therefore, regulate intelligently and prevent abuses from happening. The S&L crisis, costing the taxpayers roughly $200 billion, foreshadowed the far greater financial Panic of 2008 resulting with much the same dynamic: too much money to lend, too much greed, too many cut corners, too little regulatory supervision of lending practices. "Those who cannot remember the past are condemned to repeat it." (Santayana) How true.

3. **Strong defense**: Reagan's advocacy of growth in military spending went beyond mere job creation to something far more visceral, and, therefore, essential to his political success: fear and wounded pride within the electorate. Reagan's pitch for military spending resonated with that segment of Americans still smarting from the humiliation of the U.S. defeat in Vietnam, blamed on "Peaceniks," "Jane-Fonda liberals," and left-leaning allies in Congress who had "stabbed the military in the back" by pressuring Johnson and Nixon to "bug out" and later passing the War Powers Act (reaffirming Congress' primacy in matters of war and peace), and refusing President Ford's request for $722 million to support the Thieu regime after American troops had been withdrawn. (This appeal to fear and wounded pride is the same

political dynamic harnessed by Hitler half a century earlier following Germany's humiliating defeat in World War I and subsequent forced disarmament – and, yes, I know Hitler comparisons have become cliché, but that does not diminish their relevance. The tragedy of the twentieth century German experience, occurring within a culture at the apex of civilization, affords history's most profound cautionary tale about doomsday politics.)

Reagan discovered this resonance when campaigning against Ford for the Republican nomination in 1976, opposing the "giveaway" of the Panama Canal. ("We bought it, we paid for it, we built it, and we intend to keep it!" – a guaranteed jingoistic applause line trumped, some might say, by fellow Californian Senator S. I. Hayakawa's sarcastic quip during the Senate debate on the Canal: "Of course we should keep it. After all, we stole it fair and square.") Consequently, Reagan played on the electorate's fears by wildly exaggerating the supposed threats (implied by the return of the Panama Canal, of the military prowess of the Soviets and, absurdly, of the Marxist-Leninist governments of Nicaragua and Grenada, a member of the British Commonwealth), and allayed such fears while soothing wounded pride by promising "Peace through strength," doubling the Defense Department's budget, including the failure-prone "Star Wars" intercontinental ballistic missile defense.

Such fears were exacerbated by the Soviet invasion of Afghanistan in 1979, followed by the Soviet military occupation spanning Reagan's time in office. The Iranian takeover of the U.S. embassy in Tehran and the failed attempt to rescue the hostages during Carter's watch rekindled smoldering resentments against being "pushed around," leading conservatives to believe Reagan's hard line on military preparedness prompted the release of the hostages the instant he was sworn in, rather than the Iranians' desire to humiliate Carter.

It's hard to say whether Reagan truly believed in his appeal to emotion, or whether he was, as Gore Vidal put it with characteristic venom, "The best cue-card reader they could find."

We do know that doubling the Department of Defense budget during the Reagan years did, in fact, mean jobs in defense-related industries. However, these too were incidental to the enhancement of corporate profits, dividends and C-suite compensation, and the "acquisition of unwarranted influence . . . by the military-industrial complex. . . [and] the potential for the disastrous rise of misplaced power" at the heart of the Reagan Revolution on behalf of the Republican base.

Reagan's evisceration of union power merits mention (although not inclusion in the "3 pillars"), inasmuch as it dovetails with the primary thrust of Reaganomics' favoring corporations as the funnel for the upward distribution of income and wealth. In August of 1981, when confronted by a strike by the Professional Air Traffic Controllers' (PATCO) Union, Reagan fired 90 percent of the nation's air traffic controllers who failed to heed the administration's ultimatum to return to work within 48 hours or be fired. This show of anti-union resolve – mirroring Margaret Thatcher's uncompromising stand against miners' and garbage collectors' unions in the U.K. – broke the back of the union and, according to Alan Greenspan, "gave weight to the legal right of private employers, previously not fully exercised, to use their own discretion to both hire and discharge workers." Reagan's successful stand against PATCO furthered the ongoing decline of unions as the sole remaining organized counterweight to corporate political influence. (Wisconsin's Governor Walker's attempt to emulate this feature of Reaganomics three decades later would spark what arguably may be called the beginning of a liberal/progressive counter-revolution against Reaganomics.)

To be sure, after bottoming in December 1982, nearly two years after Reagan took office, the U.S. economy prospered for the remainder of his presidency: gross domestic product surged, averaging 3.56 percent growth during the Reagan years; 16 million new jobs were added overall (an average of 2 million per year); unemployment declined to 5 percent (according to the Federal Reserve Bank of St. Louis). Republicans routinely attribute the improvement to Reaganomics, especially the Reagan tax cuts.

However, while tax policy unquestionably impacts the distribution of wealth, its impact on overall economic growth tends to be vastly overstated. As we shall see, the raising of tax rates during the Bush 41 administration did not slow the economy, nor did even higher tax rates during the Clinton administration dampen economic growth and job creation, which exceeded that experienced during the Reagan years. Conversely, the lowering of tax rates during the G. W. Bush administration and the extension of those low rates during the Obama administration failed to rouse the economy from lethargic growth. Moreover, to the extent that Reagan's tax reductions for the wealthy were offset by payroll tax increases on the working class, the dampening effect of the latter largely negated the stimulus of the former, according to supply-side dogma. No matter. With Reagan begins the era of divergence between dogma and reality, to be perfected later by Karl Rove during the Bush 43 administration.

Accordingly, it makes more sense to attribute Reagan-era prosperity to the following macro-economic factors:

- Recovery from a deep economic trough (11 percent unemployment and 72 percent total industry capacity utilization in 1982) left lots of slack in the economy and, therefore, room to grow briskly before running into inflationary capacity constraints.

- A collapse in oil prices in 1986 engineered by the Fed, dispelling inflation and increasing household and business spendable cash to drive economic growth with cheap fuel and lowered interest rates. By my calculation, cheap oil was the dominant factor stimulating the economy in the late 1980s, just as expensive oil was the primary cause of the economic and financial "malaise" in the 1970s.
- Strong monetary stimulus from the Fed after oil prices collapsed, made possible by the previous two factors driving economic growth without fear of re-igniting inflation, at least in the early stages of recovery.
- Much lower levels of household debt: In the early 1980s, household debt was 45 percent of GDP. In 2008, it was 110 percent, meaning (unlike 2008) consumers in the 1980s had unused debt capacity allowing them to borrow and spend in response to Fed-lowered interest rates.
- The beginnings of the Electronic Revolution in the early 1980s when personal computers became ubiquitous, stimulating capital spending and improving productivity.

Nevertheless, in a classic case of "*post-hoc, ergo propter hoc*,"[7] Reagan Republicans became unalterably convinced of an inverse correlation between changes in tax rates and economic growth, even to the point of asserting that tax cuts would "pay for themselves" (a contention Alan Greenspan and ample factual evidence would later rebut). This article of faith reached the point where raising taxes on the wealthy jeopardized one's chances for re-election (as for G.H.W. Bush) and pledging tax cuts became a Republican prerequisite to run for office (as for G.W. Bush and, most recently, Mitt Romney).

One of the most Machiavellian components of Reaganomics was the demonization of the U.S. Government: "Government is not the *solution* to the problem; government *is* the problem," said Ronald Reagan, teeing up his proposals to both reduce and reform government (neither of which he accomplished). While "limited government" sounds appealing in principle, in practice, the demonization of government served three critical purposes essential to the Reagan Revolution: 1) It supported the supply-side argument for lower taxes to "starve the beast," legitimizing cuts in government benefits and less regulation and 2) It misdirected the electorate's anger toward "faceless bureaucrats in Washington" and away from the rich ruling

---

[7] ***Post hoc ergo propter hoc***, Latin for "after this, therefore because of this," is a logical fallacy (of the questionable cause variety) that states, "Since that event *followed* this one, that event must have been *caused* by this one." It is often shortened to simply *post hoc* and is also sometimes referred to as false cause, coincidental correlation, or correlation not causation. (Wikipedia)

elite who promoted and alone stood to benefit from Reaganomics. 3) It undermined public support for public employee unions, one of the few remaining bastions of organized labor left to oppose corporate political influence.

Right-wing demonization of government has been wildly inconsistent -- giving Defense a free pass and relying on government to enforce the right-wing social agenda, like criminalizing street narcotics, prohibiting same-sex marriage, hindering women's access to abortion, and restricting stem-cell research. Maligning government also sharpened the political polarization, ill will and incivility between left and right (presently embodied in the Occupy Wall Street and Tea Party movements and their corresponding allies in Congress). In a consummate act of hypocrisy, the same folks trumpeting free-markets and insisting "government is the problem" would elbow their way to the head of the line for government handouts when the wheels came off the wagon in 2008, as we will see.

To be fair, the left does its share of demonizing government too, though in opposite ways. Whereas the right demonizes the safety-net/social spending side of government and enthusiastically supports the military/security/law-enforcement side, the left reveres the former and demonizes the latter. The appropriate resolution of these conflicting perceptions of government, I suggest, lies in avoiding extremes on both sides of government, as I will discuss at greater length in Chapter 8.

Despite his distaste for big government and lip service paid to fiscal conservatism, Reagan made big government bigger, never submitted a balanced budget, and piled up more national debt than had been accrued in all the United States' prior history, due precisely to pathologically low taxes on the wealthy and bloated defense budgets underpinning "peace through strength." The United States, once the world's largest creditor nation became the world's largest debtor nation during Reagan's watch, in large part to finance the Reagan deficits, thereby forfeiting American financial sovereignty. Reaganomics launched three decades of unprecedented upward-redistribution of income and wealth. The share of the growth in national income going to the top 10 percent of income earners shot up from an average of 35 percent in the post-war period before Reagan, to 87 percent during Reagan's watch. Conversely, the share of the growth in national income going to the remaining 90 percent of income earners fell from 65 percent to 13 percent. The ultimate consequences of this tectonic shift in class rewards would not become fully apparent for another 20 years, during most of the Bush 43 administration, when the growth in national income would be divided 98 percent for the top 10 percent of income earners, leaving only 2 percent for the rest. ***The seeds of wealth inequality sewn by Reaganomics would germinate under Bush 43, blossoming into***

the stinkweed of the financial and economic meltdown in 2008, as we shall see.

The G.H.W. Bush Years (1989-1993): President George Herbert Walker Bush navigated the transition between the old antagonist, the collapsed Soviet Union, and the new, unfriendly Muslim regimes. When Saddam Hussein invaded Kuwait in August of 1990, Bush announced, "This aggression will not stand." He then sent his able Secretary of State, James A. Baker, III, to round up a broad coalition consisting of 32 countries, including 7 members of the Arab League, and promptly kicked the Iraqis out. Needless to say, the protection of the world's oil lifeline in the Middle East figured prominently in the calculus of war.

In his book, *A World Transformed* (1998), Bush 41 explained why he did not invade Iraq and eliminate the Iraqi dictator:

> "Trying to eliminate Saddam . . . would have incurred incalculable human and political costs. Apprehending him was probably impossible. . . . We would have been forced to occupy Baghdad and, in effect, rule Iraq. The coalition would instantly have collapsed, the Arabs deserting it in anger and other allies pulling out as well. Under the circumstances there was no viable 'exit strategy' we could see, violating another of our principles. . . . Furthermore, we had been self-consciously trying to set a pattern for handling aggression in the post-Cold War world. Going in and occupying Iraq, thus unilaterally exceeding the United Nations' mandate, would have violated the precedent of international response to aggression that we hoped to establish. Had we gone the invasion route, the United States could conceivably still be an occupying power in a bitterly hostile land. It would have been a dramatically different – and perhaps barren – outcome."

Too bad his son, "Dubya," doesn't read books.

The Election of 1992: You would think G. H. W. Bush's re-election would have been a foregone conclusion given the euphoria surging from the collapse of the Soviet Union and Bush's quick victory in ejecting Saddam Hussein from Kuwait in the First Gulf War. But no.

Bush 41 inherited an economy in January 1989 operating at full tilt and on the verge of overheating, pushing inflation up to a worrisome 5 percent. Bush's major international challenge, the First Gulf War, produced a mini-oil shock when Saddam Hussein invaded Kuwait in August 1990.

War fear and the Kuwaiti oil cutoff spiked oil prices briefly from $20 to $37/barrel, pushing inflation up even further to 8 percent, enough to spook the stock market and tip the economy into a six-month recession ending around the same time as the war did, in March 1991.

The recession ending in March 1991 and a weak recovery for the remaining three quarters of 1991 (real GDP growth 2.7, 1.7 and 1.6 percent, respectively) pushed unemployment up as high as 7.3 percent in the year leading up to the 2002 presidential election. Consequently, the economy dominated the political discourse, to William Jefferson Clinton's advantage, giving the Democrats campaign a simple, devastatingly effective slogan: "It's the economy, stupid."

By rights, "It's the economy, stupid," should have lost its sting in the run-up to the election in 1992, since real GDP growth picked up to a very respectable 4.5, 4.3 and 4.2 percent, respectively, during the first three quarters of 1992. However, despite strong economic growth in the months leading up to the November 1992 elections, unemployment remained stubbornly high, between 7.3 and 7.8 percent, because of an unusual surge in productivity during the first three quarters (7.8, 2.6 and 4.1 percent, respectively, compared to rates ranging between 1 and 2.1 percent in the three preceding years). In short, productivity gains associated with the blooming high-tech revolution produced the strong growth in GDP without the need for businesses to add employees.

GDP numbers are reported quarterly, whereas unemployment numbers are reported every month. So every month the Clinton campaign had fresh ammunition in the unemployment numbers with which to assail Bush. For its part, the Bush campaign countered once a quarter, saying GDP growth was strong – to no avail, since the reality of unemployment is stronger than the abstraction of GDP in the minds of voters.

Bush also faced an uphill climb due to resistance within the Republican base. The base objected to some of the laws Bush 41 signed, viewed as liberal and not in keeping with the "government-is-the-problem" trope: The Americans with Disabilities Act of 1990 (one of the most pro-civil rights bills in decades), increased federal spending for childcare and advanced technology research, the reauthorization of the Clean Air Act, the Immigration Act of 1990 (increasing legal immigration by 40 percent), and a temporary ban on the import of certain semiautomatic rifles (producing a hissy fit within the National Rifle Association). Bush also nominated David Souter to the U.S. Supreme Court. Souter seemed like a reliably conservative choice, but turned out to be a stealth-liberal, adding to the base's disenchantment with the President. Bush successfully waged a brief war in the Gulf, promptly achieving limited objectives and then withdrawing. That too did not sit well with MITP-complex Republicans who thrive on Long Wars. However, Bush's unforgivable sin was to raise tax rates for the wealthy (from a top rate of 28 to 31 percent) after having campaigned on the slogan, "Read my lips: No new taxes." Bush did the sensible and honorable thing in raising taxes to narrow the systemic budget deficits introduced by Reagan's tax cuts, appropriately dubbed "Voodoo Economics," by Bush himself during the Republican primaries in 1980. The rich and powerful elite never forgave him, making him the poster boy for what happens to rogue Republicans who attempt to balance the budget on the backs of the base – a point recently publicly reiterated by Grover Norquist, instigator of the Republican congressional pledge never to raise taxes.

The nail in the coffin of Mr. Bush's re-election ambitions, however, came from Ross Perot, who ran the most successful third-party candidacy since Teddy Roosevelt's Bull Moose run in 1912. While he won no electoral votes, Perot garnered 18.9 percent of the popular vote, a majority of which would otherwise have probably voted for Bush. Clinton won with 43 percent of the vote, with G. H. W. Bush trailing at 37.4 percent.

The Clinton Years (1993-2001): Bill Clinton, former governor of Arkansas, became U.S. President on January 20, 1993 and had the privilege and good fortune, history may say, of presiding over the United States of America at its peak, relatively speaking. The Clinton years coincided with a tectonic economic shift: the rise to dominance of electronic technology.

Megacycles

Throughout history, changes in dominant forms of energy and technology have combined to create what I call economic Megacycles, such as the Industrial Revolution, combining mechanical technology and coal, and what I call the Petro-Industrial Revolution (usually referred to as the "Second Industrial Revolution"), combining electro-mechanical technology and oil. Each of these Megacycles produced radical changes in occupations, habitat, modes of transport, diet, lifestyle, politics. In short, almost every facet of human existence changes with each Megacycle.

(See: www.cassandra-chronicles.com/Presentations/megacycles.ppt)

Historically, Megacycles have progressed in three phases:

I. Rapid economic growth and job creation to adapt to the new economic paradigm, overinvestment in the new technology and energy, and euphoria creating a bubble in stock prices.
II. Stock market crashes undermining investor confidence and investment, resulting in a Great Depression, skyrocketing unemployment and political discontent, followed by war.

III. Postwar, peace and prosperity, based on mature growth of the new energy-technology combination, and relatively benign economic and investment cycles trending upward in an extended period of generally good times – until the next Megacycle comes along.

In the 1990s, we enjoyed the fruits of the first phase of a new Megacycle, the Electronic/High-Tech Revolution, completing the shift in dominance from electromagnetic technology to electronic technology (begun in the 1950s with the introduction of transistors), giving rise to the personal computer, the Internet, smart cell phones, iPods, flat-screen TVs, GPS navigational systems and myriad other commonplace electronic devices and services we never imagined back in the sixties. Burgeoning biotechnology, nano-technology and other forms of technology complemented the Electronic/High-Tech Revolution. However, since oil remains the dominant form of energy, the current Megacycle must be considered only partially realized, awaiting the development of substitutes for hydrocarbons to complete the transformation.

Even without a shift to a new energy source, during the 1990s the first phase of the current Megacycle unfolded in typical form with rapid economic growth, surging investment in the new technologies, full employment, investment euphoria ("This time it's different!") and soaring stock prices, particularly in the new technology. The euphoria typical of the first phase, as it always has, led to overinvestment in new technology and a stock market bubble, setting up the second phase of the Megacycle, presided over by G. W. Bush (further described below) in which the bubble bursts, stock markets crash, the economy stumbles *twice*,[8] unemployment soars and civil unrest is accompanied or followed by war.

President Clinton's first order of business was to pass a stimulus package – in reality, not big enough to make much of a difference, but in the *post-hoc, ergo propter hoc* Washington mindset, a plausible political ploy to take credit for the ensuing burst of economic growth, soaring stock prices and sound fiscal policy. Naturally, no Republicans voted for it. Nor did any Republicans vote for Clinton's 1993 tax increase, which, among other things repealed the cap on Medicare taxes, raised transportation fuel taxes by 4.3 cents a gallon, extended limits on itemized deductions and, to the great consternation of the rich, raised the top income tax rate from 31 percent to just under 40 percent. "The largest tax increase in history," according to horrified supply-siders, would send the economy into a tailspin, creating huge federal deficits. Instead, up-ending supply-side theory, the economy boomed ("the longest period of peacetime expansion in American history"), with GDP expanding at a brisk 3.73 percent rate, creating 17.8 million jobs

---

[8] As described by Nikolai Kondratieff in "The Major Economic Cycles" (1925)

(an average of 2.2 million per year) – numbers narrowly exceeding those of the Reagan administration and those of both Bush administrations by a substantial margin. Economic stimulus during the Clinton years resulted mainly from the tech revolution and the accompanying surge in stock prices in the late 1990s, lowering the cost of capital for business investment; moderate oil prices; accommodative monetary policy; and abundant supplies of cheap foreign capital from trading partners recycling their trade surpluses back into the American economy. The combination of a vibrant economy and higher tax rates produced a surge in federal revenues, while the "peace dividend" from the end of the Cold War restrained the growth in federal spending. Consequently, Clinton's fiscal policy produced the very conditions Reaganomics promised but failed to deliver: not only a balanced budget within a few years, but also substantial surpluses for the last four Clinton budget years. During the Clinton years we also witnessed a marginally more even-handed distribution of the *growth* in national income with the top 10 percent of income earners garnering 70 percent as compared to 87 percent and 98 percent, respectively, under Reagan and G.W. Bush.[9]

Early in his presidency, Clinton signed groundbreaking legislation including the Family and Medical Leave Act of 1993, the Brady Handgun Violence Prevention Act, the Violent Crime Control and Law Enforcement Act (providing funding for 100,000 new police officers, prison expansion and crime prevention programs), and the Communications Assistance for Law Enforcement Act (enhancing the ability of law enforcement agencies to monitor all telephone, broadband Internet and VoIP traffic in real time).

Mid-term elections 1994, Republican Congress: Before the robust economic results during the Clinton presidency were known, Republicans succeeded in alarming the electorate – needlessly as it turned out – about the potential consequences of the Clinton tax increase. There is nothing quite like a tax increase to mobilize the Republican base to recycle Reaganomics. Sparked in part by Newt Gingrich's "Contract with America," (http://en.wikipedia.org/wiki/Contract_with_America) drawn largely from Reagan's 1985 State of the Union Address and fueled also by the residue of Reagan's "government-is-the-problem" rhetoric, a growing religious conservative movement, and Clinton's failed attempt to provide universal health care, Republicans gained control of both houses of Congress for the first time since 1954 during the Eisenhower administration.

Divided government during the Clinton administration proved to be surprisingly productive, forcing Clinton to "triangulate," seeking common ground to pass legislation, much of it right-leaning. President Clinton and

---

9 http://stateofworkingamerica.org/who-gains/#/?start=1993&end=2000

Speaker Gingrich developed a working relationship resulting in significant legislation including: the Lobbying Disclosure Act of 1995 (requiring greater accountability, including registration, in federal lobbying practices), the Interstate Commerce Commission Termination Act (abolishing the ICC and replacing it with the Surface Transportation Board), the Telecommunications Act of 1996 (allowing media cross-ownership, deregulation of the broadcasting market), the Antiterrorism and Effective Death Penalty Act of 1996 (modifying the law of *habeas corpus*, and limiting the appeals process for death-penalty sentences), the Small Business Job Protection Act of 1996 (giving tax breaks to small businesses and raising the minimum wage), the Health Insurance Portability and Accountability Act (protecting patient privacy and protecting health insurance coverage for workers when they change jobs), the Personal Responsibility and Work Opportunity Act (reforming welfare by giving states more autonomy over welfare delivery and reducing the federal government's responsibilities by placing time limits on welfare assistance, and increasing work requirements), the Defense of Marriage Act (a highly controversial act, pushed by the Religious Right, codifying the non-recognition of same-sex marriage for all federal purposes), the North American Free Trade Agreement (NAFTA), the "don't ask, don't tell" (tolerating gays in the military) initiative, the Taxpayer Relief Act of 1997 (a largely Republican-favored act reducing the capital gains tax from 28 to 20 percent, raising the estate tax exemption to $1 million, and exempting from taxation the profits on the sale of a personal residence up to $500,000 for married couples and $250,000 for individuals), the Securities Litigation Uniform Standards Act (lobbied for by Wall Street, restricting the use of class-action lawsuits in federal court), the Gramm-Leach-Bliley Act also known as the Financial Services Modernization Act of 1999 (another Republican initiative, heavily supported by bankers, repealing the Depression-era Glass-Steagall Act separating commercial from investment banking) and the Commodity Futures Modernization Act of 2000 (deregulating financial derivative products, also lobbied for by Wall Street). These last two acts were in large measure responsible for opening Pandora's box of Wall Street's excesses creating the Panic of 2008 and subsequent Great Recession.

With the Cold War over, President Clinton's foreign policy took on a regional character, dealing mostly with the ongoing confrontation between Muslims and the West:

- Mediation of secret negotiations between Israeli Prime Minister Yitzak Rabin and Palestine Liberation Organization Chairman Yasser Arafat culminating in the Oslo Accords in September 1993, allowing limited Palestinian self-rule in the Israeli-occupied West

Bank and Gaza Strip. As implementation of these peace initiatives stalled, Clinton mediated yet another agreement, the Wye River Memorandum, between Israeli Prime Minister Netanyahu and Yasser Arafat, calling on Israel to cede more West Bank territory and establishing a timetable for the establishment of a Palestinian state. Violence following the agreement prompted Netanyahu to backtrack and contributed to his replacement by Ehud Barak who supported the resumption of the peace process.

- A June 1993 cruise missile attack on the Iraqi Intelligence Services' command and control complex in Baghdad in retaliation for an assassination attempt on ex-President Bush while he was visiting Kuwait.
- A vain attempt to relieve the starvation menacing Somalia (a policy initiated by his predecessor), resolved by an ignominious withdrawal of troops in 1994, after the Battle of Mogadishu (of *Blackhawk Down* fame).
- Refusal to intervene in the genocidal 1994 war in Rwanda resulting in the killing of an estimated 500,000 to 1 million mostly Tutsi Rwandans. A belated attempt to relieve suffering in refugee camps by airdrops of food and supplies ended in October 1994.
- Ineffectual air attacks in Afghanistan (headquarters of al-Qaida) and Sudan (site of a pharmaceutical factory allegedly owned by al-Qaida) in retaliation for an al- Qaida attack on the U.S. embassies in Nairobi, Kenya and Dar es Salaam, Tanzania (further steps in the escalation of conflict between Radical Islam and the U.S.).
- Successful intervention in the Balkans through the use of air power against Serbs in 1995 to end the civil war between them and Bosnians Muslims and Croats, formalized in the Dayton Peace Accords brokered by the U.S..
- Another NATO air campaign in the Balkans in 1999 succeeded in preventing former-Yugoslavian Serbs from carrying out brutal ethnic cleansing of Muslims in Kosovo.
- A wavering policy toward Iran alternating between the stick (trade sanctions) and the carrot, (in effect apologizing for the 1953 CIA-assisted coup deposing Mohammed Mossadegh and installing Shah Reza Pahlavi), easing restrictions on U.S. sales of food and medical supplies while allowing the purchase of certain Iranian goods, and attempting, unsuccessfully in the end, to establish a diplomatic dialogue.
- A conciliatory policy toward China, resulting in permanent normal trade relations.

Sadly, lacking self-control, good judgment and a sense of his place in history, Clinton tarnished an otherwise impressive legacy with a tawdry interlude with a young intern, Monica Lewinsky, about which he lied, resulting in his impeachment by Republicans in the House of Representatives bent on his political destruction. Cooler heads prevailed in the Senate and he was not convicted.

Chapter 6: The G.W. Bush years (2001-2009) – Reaganomics *redux*. How Reaganomics caused the Panic of 2008 and Great Recession. A final reckoning for Reaganomics

The Bush 43 administration began with raging controversy over the legitimacy of his election in 2000; suffered the disastrous consequences of intelligence failures on 9/11 and in Iraq; launched two counterproductive, expensive and unfunded Long Wars; passed The Patriot Act, vastly expanding government's powers of surveillance, arrest and imprisonment without trial, abrogating many freedoms enshrined in the Constitution and Bill of Rights; practiced torture; unilaterally withdrew from a number of international treaties, notably the Kyoto Protocol on global warming; fumbled recovery from the Hurricane Katrina disaster in New Orleans. In addition, the younger Bush reinstituted Reaganomics, thereby exacerbating inequality of wealth; shrinking household income after decades of steady growth and raising poverty rates after decades of decline; increasing by 6 million the number of Americans without health insurance; squandering a budget surplus inherited from the Clinton administration, thereby doubling the gross national debt with an additional $6.1 trillion; incurring massive deficits in the international balance of payments, vastly expanding U.S. foreign debt with corresponding loss of financial sovereignty; creating financial and economic disaster and a humiliating loss of U.S. prestige and respect on the world stage. Compared with 68 percent approval ratings for Reagan and Clinton, 54 percent for his father, 44 percent for Carter, Bush left office with an approval rating of 22 percent, the lowest rating for an outgoing president since Gallup began asking about presidential approval more than 70 years ago. Cheney's outgoing approval rating was 13 percent.

"Other than that, Mrs. Lincoln, how did you enjoy the play?"

From an economic and financial standpoint, Bush was unlucky, inheriting a dot-com "bubble economy" nearing the crest of the economic cycle as he took office in early 2001, marking the beginning of the turbulent Phase II of the Electronic Age Megacycle. (By now the recurring theme of fortunate or unfortunate timing as the primary factor in the success or failure of a presidency should be apparent.) The tech-led boom during the latter Clinton years had produced robust real GDP growth averaging close to 5 percent, pushing capacity utilization and employment near their upper limits, driving unemployment down to around 4 percent, generally regarded as "full employment." Strong oil demand from a vibrant economy began driving up oil prices. The combination of these factors began rekindling inflation from below 2 percent, regarded as acceptable, to an uncomfortable 3.5 percent in the run-up to the 2000 election, prodding the Fed to cool down the economy by raising short-term rates by about two points to 6.5 percent – all typical symptoms of an economy on the verge of a recession

As is typical in the first phase of a Megacycle, over-investment in new technology had produced a bubble known as the "Dot-Com Boom" during the Clinton administration. Technology stocks in particular became grossly overvalued – justified by financial pundits with the lethal phrase "This time it's different".

"Things couldn't be better," the pundits said at the turn of the millennium, to which I replied in my cautionary lectures and writings: "If things couldn't be better, then they are bound to get worse." (www.cyclical-investing.com)

And so they did, just as I predicted in 1999. The dot-com bubble burst in March 2000, followed by three years of declining stock prices in which the tech-heavy NASDAQ lost 75 percent of its value, wiping out the life savings of many who unwisely went along with "This time it's different." (Those who followed my advice to exit the stock market on January 4, 2000 and stay out until the spring of 2003 avoided this financial calamity.)

Bush 43, therefore, had the misfortune of taking over just two months before the economy peaked in March 2001, and then slumped into a mild 8-month recession, ameliorated by an accommodative Fed chaired by Alan Greenspan. The recession popped the dot-com bubble, prompting a 3-year stock-market meltdown, exacerbated by the turmoil of 9/11, revealing the beginning of the turbulent Phase II of the current Megacycle.

Bush's first priority was to reinstitute Reaganomics – cut taxes, undermine regulation, and increase defense spending. During the 2000 campaign, with the economy still booming, Bush pitched the tax cuts as returning to the people the surpluses generated by Clinton's higher tax rates (rather than leaving rates where they were and applying the surplus to the reduction of the national debt and providing for future retirement needs of the Baby Boomers, as Al Gore had prudently advocated). Bush positioned the cuts as a "refund" of "overpaid taxes." ("It's your money," he said.) However, by the time Bush got around to passing the tax cuts, the economy had soured, so he changed his pitch back to the supply-side rationale, arguing for tax cuts as a source of job-creating stimulus. It was a tax cut for all reasons – the main unspoken one being to "serve the base."

As with tax cuts, Bush offered wars for all reasons too. The war in Afghanistan was originally pitched as a campaign to bring the "perpetrators of 9/11 to justice." When that failed, the pretext then morphed into nation-building to prevent Afghanistan from becoming a "failed state" from which further attacks on the U.S. might be launched. "Fight them there so we don't have to fight them here," was proffered as another questionable rationale. He did much the same thing with the justification for the war in Iraq.

Initially it was pitched (without foundation) as reprisal against al-Qaida in Iraq, and as pre-empting Saddam Hussein from deploying the weapons of mass destruction George Tenet's CIA assured the administration Iraq possessed. When we later learned no such weapons existed, Bush shifted his rationale for the war variously as "establishing Iraq as a beacon for democracy in the region," or "regime change" and "nation-building" (despite having campaigned against nation-building in 2000).

What seems painfully clear from these examples is Bush's unswerving commitment to implement policies demanded by his wealthy "base," making up dubious, yet superficially plausible reasons for them as he went along. That such reasons were divorced from reality mattered not to an administration skilled in manufacturing its own self-serving, separate reality in a news terrarium crafted by its ministry of propaganda, Rupert Murdoch's Fox News and *The Wall Street Journal.*

Reaganomics under Bush 43 proved to be considerably less successful in reviving the economy than under President Reagan, debunking the efficacy of tax cuts as an effective economic stimulus. However, until the wheels came off the wagon in 2008, no doubt existed as to the efficacy of Bush's Reaganomics *redux* in feathering the nests of his wealthy "base." Not only did the wealthy enjoy significant cuts in income tax rates, they also benefited from reductions in estate taxes and in capital gains and qualified dividend tax rates from 20 to 15 percent. Since capital gains and dividends represent the bulk of income for the very wealthy, the top 400 households, for example, wound up paying effective federal tax rates of between 16 to 18.6 percent (according to the IRS), a far lesser rate than middle-income taxpayers. Mitt Romney paid an even lower rate of around 14 percent in 2010 and 2011, according to the two tax returns he released. The inequitable disparity between the cost of the federal government equaling about 25 percent of national income and Romney's contribution of only 14 percent of his income toward paying for a government essential to his accumulation of wealth did not appear to register with either him or his party.

The Bush tax cuts dovetailed effectively (for the rich) with Reagan's plan to shift income to the wealthy. Reagan shoveled income into the coffers of the wealthy by slashing their income tax rates and funneling profits into corporations by reducing regulations and pumping up defense contracts. The main beneficiaries of blossoming corporate profits were wealthy C-suite executives and shareholders, inasmuch as employee compensation remained largely stagnant in real terms. Having thus accumulated vast fortunes in the wake of the Reagan income tax cuts, the wealthy then turned to Bush 43 to cut their capital gains and dividend taxes so these fortunes could grow even more rapidly. And, capping off the process, to ensure these fortunes remained "in the family," Bush's wealthy base demanded that estate taxes be cut progressively to zero by 2010 with a proviso similar to the Bush income tax cuts, decreeing taxes would be restored to pre-Bush levels unless extended or made permanent. Obviously, the plan was to make the reductions permanent toward the end of the Bush administration, as Bush often urged Congress to do. The cuts for the wealthy were the main bone of contention as the nation approached the "fiscal cliff" on December 31, 2012. But I'm getting ahead of myself.

The Bush reprise of Reaganomics produced the effects desired by his base: the top 10 percent of income earners scooped up 98 percent of the growth in national income during the first 7 years of the Bush 43 administration, exacerbating inequality of not just income, but also wealth, with the richest 10 percent controlling a reported two-thirds of the nation's net worth. The top quintile owns about 84 percent of the nation's wealth, while the bottom 60 percent owns only about 5 percent – the most unequal distribution of all major advanced nations.

The Panic of 2008, followed by the trough of the Great Recession in early 2009, marked the ignominious end to the most economically disastrous presidency since Herbert Hoover. Inequality of income and wealth, coupled with inadequate regulatory supervision of the financial sector, both end-products of Reaganomics, eventually led to these calamities – a conclusion not generally understood, so I will explain.

How Reaganomics caused the Panic of 2008 and the Great Recession:

Fundamentally, Reaganomics makes the rich stupendously richer, the poor desperately poorer, and forces the middle class to mark time and, eventually, lose ground when the financial system implodes.

Three decades of data support this outcome unequivocally. For a scathing account of how the rich garnered virtually all the *growth* in national income from the time of Reagan on, see the "Guide to Statistics on Historical Trends in Income Inequality" by Chad Stone, Hannah Shaw, Danillo Trisi and Arloc Sherman at the Center on Budget and Policy Priorities.[10] Study the graphs below (reproduced with permission), in particular, revealing the following eye-opening statistics:

- Real family income between 1981 and 2010 increased:
  - For the 95th percentile: Nearly 50 percent
  - For the 50th percentile: About 5 percent
  - For the 20th percentile: Not at all. Nada. Zip.

[10] http://www.cbpp.org/cms/index.cfm?fa=view&id=3629.

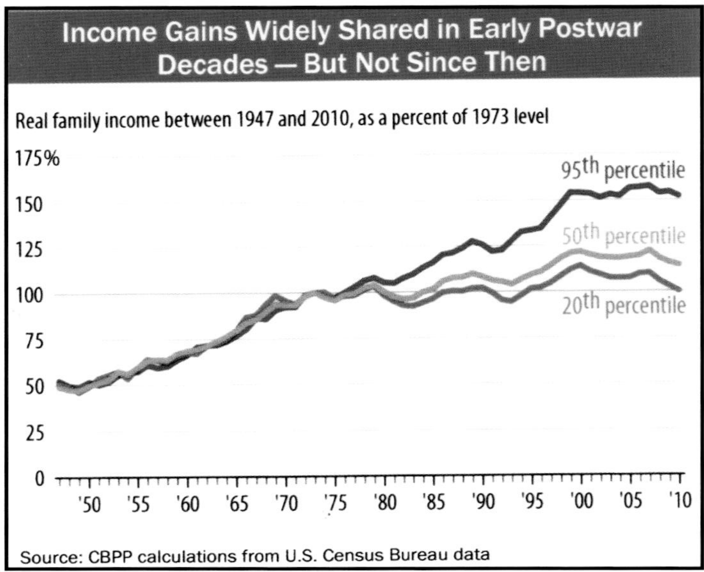

The data on income concentration and gains at the top clearly reveal a turnaround in favor of the rich beginning during the Reagan adminstratiion and accelerating during G. W. Bush's reprise of Reaganomics. The graph on the left, below, reveals an eroding share for the top 1 percent from the peak attained in 1929 (just before the stock market crash and Great Depression) until Reagan came to power in 1981, followed by rapid gains thereafter. The stock market crashes and ensuing economic contractions occurring at comparable peaks of income concentration in 1929 and 2008 provide persuasive clues as to the connection between concentration of income at the top and economic calamity. The graph on the right demonstrates how the income gains for the top 1 percent dwarf those of the rest of society.

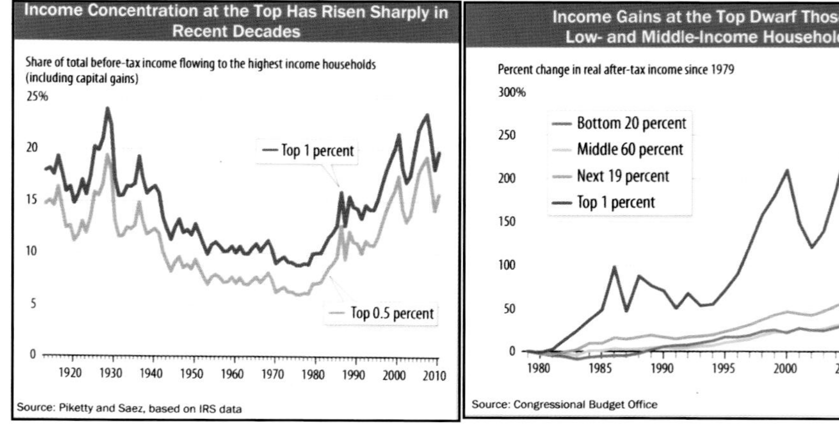

With the rich scooping up virtually all the fruits of economic growth, the stagnant middle class, and as many of the poor as were able, made up the shortfall between their aspirations for consumption and their stagnant "trickle-down" incomes by going into debt. To keep their American Dream alive, they borrowed from the rich who, after all, were the ones with plenty of money to lend, thanks to Reaganomics. Through the intermediation of the banks, the rich recycled their vast fortunes into the mortgage, student loan and credit card markets. (Foreigners and the Fed are also sources of credit, but for purposes of illustration I will concentrate on wealthy American lenders.)

The superabundance of cheap, available credit fueled the housing boom in the 1980s leading to the bubble in the 1990s. Homeowners used the growing equity in their homes as ATM machines to support consumption. They assumed what was then "common wisdom" (seconded by none other than then-Fed Chairman, Alan Greenspan), that houses always rise in value (the growing equity representing, in effect, a reliable source of savings), and tomorrow will be better than today, enabling mortgagers to pay off the debt. So households kept taking on what by 2007 became a crushing burden of debt.

The superabundance of lendable funds from the rich, from foreign creditors and from an over-accommodative Fed, eventually swamped the banking system resulting in the lowering of lending standards and, with regulators asleep, the over-extension of credit to un-creditworthy borrowers. "Sub-prime" borrowers, in Wall Street-speak, were inveigled by unscrupulous (and under-regulated) mortgage brokers into taking on variable-rate mortgages at a time of unusually low mortgage rates following the 2001 recession. In the trade, such loans were known as NINJA mortgages (**N**o **I**ncome, **N**o **J**ob, No **A**ssets), often obtained with fraudulent information supplied by unscrupulous mortgage brokers and based on over-inflated appraisals from accommodating appraisers. Banks processed the paperwork, collected processing fees and then (because of the repeal of Glass-Steagall) passed the loans on to their Wall Street confreres, indifferent to the quality (or lack thereof) of the loans they processed because they retained little, if any financial interest in them.

Lacking adequate regulatory restraint, Wall Street's Masters of the Universe "securitized" billions in dodgy debt, miraculously "sliced and diced" into "collateralized debt obligations" (CDOs) rated triple-A by clueless, compliant rating agencies on Wall Street's payroll, and then distributed to investors worldwide. Unconscionably, even as they sold what in time would be worthless paper to their best customers, Wall Street titans, like Goldman Sachs, placed bets ("short sales") enabling them to profit from the CDOs' anticipated subsequent decline in value.

When mortgage rates climbed back to normal levels, marginal, "sub-prime" borrowers could not make the increased payments, defaulted and started a cascade of foreclosures undermining the housing market, creating the Panic of 2008 and the ensuing Great Recession at home, and financial and economic turmoil globally from which the world economy is still struggling to recover.

In short, inequality of income and wealth prompts the middle class to borrow unwisely because they have too little money and the rich to lend imprudently because they have too much. The very existence of excessive household debt is incontrovertible evidence of income inequality, fueling bubbles in the stock and real estate markets, which eventually burst, creating cascading defaults, financial panic and economic entropy. Get it: extreme inequality of wealth = financial panic and recession, or worse.

Perhaps it should come as no surprise, then, that the levels of debt relative to GDP prevailing in 2008, just before the financial meltdown and the Great Recession, were almost identical to those prevailing in 1929, just before the stock market crash and Great Depression.

Bottom line: Inequality of wealth created by Reaganomics produced the Panic of 2008 and Great Recession.

Republican attempts to shift the blame:

Republican conservatives have been attempting to exonerate the Bush 43 Reaganomics policies as a causal factors in the 2008-2009 financial and economic meltdown ever since it began, spuriously laying the crisis on Democrats Barney Frank's and Chris Dodd's support in Congress for Fannie Mae and Freddie Mac in 2003 (despite their being *in the minority* at the time), Carter's passing the Community Reinvestment Act (CRA) (*31 years before the crisis!)*, and Clinton's passing the Gramm-Leach-Bliley Act repealing Glass-Steagall (notwithstanding that *the law's three sponsors were Republicans* at a time when Republicans controlled both houses of Congress). And while there is a slight grain of truth in these assertions, these right-wing palliatives are the equivalent of blaming the train for a derailment when the tracks were twisted.

As previously explained, the train went off the rails because of the inequality in the distribution of income and wealth created by Reaganomics. Deregulation allowing the issuance of NINJA adjustable-rate mortgages, the CRA's directive to lend locally, the Fed's manipulation of interest rates, the lack of a Glass-Steagall firewall, Wall Street's securitization of mortgages backed by Freddie and Fannie, the spurious AAA-ratings by the credit rating agencies all aggravated the 2008-2009 crisis, *but did not cause it.* The primary cause was inequality of income and wealth prompting the middle classes to borrow beyond their means, accommodated by obliging rich folks with lots of money to lend, thanks to Reaganomics. The surfeit of lendable funds as a result of this inequality created the housing and accompanying debt bubbles, which, when punctured when overburdened debtors defaulted, created the Panic of 2008 and Great Recession.

A final reckoning for Reaganomics:

With 30 years of hindsight since the introduction of Reaganomics as the dominant fiscal paradigm, we are now in a position to evaluate its ultimate results:

1. The rich became stupendously richer, the poor became desperately poorer, and the middle class marked time. Or as Bill Moyers put it recently: **". . .** our political and financial class [shifted] the benefits of the economy to the very top, while saddling us with greater debt and tearing new holes in the safety net." When liberals have the temerity to point out these inequities, the right, lacking a reasonable rebuttal, immediately resorts to misdirection by crying out "class warfare," as if the mere mention of class warfare in the land where "all men are created equal" should end the discussion. Billionaire Warren Buffet best expressed the truth of the matter: "There's class warfare, all right, but it's my class, the rich class, that's making war and we're winning." The following graph contained in a paper by Michael Norton (Harvard) and Dan Ariely (Duke) "Building a Better America – One Wealth Quintile at a Time" published in *Perspectives on Psychological Science* (2012) affords a stunning visual depiction of just how far out of whack the distribution of wealth has gotten, according to a recent survey of 5,000 Americans. The graph shows:

    a. What Americans believe the distribution of wealth *ought to be*: about 30 percent of wealth going to the top fifth, 10 percent to the bottom fifth and the remainder divided among the rest.
    b. What Americans *think* the distribution of wealth *is*: About 58 percent going to the top fifth, about 3 percent to the bottom fifth and the remainder divided among the rest.
    c. What the *actual* distribution of wealth is: About 84 percent concentrated in the top fifth, about 12 percent to the second fifth, about 4 percent to the third fifth, 0.2 percent to the fourth fifth and 0.1 percent for the bottom fifth.

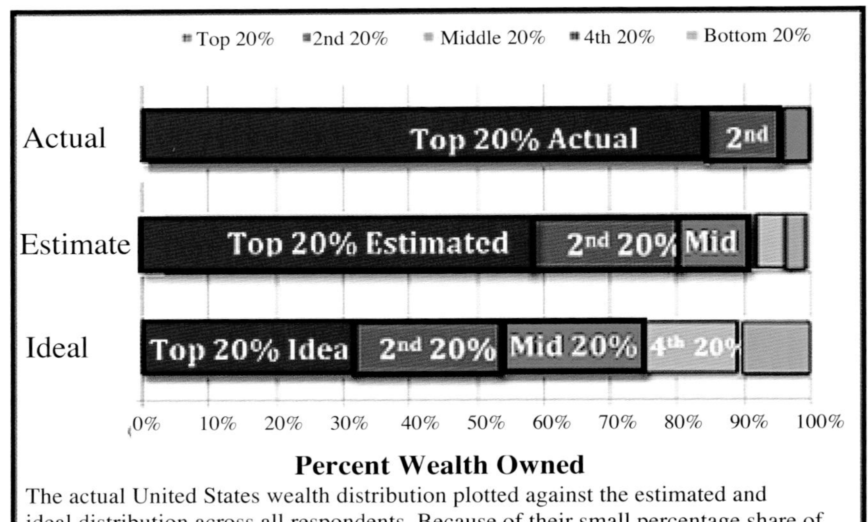

The actual United States wealth distribution plotted against the estimated and ideal distribution across all respondents. Because of their small percentage share of total wealth, both the 4th 20% value (0.2%) and the Bottom 20% value (0.1%) are not visible in the actual distribution.

d. This graph, (stunningly explained in a video gone viral at http://mashable.com/2013/03/02/wealth-inequality/) put in context along with other statistics cited elsewhere in these pages regarding the distribution of income and taxes reveal the absurdity of the right-wing handwringing about government "taking money from productive members of society and redistributing it to the undeserving poor." The distinguishing feature of economic policy for the past 30 years has been the unprecedented *upward* redistribution of wealth and income. So to the extent that government *borrows* money from the rich (since they refuse to give it up in taxes) and gives it to the poor it is because the rich have sucked the oxygen out of a system they have mismanaged, leaving government no alternative but to provide a measure of sustenance to the poor if we are to avoid massive homelessness and starvation in America. When Republicans deride Obama for being "the food-stamp President," they are really indicting their own policies giving rise to the increased need for food stamps. The bill for such support, I might add is, being passed on to "our children and our children's children" for whose benefit the ruling elite claim to be running the country.

2. As just explained, the mal-distribution of income and wealth prompted the over-extension of credit, creating the housing boom and bust at the core of the Panic of 2008 and Great Recession.
3. This same mal-distribution provided Wall Street, as custodians of the resulting wealth, with unprecedented power and influence over not only the allocation of scarce resources in the economy, but also over the political process as major political benfactors.
4. Wall Street lenders protected themselves against the consequences of anticipated loan defaults by successfully lobbying for revisions in the bankruptcy laws making it harder for working class individuals to wipe out debts through bankruptcy, and in the case of student loans, impossible to do so (!) – all in the name of avoiding "bankruptcy abuse." These same revisions gave claims of obligations due the wealthy (such as derivatives) seniority over claims due the working classes, like wages and retirement benefits. Corporations routinely shuck their obligations to retirees by underfunding retirement and health benefit plans (while declaring large bonuses for management), declaring bankruptcy (leaving retirees in the lurch or saddling taxpayers with the burden through the Pension Benefit Guaranty Corporation), and later resuming operations free of these contractual obligations. All perfectly legal, if blatantly immoral.
5. Popular discontent with the economic and financial calamities and inequities wrought by Reaganomics resulted in mounting civil unrest, creating potentially explosive political polarization as exemplified by the Occupy Wall Street movement (on the left, justifiably excoriating the "1 Percent") and the Tea Party movement (on the right, blaming the government, oblivious to the role of the 1 Percent in manipulating government for their own advantage to the detriment of middle-class Tea Party supporters).
6. The burden of taxation shifted significantly from the corporate rich to working Americans, as the proportion of the federal budget funded by corporate income taxes and corporate excise taxes dwindled, individual tax rates at the very top were cut by 50 percent, and payroll tax rates rose, further exacerbating inequality of wealth. From the time Reagan became President in 1981 until 2011 (an interval largely dominated by Reaganomics tax policies), the portion of the federal tax burden borne by payroll taxes jumped from 30.4 percent to 35 percent, while the burden borne by corporations in the form of corporate taxes and excise taxes fell from 17 percent to 11 percent. As previously explained, the payroll tax burden falls most heavily on working Americans, rather than the very rich who stop paying into Social Security on all income in

excess of $110,100 currently. Right-wing critics who profess to be alarmed by the fact that nearly 50 percent of taxpayers pay no income tax, and therefore supposedly have "no skin in the game," always fail to mention the substantial, regressive payroll and sales taxes they do pay.

7. Whereas they had enormous impact on the distribution of wealth, changes in tax rates proved to have little discernible effect on economic growth or employment,

President	GDP Growth Compound Annual Rate	New Jobs Added Millions	New Jobs Added Avg. Ann. Rate (millions)
Reagan	3.53%	16	2
G.H.W. Bush	1.97%	2.4	0.6
Clinton	3.73%	17.8	2.2
G. W. Bush	1.59%	3.6	0.45

Clinton, who raised both income and capital tax rates, enjoyed an interval of faster economic growth and job creation than the low-tax regimes of Reagan or Bush 43.

8. The government's Reaganomics-inspired propensity to overspend on defense and under-tax the wealthy created federal deficits that not only inhibited needed emergency spending after the Panic of 2008, but also forced the government to borrow heavily from foreigners. Once the world's foremost creditor nation, the U.S. became the world's largest debtor nation on Reagan's watch. Consequently, the U.S. has surrendered financial autonomy to foreign creditors, leaving the U.S. financial markets and economy vulnerable to external manipulation.
9. The means by which inequality of wealth is produced -- namely tax cuts favoring the rich, reduced regulation and costly Long Wars favoring corporations as funnels for income to the rich — contributed to huge federal deficits, starting with Reagan. At the end of the Carter administration, the national debt as a percent of gross domestic product stood at around 35 percent at the end of a long descent from the World War II peak around 120 percent. With the adoption of Reaganomics, the ratio began climbing during the Reagan administration reaching around 65 percent by the end of the

Bush 41 administration, then declined by almost 10 percentage points during the Clinton administration. With the return to Reaganomics during the Bush 43 administration, the ratio began climbing again to around 80 percent by the time Bush left office with the economy in shambles. The ratio has continued to climb during the Obama administration, forced to resort to modest emergency spending measures to rescue the economy without the ability to raise taxes or cut defense spending due to Republican refusal to consider tax increases or defense spending cuts of any sort.

10. Under-investment in social spending (following Reaganomics' "government-is-the-problem" line of reasoning) has caused America to slip into the company of the Third World in rankings of social progress and justice, in areas like education, health care, the prevalence of poverty, hunger, incarceration of its citizens, and inequality of wealth. Consequently, the U.S. now has the dubious distinction of exhibiting the greatest inequality of wealth of all major advanced nations. Conservatives say, in effect: "Let the free-markets guide and private enterprise provide," while liberals point out the private sector has failed to provide adequate health care, nutrition, education and income for unacceptably large segments of the population for more than 3 decades since Reagan began dismantling the Great Society. Whereas in 1962 the U.S. was indisputably "Number 1," now, fifty years later, by many measures it no longer is, as readily available statistics will attest – not an enviable record for a country priding itself on its "exceptionalism."
11. The accumulation of federal deficits, dating back to Reagan, expanded the national debt in the hands of the public to around $11 trillion ($16 trillion including inter-agency debt), an unjustifiable burden placed on younger generations, raising the specter of generational warfare, as my late classmate, Senator Paul Tsongas, warned years ago.
12. The U.S. remains unquestionably the world's most formidable military power, thanks to Reaganomics' commitment to "strong defense" and Bush 43's commitment to Long Wars, spending more on defense than the rest of the world combined. However, a significant portion of DoD spending is invested in expensive weaponry – nuclear submarines, aircraft carriers, bomber fleets, for example – suited to the Cold War, rather than the small-scale, asymmetrical threats faced by the U.S. today. Such threats are better met with action by special forces, black ops, intelligence-gathering services and both domestic and international law enforcement and forensic financial tracking, rather than full-scale armored

amphibious invasions and long military occupations wasting precious blood and treasure on both sides. The U.S. armaments industry also pumps tons of weapons into the hands of primitive people who exhibit a distressing propensity to use them – often against Americans – contributing to the escalating level of violence in the world today.

13. The U.S. response to the ongoing escalation of the current Long War of Religion has created conditions imperiling cherished American freedoms. In the name of the War on Terror against radical Muslims, Americans have forfeited a hefty chunk of the Constitution and Bill of Rights in exchange for the uncertain promise of security. The decks have been cleared for dictatorship.
14. Continuing escalation of conflict between historical religious antagonists presents a clear and present danger of irreversible escalation with unforeseeable, potentially catastrophic consequences.

Reaganomics and its aftermath:

On two occasions, Ronald Reagan publicly cited a famous quote, originating not long after the United States established its democracy, (variously attributed to Prof. Alexander Tytler (Scottish-born British academic), Benjamin Disraeli, Alexis de Tocqueville and others): "A democracy cannot exist as a permanent form of government. It can only exist until the voters discover that they can vote themselves largesse from the public treasury. From that moment on, the majority always votes for the candidates promising the most benefits from the public treasury with the result that a democracy always collapses over loose fiscal policy, always followed by a dictatorship." (Reagan omitted "then a monarchy.")

In using the quote, Reagan intended to bolster his case for smaller government by warning of the dangers of "largesse from the public treasury" being expended on the majority of voters at their insistence. Ironically, the danger of "democracy [collapsing] over loose fiscal policy" has materialized not so much from the public voting itself "largesse," as from the ruling elite suborning the democratic process for its own benefit with tax cuts, lax regulation and bountiful defense spending. The truth of this assertion is clearly evident in the data on distribution of wealth and income. For the past 30 years, ever since Reagan sold the electorate on Voodoo Economics, the rich have been the only ones benefiting from economic growth, getting stupendously richer while the poor have grown desperately poorer and the middle class, beset since 2008 by collapsing house prices, unsustainable amounts of debt, high unemployment and stagnant wages, has lost ground.

In effect, Reaganomics painted the U.S. government into a corner: By disproportionately favoring the rich at the expense of the rest, Reaganomics created the preconditions for an economic meltdown, as previously explained, while concurrently pumping up the federal debt by increasing defense spending while reducing taxes – a formula repeated twelve years later by G.W. Bush.

When the economy then crumbled, consumers were forced to trim spending. The Obama administration attempted to fill in the resulting void in demand with emergency government spending with a modest stimulus package totaling just over 5 percent of GDP spread over 2 years. The emergency spending was intended to supplant flagging consumer demand so as to provide incentives for business to hire and invest. Coupled with the natural resiliency of the American economy, the modest fiscal stimulus managed to reverse the economic slump, generating lackluster growth in GDP and employment, reducing the unemployment rate from around 10 percent to a still-troubling 7.8 percent recently.

Going forward, the Obama administration has been thrust on to the horns of a dilemma, aptly captured by former Obama economic advisor, Lawrence Summers in *The Financial Times*, October 14, 2012:

> While there is agreement on the need for more growth and job creation in the short run and on containing the accumulation of debt in the long run, there are deep differences of opinion both within and across countries as to how this can be accomplished. What might be labelled the 'orthodox view' attributes much of our current difficulty to excess borrowing by the public and private sectors, emphasises the need to contain debt, puts a premium on credibly austere fiscal and monetary policies, and stresses the need for long-term structural measures rather than short-term demand-oriented steps to promote growth.
>
> The alternative 'demand support view' also recognises the need to contain debt accumulation and avoid high inflation, but it pushes for steps to increase demand in the short run as a means of jump-starting economic growth and setting off a virtuous circle in which income growth, job creation and financial strengthening are mutually reinforcing. International economic dialogue has vacillated between these two viewpoints in recent years. [With due allowance for British spelling.]

Reducing the national debt by curtailing spending -- "austerity" -- risks economic relapse and rising unemployment, as we are seeing in Europe. Increasing emergency spending to spur the economy and create jobs

– "stimulus" -- increases the national debt and eventually risks either inflation if the debt is monetized by the Fed, or severe economic contraction and default if it is not. Therein lies the dilemma. There is no free lunch.

Bottom line: Reaganomics caused economic distress prompting the need for fiscal stimulus while at the same time creating the national debt now preventing such stimulus from being applied. In short, Reaganomics both got us into this mess and prevents us from getting out of it.

The quandary persists largely because of the dogged determination of the rich ruling elite to preserve and, indeed, enhance vast fortunes accumulated thanks to Reaganomics. Having enjoyed the benefits of massive, state-legislated upward redistribution of income and wealth during the past three decades, the rich vehemently oppose any attempt to redistribute income and wealth downward. They hide it in the rhetoric of "preserving freedom" and "protecting small business" and "creating jobs" for the middle class when what they intend is to bolster corporate profits (the funnel of income for top management and shareholders) and to protect the wealth of the richest Americans.

Massive debt, the tangible manifestation of wealth inequality, is the bone of contention between the rich and the rest. While both the working classes and the government struggle with the burden of too much debt owed to wealthy creditors at home and abroad, creditors manipulate the political process to ensure repayment. Here's how:

Since too much debt, both personal and federal, is the problem, then debt reduction is the solution. There are only three ways to relieve debt burdens: 1) Earn more and/or spend less, and repay debt with the surplus 2) Sell assets and 3) Default.

Rich creditors resolutely insist on being repaid by either #1, repayment from income, or #2 repayment from sale of assets (as in foreclosures and repossessions), and just as resolutely seek to avoid the possibility of default, #3. Ensuring payment from income while voiding default is why debt collectors proliferate and why bankruptcy laws are amended to make it harder for individuals – but not corporations – to shed debt through bankruptcy. For example, student loans cannot be shed by bankruptcy but instead *must* be paid off, if necessary by docking Social Security benefits if still owing by retirement age. The Bankruptcy Abuse Prevention and Consumer Protection Act of 2005 (BAPCPA) makes it more difficult for some consumers to obtain immediate and complete debt relief through bankruptcy under Chapter 7, forcing them instead to resort to financial reorganization under Chapter 13, requiring repayment of consolidated debts over a 3-5-year period for those the Court deems able to do so.

On the other hand, despite their owners' vast reserves of personal wealth available to settle "debts of honor," corporations can readily shed debt through bankruptcy. That's the leverage Mitt Romney used settle Bain Corporation's debt to the Federal Deposit Insurance Corporation (FDIC) at 35 cents on the dollar, sticking the taxpayers with a $10 million loss in 1992. In addition, Bain Capital repeatedly bought companies, loaded them up with debt to pay for large management fees and dividends to Bain, and, if the acquired company could not lift the debt, promptly declared the company bankrupt and walked away from the debt with a tidy profit.[11]

Perhaps more to the point, the rich will resort to extraordinary measures to protect their wealth when faced with a financial collapse (of their own making) by demanding that taxpayers bail out the banks holding their deposits or face the threat of financial and economic chaos associated with massive bank failures. Rather than bailing out homeowners, Congress bails out the banks.

What does all this tell you about whose side Congress is on?

Here's the point the extreme right misses about changing the rules to stop the ineluctable campaign by the rich to gather up all the marbles: It is not just fair, but also good business for them to "spread the wealth." Concentration of wealth has three undesirable side effects *for rich people:*

1. The middle class, forced to mark time with no real pay increases in over three decades, tends to borrow beyond their means to repay, just to keep up with what has become the chimera of the American Dream. To the extent that the middle class then defaults, the rich suffer, since they are the main ones doing the lending. (Although as previously described, the rich will go to extraordinary measures to avoid such defaults by amending bankruptcy laws, forcing foreclosures and standing first in line for government bailouts when financial collapse imperils their bank deposits.)
2. The lack of growth in real income for the middle and lower classes, particularly when combined with the deleveraging that follows a credit meltdown, means a lack of growth in consumer spending, in turn causing a lack of growth in corporate sales, income and investment, producing a corresponding damper on the prices of common and preferred stocks mostly owned by the rich.

---

[11] Rolling Stone: "The Federal Bailout that Saved Romney" by Tom Dickinson, August 29, 2012
Rolling Stone "Greed and Debt, The True Story of Romney and Bain Capital" by Matt Taibbi, August 29, 2012

3. If "the rest" are economically oppressed beyond endurance, they will eventually revolt and redistribute wealth by either ballots or bullets, depending on their options.

Early on, Henry Ford had the foresight to pay his workers well because he wanted them to be able to afford to buy the cars they were making. The rich today demonstrate no such enlightened self-interest. They do, however, demonstrate enlightened self-interest of a more sinister variety, namely in the adroit manipulation of the political process in the single-minded pursuit of wealth and power with scant regard for the commonweal.

Despite Governor Romney's penchant for playing political air-guitar when describing his proposals, as a card-carrying member of the 1 Percent, Romney's "new plan" for America was quite obviously a replay of the old plan of Reaganomics: tax cuts for the rich (now beatified as "job creators"), lax regulation and high levels of defense spending – the same formula that brought us the greatest inequality of wealth in our history, the evisceration of the middle class, and the attendant economic and financial calamities of the Bush administration.

The question resolved by the 2012 election, then, was whether Charlie Brown would let Lucy hold the ball again—a topic we will take up in detail again later in Chapter 8.

Chapter 7: Barack Obama and the aftermath of the Panic of 2008 and the Great Recession. The elections of 2008 and 2010. Frustrated liberalism. The leftward shift of the pendulum begins, confronted by strong Republican resistance.

President Barack Obama's first term (January 2009 to January 2013, the time of this writing): In a long line of recent "unlucky presidents" assailed by economic headwinds during their term in office – since Nixon, all but Clinton – Barack Obama is surely the unluckiest, having inherited from Bush the Younger what is widely regarded as "the worst economy since the Great Depression." The recession began gently in December 2007, gathered momentum as oil prices spiked above $145/barrel during the summer of 2008, followed by the financial meltdown reaching a crisis panic in September 2008, less than two months before the election. The financial crisis devolved into what was dubbed as the Great Recession during Bush's lame-duck interregnum and, shortly after President Obama took office, the economy bottomed in the first quarter of 2009 after real GDP contracted by 5.1 percent from its earlier peak. Unemployment peaked at 10 percent in October 2009. Less than two months after inauguration Obama was faced with the Dow crashing to a low of 6,443.27 on March 6, 2009, having lost over 54 percent of its value since the October 9, 2007 high of 14,164.53. The world stood on the edge of the precipice and stared into the abyss.

President Obama also inherited from G. W. Bush a fiscal policy in disarray:

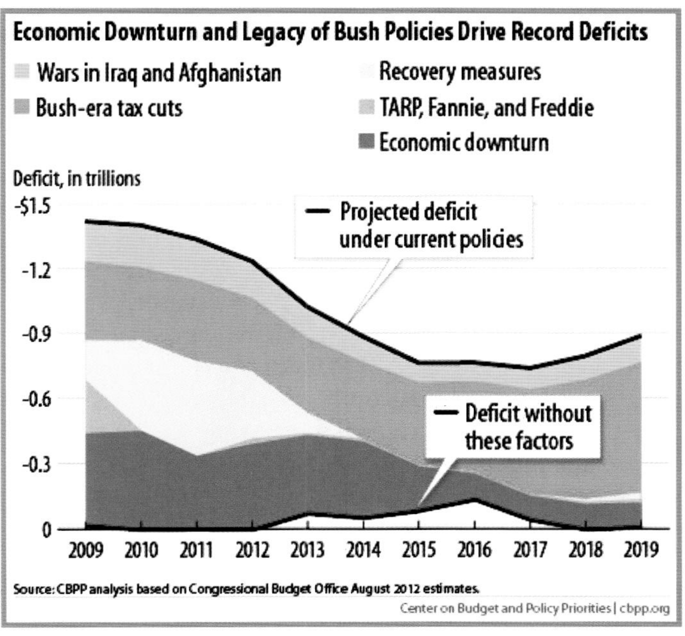

The combination of spending on two wars combined with the Bush era tax cuts produced huge, ongoing federal deficits. These were further swollen by a) the falloff in federal revenues caused by Bush's financial crisis and Great Recession, and b) the increase in federal spending occasioned by the emergency measures required to rescue the banks, Fanny Mae and Freddy Mac and restore economic growth and employment with the American Recovery and Reinvestment Act (ARRA). Absent these factors, the Obama deficits would have been negligible, as shown by the preceding graph from the Center on Budget and Policy Priorities. Needless to say, Republicans fail to take Bush's contribution into account when decrying the deficits incurred during the Obama administration.

Obama entered office as a liberal "agent of change," supported by what appeared to be comfortable majorities in both houses of Congress (257-178 in the House, 59-41 in the Senate, including 2 independents). However, the legislative honeymoon proved to be surprisingly short-lived. Ted Kennedy (D-MA), forced by terminal illness to withdraw from the Senate about 40 days into the Obama administration, reduced the Democratic majority to 58. Kennedy died the following August, triggering a special election in January 2010, won by Republican Scott Brown in a stunning upset. The Democratic majority was later increased to 59 with Sen. Arlen Specter's switch from Republican to Democrat. Ironically, Senator Brown's success in winning what had been a reliably Democratic seat for decades, provided Republicans with the 41 votes they needed, according to Senate rules, to successfully filibuster any Democrat-sponsored legislation they didn't like – a privilege "the Party of No" (or the GNoP) would abuse liberally, no pun intended.

Obama began with a flurry of liberal-leaning legislation and executive orders – low-hanging fruit – including directing the military to draw up plans to withdraw from Iraq and ordering the closing of the Guantanamo Bay detention camp no later than January 2010 (yet to be funded by Congress or insisted upon by Obama). He suspended last-minute federal regulations pushed through by his predecessor, reversed the Bush ban on federal funding of foreign establishments that allow abortions, reversed Bush's policy on embryonic stem cell research, signed an executive order banning waterboarding and other "harsh interrogation methods" not sanctioned by the Army Field Manual, signed the Lilly Ledbetter Fair Pay Act of 2009 extending the statue of limitations for equal-pay lawsuits, signed the Children's Health Insurance Program Reauthorization Act providing additional matching funds to states for health insurance to families with children to expand the program's coverage from 7 to 11 million children and, over strong objections from Wall Street and

Republicans in Congress, signed the Dodd-Frank Wall Street Reform and Consumer Protection Act creating the Consumer Financial Protection Bureau regulating consumer protection with regards to financial products and services.

Within a month of taking office, Obama signed his first major economic initiative, the American Recovery and Reinvestment Act. ARRA provided an estimated $787 billion in emergency spending and tax relief over two years, intended to create and preserve jobs as well as stimulate household spending and de-leveraging. The Act passed without a single Republican vote in the House and only made it past the filibuster hurdle in the Senate thanks to three Republican senators (Susan Collins, Olympia Snowe and Arlen Specter) who broke the partisan gridlock.

ARRA revived Keynesian economics, largely dormant during the era of Reaganomics, attempting to fill with government emergency spending the void in aggregate demand left by the crippled private sector. Keynesians, like Nobel laureate, Paul Krugman, writing for the *N. Y. Times* applauded ARRA, but viewed it as inadequate to the task. At 5.6 percent of GDP spread over two years, ARRA, could not reasonably be expected to ignite a vigorous, sustained recovery. Nevertheless, combined with the U.S. economy's natural resilience, Bush's TARP rescue and the support of a hyper-accommodative Fed, ARRA did manage to stabilize the economy and foment moderate economic and job growth, gradually reducing the unemployment rate to 7.7 percent by November 2012. By the second quarter of 2011, gross domestic product recovered all lost ground.

On the other hand, Reaganauts, who previously dismissed the Bush deficits saying, "Reagan taught us deficits don't matter," suddenly became imbued with profound fiscal conservatism and decried ARRA as wasteful, ineffective and irresponsible. In essence, Republicans behaved like arsonists who set the building ablaze and then derided the fire department for wasting water. Stupidly, Democrats bolstered Republican criticism of the effectiveness of ARRA by citing an earlier report by Christina Romer, then Chair of the President's Council of Economic Advisers, claiming ARRA would prevent the unemployment rate from rising above 8 percent. Never mind that unemployment already exceeded 8 percent at the time ARRA became law, Republicans gleefully seized on the continued increases in unemployment (to a high of 10 percent in October 2009), as conclusive evidence that ARRA, and, more broadly, Keynesian economics "doesn't work," rather than the more plausible conclusions that a) Romer simply erred in her forecast and b) the weight of "the worst economy since the Great Depression" created by Bush 43, like its namesake in the 1930s, would persist for several years.

One cannot help but wonder at the many Republican ironies of the situation:

- Deficits didn't matter when Reagan and the two Bushes collectively added $9.5 trillion to the gross national debt (standing at $16 trillion currently according to the Treasury Department). Clinton added $1.4 trillion and ended with 4 fiscal years of budget surpluses. Now that Obama has been forced to add about $6 trillion, as just explained, Republicans are seizing on the deficits as a pretext for cutting government spending (and, therefore jobs, at a time of high unemployment and safety net spending at a time of dire need) rather, than, heaven forbid, raising taxes on the wealthy who have been the only ones to prosper under Reaganomics. Consequently, at a time when the American people say jobs should be the government's top priority, Republicans insist deficit reduction be placed at the head of the list, and then promptly deny the Obama administration two out of the three policy measures – tax increases and defense spending cuts – capable of narrowing the deficits, leaving cuts in social spending and income transfers as the only alternatives.
- Republicans demonize social spending and income transfers ("entitlements" in Republican-speak) in their campaign to shred the safety nets created during the Great Depression (the New Deal) and thereafter, particularly during the days of Johnson's Great Society. They do this to set the stage for cuts in such spending so as to preserve the Bush 43 tax cuts and high levels of military spending. It does not occur to them that the heightened need for social spending arises from three decades of Republican policies diverting nearly all the growth in national income to the very wealthy, leaving the poor and much of the middle class in dire need of a safety net. For Republicans it's "Pull up the ladder, I've got mine."
- Republicans get to blame Democrats for the mess Republicans themselves created, while, in single-minded pursuit to regain power, obstructing virtually all Democratic initiatives to remedy the situation. It makes one suspect the Republicans deliberately threw the 2008 election to shift blame for the mess they created into the laps of the Democrats.[12]

---

[12] I attribute the 2008 election of Obama to astute political strategy by the Republicans who wanted no part of the presidency in light of the shitstorm about to blanket the country as a result of the base-serving policies of George W. Bush. Consider the evidence:

- They put up two goof balls to head the Republican ticket — self-styled "mavericks" who would fail to rally the Republican base.
- Underfunded the McCain/Palin campaign

- Republicans claim $787 billion in Keynesian stimulus "didn't work" when the Republican cure-all for unemployment, the Bush tax cuts, has remained in place for the past decade, adding up to a revenue loss exceeding $3.5 trillion (according to the non-partisan Congressional Research Service) with little discernible effect on employment. Undeterred, Republicans still profess faith in the job-creating efficacy of tax cuts favoring the wealthy "job creators," despite their manifest ineffectiveness in creating jobs ever since the Bush tax cuts in the early 2000s, largely still in effect as of this writing.
- It's a Republican article of faith that raising taxes, especially on the rich "job creators," will "kill jobs" because, the theory goes, money will be taken out of the private economy, reducing private spending and investment, thereby reducing aggregate demand and producing a commensurate reduction in employment. The theory is flawed on three counts:

   1. There is no evidence to support the theory. The economy thrived when taxes were raised during and after World War II, when Bush 41 raised tax rates, and the Clinton administration raised taxes in 1993.
   2. The money taken out of the private economy through higher taxes doesn't disappear down some black government hole never to be seen again. The government puts it right back into the economy as a current expense or transfer payment (which also gets spent or invested) or government investment in things like roads, bridges or aircraft carriers. Now we can argue about whether the money is better spent by leaving the money in private hands or allowing the government to determine the spending and investment priorities for the funds in question. The reality is both are necessary. The trick

---

▪ I suspect they secretly funded the Obama campaign inasmuch as Obama (a black man with a Muslim-sounding name, questionable birthplace and limited political experience) would be easier to wrest power from in 2012 than Hillary Clinton. Obama raised $745 million, much of it from Big Money sources, twice as much as McCain's $368 million (according to the Center for Responsive Politics).

By deliberately throwing the 2008 election, Republicans avoided taking the heat for Bush 43's disastrous policies and instead got to blame Obama for the mess they themselves created. Republicans allowed an inadequate Keynesian stimulus to be enacted and then torpedoed any further efforts to revive the economy so they could then discredit not only Obama but also Keynesian economics in the bargain, thus setting up the Republican "1 Percenters" to win back the House in 2010 and a to have good shot at regaining control of Congress in 2012 along with the presidency in the hands of one of their own. This all makes too much sense not to be true.

is to find the optimal balance between the two and allocate resources to whatever sector can best do the job. As is often the case, the money routed through the government often gets rerouted directly back to the private sector through outsourcing. However, it cannot be argued, as Republicans do, that tax increases kill jobs by dampening consumption and/or investment inasmuch as aggregate demand remains essentially unchanged.

3. Rich Republicans want to perpetuate the raising-taxes-kills-jobs myth simply because they want to get richer by paying less taxes. Strange isn't it? The rich don't have the money to give up in taxes to close the deficits, lest "jobs be killed," but they do have it to *lend* for the same purpose with no mention of jobs lost. The money is siphoned from the private through the public sector of the economy just as surely either way. The difference is the older-generation rich get richer if they lend rather than pay higher taxes, while younger generations wind up shouldering the debt. So much for "We're doing it for our children and our children's children."

Notwithstanding the tendency toward political gridlock in Washington, President Obama has signed into law 38 Acts ranging beyond economic stimulus and budgets to social issues (hate crimes, repeal of "don't ask, don't tell," veterans care, Haiti relief, child nutrition), reforms in credit cards and Wall Street (though watered down), and, most contentious of all, the Patient Protection and Affordable Care Act (derisively dubbed "ObamaCare" by Republicans) recently reaffirmed as constitutional by the Roberts Supreme Court.

Most of this legislation promotes limited left-of-center objectives while making huge concessions to Republicans wielding the threat of a government shutdown if they didn't get their way. For example: the first Obama extension of the Bush tax cuts for the middle class also included their extension for the wealthy despite huge deficits. Some of the more egregious abuses by credit card issuers have been curtailed while allowing lenders to charge interest rates that would make a loan shark blush. While partly restrained by Dodd-Frank regulation, Wall Street can still gamble on risky derivatives and other financial "innovations" with reckless impunity. The worst abuses by health insurers have been prohibited in exchange for which the insurance companies get to sign up some 40 million new customers required to obtain coverage (some with subsidies) according to the much-maligned "mandate."

In foreign policy, Obama seems to be belatedly earning the Nobel Peace Prize he received in 2009 "for his extraordinary efforts to strengthen international diplomacy and cooperation between people." (I suggested as much in my blog www.cassandra-chronicles.blogspot.com "Behind the Nobel Peace Prize for President Obama," October 22, 2009). In December 2011, despite ongoing political instability and sectarian violence, the war in Iraq officially ended with the withdrawal of American combat troops, fulfilling one of Obama's most important campaign promises. A similar ending to the war in Afghanistan in 2014 (or maybe 2013) has recently been announced, again bringing to mind Senator Aiken's (D-VT) formula for ending the war in Vietnam, in effect, to declare victory and bring the troops home. As in Vietnam, the U.S. Government has little to show for its massive expenditure of blood and treasure other than swollen armaments industry profits and C-suite compensation adding to the unprecedented U.S. imbalance in the distribution of wealth.

However, Obama has retained and even expanded on the Bush 43 abrogations of civil liberties, unconstitutional police-state powers and use of drones over foreign territory, making him the only Nobel Prizewinner with a kill list.

The administration was careful not to be seen as an *agent provocateur* in the various "Arab Spring" revolutions in Tunisia, Egypt and elsewhere in the Middle East.

At present it is too early to tell how the political upheaval in the region will shake out, although the election of Muslim Brotherhood candidate, Islamist Mohamed Morsi, as President of Egypt, may be cause for concern. Morsi decreed himself powers deemed dictatorial by the liberal/leftist/Christian opposition, and appears to have gained approval in the recent referendum for a new draft constitution expanding the role of Sharia law and limiting women's rights and free speech. The confrontation between the Israelis and the Palestinians recently escalated into open conflict (now subject to a tenuous cease fire) following the Israeli assassination by drone of Hamas' leader, resulting in the exchange of Palestinian missiles from Gaza and aerial and artillery fire from Israel, leaving matters between the two pathologically unresolved. Attempting to move along the stalled "peace process" toward a "two-state solution," for the first time the U.N. recently elevated Palestine to a "non-member observer" state, the first time "state" has been applied to the Palestinians. The civil war in Syria continues unabated without foreign involvement.

Chris Hayes, moderator of "Up w/Chris Hayes" on MNBC recently offered a sobering critical assessment of Obama's foreign and national security policies on TV when discussing Dinesh DeSouza's 2010 film, "2016: Obama's America'. While disagreeing with most of DeSouza's rabidly right-wing criticism, Hayes added:

> I don't support Obama. You know, I wish somebody would make a documentary on what Obama's done. I just sued

> the President in Federal court over the National Defense Authorization Act, the assault on civil liberties under the Obama administration. This should not be a left-right divide. It has been far worse under Obama than it was under George W. Bush. And yet none of that is in the film. Obama's refusal to restore *habeas corpus*. Obama's supporting of the FISA Amendment Act, which retroactively makes legal what under our constitution—and I assume Dinesh is a constitutionalist — has traditionally been illegal. Warrantless wiretapping, monitoring, and eavesdropping of tens of millions of Americans. The use of the Espionage Act, six times, to shut down whistleblowers who have exposed, in some cases, war crimes committed by the U.S. government. And finally, the NDAA, Section 1021, which authorizes the U.S. military to carry out detentions, seizures, on American soil, strip American citizens of due process, and hold them in their offshore penal colonies.
>
> None of that's in the film. The craven sort of obsequiousness on the part of the Obama administration to Wall Street. The expansion of our imperial wars. Our proxy wars in Pakistan, Somalia, Yemen. I think these are pretty good criticisms of Obama.

And from Chris Hedges (We Are Change interview):

> Obama is the soft case of imperial corporate power. He's a brand. And he functions very effectively as a brand. I have long argued and believed that the personal narrative of presidential candidates is meaningless. If you look at all of the major structural issues, there is complete continuity from the Bush Administration to the Obama administration; and that's because these individual figures have very little power. The way the American political system is configured now, it is impossible to vote against the interests of Goldman Sachs. You can't do it – or Exxon Mobil, or Raytheon or all those people who profit from continuing these endless wars in the Middle East. So I think that, unfortunately, because of Obama's rhetoric, people spend a little too much time listening to his rhetoric and not watching what he does – which is all that counts. And what he does is really repugnant and awful. I'm less forgiving of Obama because he's a constitutional lawyer. Unlike our previous president, he's not a moron. He understands what he's doing. He's conscious of what he's doing in a way that George Bush was pretty checked out on most stuff. And that makes him for me a deeply cynical figure. I have long railed against the

liberal class on the left for not standing up. One day they are going to deeply regret it.

Bottom line: Obama's report card shows mixed results so far. His major accomplishment: arresting the dangerous rightward swing of both political pendulums initiated by Ronald Reagan and pushed to the limit by George W. Bush. President Obama demonstrated sound liberal instincts in his attempts to reform health care, energy, credit card abuses, Wall Street, consumer financial protection, gender pay disparities, discrimination against gays, harsh interrogation methods and limits on abortions and stem cell research. However, compromises necessary to overcome intractable reactionary corporate and Republican congressional resistance frustrated the scope of reform. Therefore, in these areas, the President gets an "incomplete." The administration's attempts to revive the economy proved moderately successful in restoring economic growth and reducing unemployment, but these efforts were also hampered by Republican obstructionism and the weight of previously accumulated debt on the economy. The same can be said for restoring sound fiscal policy. In foreign policy, Obama must be credited with ending the war in Iraq, taking out Osama bin Laden and setting a timetable for withdrawing from Afghanistan within the next two years. However, as Chris Hayes rightly states, civil liberties curtailed by the Bush administration in the name of the War On Terror, remain under assault by the Obama administration – perhaps, to some extent, a necessary evil to be endured until the completion of the U.S. military withdrawal from the Middle East deprives the jihadist conflagration of oxygen.

While the rightward swing of the political pendulums may have been stopped, as yet little leftward momentum has emerged, given the dependency of both parties on campaign contributions from corporations and wealthy individuals. For all his laudable liberal instincts, President Obama remains, like Laocoön, bound by powerful snakes, in this instance, Wall Street and the military-industrial-technological-political complex.

Consider as self-evident truth that American politics will remain the same vicious, venal game in the service of Big Money depicted in Netflix' "House of Cards" until such time as politicians can get elected on the strength and popular appeal of their ideals and ideas, rather than their ability to raise money. You cannot expect political contributors to fund candidates' campaigns and expect nothing in return; nor can you expect political officeholders to serve interests other than of those whose contributions placed them in office. For this reason, in Chapter 10 I propose a new political process for the cultivation, dissemination and implementation of political ideas germinating from within the population, funded exclusively by We the People to achieve the critical mass of public opinion required to elect public officials from within our midst to serve our interests.

Chapter 8: The election of 2012. Obama re-elected. Republican Big Money trounced. The leftward displacement of the pendulum confirmed. Republicans fight a desperate rearguard action. Need for a new political model. The argument for centrism.

Ugly. There's no other way to describe the 2012 elections. Not democracy's finest hour by any means. For a country aspiring to lead the world as the prime exponent of democratic statesmanship and compromise and to inspire fledgling democracies to secure the consent of the governed through the democratic electoral process, in 2012 the United States set an abysmal example of democracy in action. Why would other countries want to emulate American democracy when the main object of the exercise is to elevate leaders characterized during the course of the electoral campaigns as entirely unsuitable for office? Leaders, I might add, who when in office, collectively amply merit such characterization by their inability to achieve the compromises needed to govern on behalf of the electorate.

As is always the case in U.S. elections, the process was unconscionably long and expensive, redolent of the effluvium of Barnum & Bailey. Whereas Britons and Canadians get the job done in a couple of months, U.S. elections drag on for a couple of years, through interminable meetings in "smoke-filled rooms," straw polls, canvasses, campaign rallies, town-hall meetings, primaries, debates, conventions, media polls, robo-calls, and barrages of campaign advertising, most of it negative and misleading. Political insiders say, only half jokingly, the next election campaign begins the day after inauguration.

The Center for Responsive Politics, estimates the 2012 national elections cost a record $5.8 billion, including an estimated $2.5 billion spent in the contest for the White House, about evenly divided between the two candidates. *To my mind, the near-total failure of Republican Big Money to achieve desired results constituted the biggest surprise of the 2012 election.* The trouncing of Republican Big Money, notwithstanding the floodgates opened by *Citizens United*, demonstrated the limitations of lavish campaign spending when the message is bogus, candidate insincere and out-of-touch, and the opposition resolute and well funded.

While Democrats were spared the ordeal of a presidential primary fight, Republicans treated the nation to the spectacle of the loony right in full flight through interminable debates featuring candidates often more intent on selling books and speaking engagements than governing. Serious contenders like Governors Huntsman and Pawlenty withdrew early on, unable to meet the standards of conservative extremism set by Tea Party crazies, leaving in the running the likes of former IRS lawyer Michelle ("God told me to run") Bachmann, serial philanderer Newt ("Fly me to the moon") Gingrich, brain-frozen Rick ("Oops") Perry, gynecologist Ron ("abolish the Fed and return to the gold standard") Paul, ousted senator Rick ("intelligent design") Santorum, and, most bizarre of all, pizza-man Herman ("9-9-9") Cain whose performance-art candidacy punked America brilliantly (http://cassandra-chronicles.blogspot.com/2011/11/cain-punks-america-brilliantly.html) until he was himself punked by revelations of marital infidelity. In the end, the Democrats produced as their standard bearer, the Stepford candidate, certified 1 Percenter, vulture-capitalist Mitt ("47 percent") Romney, who chose fiscal wunderkind, PX-90 body-builder Congressman Paul ("2+2=5") Ryan as his running mate.

In its determined effort to boost political advertising, the media breathlessly called the race a dead heat right up to the eve of the election. Republican hacks, like Karl Rove and Dick Morris, foolish enough to believe the alternate reality concocted in the Fox News terrarium, thoroughly discredited themselves by predicting a Romney landslide. However, the Obama campaign prevailed handily, beating Romney/Ryan by more than 5 million, votes translating into a lopsided 332 to 206 victory in the Electoral College. The presidential victory, plus gains in the House and Senate as well as referenda favoring liberal causes like marijuana legalization and gay marriage, confirmed the reversal of the political pendulums from what mercifully now appears to have been their maximum rightward displacement during the Bush 43 administration. This is the fundamental message of the 2012 election.

Republicans suddenly found themselves out of step with changing demographics and related themes, their defeat seeming to signal an end to the political heyday of the rich, aging, angry white male. In Reagan's day white voters made up 88 percent of the electorate and minorities only 12 percent. In the 2012 election, whites, who tend to split their votes fairly evenly, receded to 72 percent, while minorities, who overwhelmingly vote Democratic, surged to 28 percent. With characteristic wry irony, Maureen Dowd captured the demographic shift in her column "A Lost Civilization" (N.Y. Times December 8, 2012).

> Who would ever have thought blacks would get out and support the first black president? Who would ever have thought women would shy away from the party of transvaginal probes? Who would ever have thought gays would work against a party that treated them as immoral and subhuman? Who would have ever thought young people would desert a party that ignored science and hectored on social issues? Who would ever have thought Latinos would scorn a party that expected them to finish up their chores and self-deport?

Romney/Ryan averted:

It is worth assessing what Americans avoided by not electing Mitt Romney and Paul Ryan, lest Americans be tempted down a similar path again. Such an exercise involves a fair measure of speculation, inasmuch as the former governor of the liberal-leaning state of Massachusetts, running for the U.S. presidency as a "strict conservative" in the primaries, then face dancing[13] as a moderate during the presidential debates, remained consistently inconsistent throughout his political career. Name virtually any issue and, over time, you will find Romney opportunistically on either side of it, depending on what he thought his audience wanted to hear. Frequently during the course of the presidential campaign he said one thing, only to have his campaign managers "clarify" his remarks the next day, saying he really meant exactly the opposite. Moreover, the positions and plans he articulated, more often than not, lacked any semblance of specificity or clarifying detail to be relied upon a foundation for predicting the policies he would have embraced as president.

For this inconsistency and vagueness critics accused Romney of having no core principles. I disagree. His overriding core principle was clear: gaining and retaining wealth and power by whatever means necessary – first financial power as a ruthless principal of Bain Capital, and later political power as the Stepford candidate for President of the United States. Had he secured the power of the presidency, we could reasonably have expected him to seek to retain and expand it by serving the interests of his wealthy base, coinciding with his own as a card-carrying member of the 1 Percent.

These interests cluster around a restatement of the premise popularized in the 1950s "What's good for General Motors is good for the U.S.A." In short, Romney touted corporations both as the sole creators of wealth and the ultimate arbiters of how such wealth should be distributed. By Romney's lights, corporate profits represent the measure of society's success, and anything – government taxes and regulations especially – likely to impair profits detract from such success. Accordingly, any attempt by government to override the dictates of corporations in allocating scarce resources, either in the process of production or distribution of the fruits of production, would not have been tolerated.

At this point, it's worth remembering Mussolini's definition of fascism as the marriage of the state and corporate power. However, where Mussolini saw corporate power as the means to achieve state supremacy, Romney saw the state as the means to achieve corporate supremacy.

---

[13] From Frank Herbert's *Dune* science-fiction novels, Face Dancers are shapeshifters, and their name is derived from their ability to change their physical appearance at will.

Therefore, to this end Romney would have fortified the already-formidable power of Corporate America by doubling down on Reaganomics.

Had Romney become President, therefore, we can reasonably assume the nation would have experienced a reprise of the Bush 43 presidency writ large: rampant inequality of income and wealth driven by Reaganomics on steroids, predictably followed by another financial meltdown resulting in a Great Depression; massive unemployment coupled with a shredded safety net to produce violent civil unrest; renewed war in the Middle East, this time with Iran, in a vain attempt to unify the country and distract it from domestic woes while serving the demands of the MITP complex; worsening federal deficits resulting from under-taxation of the wealthy and bloated military outlays, forcing the Fed to monetize the national debt, producing runaway inflation, a worthless dollar and national bankruptcy; and, ultimately, the establishment of dictatorship to stifle dissent and retain control by use of powers granted by the Patriot Acts and the National Defense Authorization Act of 2012. George Orwell would have been spinning in his grave.

The night after the 2012 election, an elated Rachel Maddow offered her list of consequences avoided on a more personal level by average citizens, implied by Mitt Romney's resounding defeat:

- We are not going to have a Supreme Court that will overturn Roe versus Wade. There will be no more Antonin Scalias and Samuel Alitos added to this Court.
- They are not going to repeal health reform. Nobody's going to kill Medicare and make old people of this generation or any other generation fight it out in the open market trying to get themselves health insurance. We are not going to do that.
- We're not going to give a 20 percent tax cut to millionaires and billionaires, and expect [cuts in] food stamps and kids programs to cover the cost of that tax cut.
- We're not going to make you clear it with your boss if you want to get birth control under the insurance plan that you're on.
- We're not going to redefine rape.
- We're not going to amend the United States Constitution to prevent gay people from getting married.
- We're not going to double Guantanamo
- We're not going to eliminate the Department of Energy, or the Department of Education or Housing at the federal level.
- We're not going to spend two trillion dollars on the military that the military does not want.
- We're not scaling back on student loans because the country's new plan is that you should borrow money from your parents.
- We are not vetoing the Dream Act.

- We are not self-deporting.
- We are not letting Detroit go bankrupt.
- We are not starting a trade war with China on inauguration day in January.
- We are not going to have a man as a president a man who once led a mob of friends to run down a scared gay kid to hold him down and forcibly cut his hair off with a pair of scissors while the kid cried and screamed for help – and there was no apology, not ever.
- We're not going to have as Secretary of State John Bolton.
- We're not bringing Dick Cheney back.
- We're not a foreign policy shop stocked with architects of the Iraq war. We're not going to do it. We had the choice to do that, if we wanted to do that as a country, and we said "no."

Amen.

So much for what we avoided. What will we likely gain from the second Obama administration? Disabused of the chimera of bipartisanship and relieved of the burden of re-election, Obama may come out swinging and genuinely lead public opinion rather than adapt to it.

Given the limiting constraints of Republican intransigence in Congress, the most anyone can do in peering into crystal balls is discern the vectors of intent within the administration, without any assurance they will be realized. These vectors are largely liberal-leaning, including a vigorous campaign for action on climate change, social justice, gay rights, equality of opportunity and pay for women, voting rights, immigration reform, gun control. Regrettably, the administration also seems committed to the decidedly non-liberal abridgements of civil liberties inherited from Bush 43.

The administration's fiscal policy will include allowing the Bush tax cuts to lapse for taxpayers earning more than $400,000, producing an increase in revenues of nearly $600 billion over 10 years, according to most estimates. The administration seems receptive to tax reform and closing unspecified "loopholes" as a source of additional revenues, mainly from the rich. (Republicans, conceding the need for the rich to pay more, yet attempting to stick to their pledges to Grover Norquist, also advocated such unspecified reform instead of higher tax rates. However at the eleventh hour they caved, allowing the Bush tax cuts to expire for taxpayers earning more than $400,000 in exchange for limiting the increase in the tax rate applicable to capital gains and dividends to 20 percent (from 15 percent) for those earning more than $400,000 and no increase for lesser incomes.)

Having wound down the war in Iraq and set a timetable for leaving Afghanistan, the second Obama administration can be expected to emphasize diplomatic engagement with potential adversaries and push for another "peace dividend" with the Army scheduled to trim its present size by 70,000 troops down to 490,000. Yet further cuts in military spending should be derived from restructuring the Army toward smaller-unit, fast-response combat brigades and special forces capabilities needed to meet the current asymmetrical warfare threat, and away from large conventional mechanized division-sized Army forces and Naval aircraft carrier task forces supported by expensive weapons systems more suited for state-to-state conflict – that is if the MITP complex can be prevented from picking a fight with Iran or China. (Ironically, higher taxes and reduced defense spending are two primary components of the "fiscal cliff" causing such fear and loathing in Washington these days. Frankly, it's just what the doctor ordered.) It's also fair to assume the administration will exhibit heightened reluctance to wage war while seeking diplomatic solutions to international tensions. In a direct affront to the MITP complex, the President stated:

> We the People still believe enduring security and lasting peace do not require perpetual war.
>
> President Barack Obama
> Second Inaugural address, January 21, 2013

The administration will also pursue additional regulations, particularly through the Consumer Financial Protection Bureau, to curb counterproductive consequences of corporate misbehavior. The President has agreed in principle to curbs on social welfare spending as a means of curbing the federal budget deficits, but has not been forthcoming with specifics of such a plan beyond cuts in Medicare fees to hospitals, nursing homes, drug manufacturers and other health-care providers. Righting the disequilibrium of wealth and income distribution between the wealthy and the rest provides the overarching liberal theme for the second Obama administration and the focus of resistance by the Republican opposition.

Before we get carried away with *schadenfreude* over the Republican post-election predicament (nice to turn the tables for a change), let us not forget that Republicans still control the House; have filibuster veto power in the Senate; preside as governors in 30 states; dominate Corporate America's C-suites; control the military-industrial complex; direct a powerful ministry of propaganda in Fox News, *The Wall Street Journal* and related media; and have a helluva lot of net worth they are determined to preserve and make grow. Consequently, regardless of his liberal inclination, Obama's efforts to move the political pendulums toward the left will continue to be opposed by formidable reactionary Republican forces fighting a desperate rear-guard action, intent on holding the political pendulums in place.

To that end, wealthy Republicans can be counted on to engage in ruthless political machinations to bend the democratic process to their will insofar as is possible. As demonstrated in the 2012 election, Republicans will use their control of the majority of statehouses to disenfranchise their opponents with contortionist gerrymandering and onerous voter identification requirements (in the name of eliminating virtually non-existent "voter fraud"), and to disempower labor unions.

We should not underestimate the effect of Republican-controlled statehouses not only on state issues, but also on the balance of power nationally. Consider Michigan, Wisconsin and Pennsylvania, states in which Republican-controlled legislatures got to redraw congressional districts after the latest census. A majority of voters in these states cast ballots for Obama and for Democratic members of Congress in the 2012 election. Yet redistricting ("gerrymandering") by Republican-dominated legislatures succeeded in sending significantly more Republicans to Congress than Democrats! In Ohio, where congressional district maps were also re-drawn by Republicans, a majority of voters cast ballots for Obama, but narrowly favored Republican over Democratic congressional candidates 52.5 percent to 47.5 percent in the aggregate. Yet Ohio is sending three times as many Republican members to Congress as Democrats (12 to 4). The same thing happened in Virginia (8 Republicans to 3 Democrats) when the overall congressional vote split narrowly, 51 percent to 49 percent.

The means of accomplishing this feat of electoral legerdemain relies on that fact that Democrats tend to congregate in densely populated cities and Republicans tend to be spread out in more thinly populated suburbs and rural areas. Therefore, the trick in Republican gerrymandering is to group large numbers of predominantly urban Democratic voters into relatively few densely populated congressional districts while grouping predominantly suburban and rural Republican voters into relatively many sparsely populated districts. Consequently, in such instances 2 to 2 ½ times as many voters are required to elect a Democratic congressman as are needed to elect a Republican. Inasmuch as the districts are of roughly comparable size, apportionment of Congressional representatives is thereby done on the basis of land area (which Republicans own more of than Democrats), rather than population (which is supposed to be the basis for representative government). In this way, gerrymandering provides Republicans representation in state legislatures and Congress far greater than their numbers would warrant, producing, in effect, minority rule. Even though in 2012 Democrats received a 49.2 to 48 percent plurality of the votes cast for the House, Republicans retained a solid majority in the lower chamber.

For their next trick in upcoming elections, Republican governors are discussing the idea of changing the apportionment of electoral votes in their states from "winner-take-all" (reflecting the will of the majority of voters in each state) to apportionment by congressional districts (again, reflecting area, not population). Had such a system been in place in 2012, Mitt Romney would have been our 45th President. Think about it.

Accordingly, given the present stalemate in Washington and the likelihood of more Republican vote-altering shenanigans in future elections, liberal Americans' relief at the prospect of arresting further rightward displacement of the political pendulums must be tempered with limited expectations of leftward movement toward equilibrium at the center and ongoing concern about potential calamities in store in the absence of such movement, given the pendulums' present displacement on the extreme right.

Lest we forget where the pendulums currently rest: Wall Street retains its unwarranted influence in the corridors of power, diligently eviscerating regulations aimed at curbing Wall Street's destabilizing speculative excesses; tax rates for the rich remain near record low levels while military/national security expenditures continue to skyrocket, creating massive budget deficits; the U.S. is still at war in the Middle East and in its quest for "adversaries," the military-industrial-technological-political complex is beating the tom-toms to extend the conflict into Iran and to lay the groundwork for confrontation with China; civil liberties remain under assault by the Patriot Acts and the National Defense Authorization Act of 2012; the Roberts Supreme Court remains right-biased; with Reaganomics still essentially in place, the rich and powerful elite continue to scoop up most of the fruits of progress and control a wildly disproportionate amount of wealth while the middle class struggles with stagnant real wages and a heavy burden of debt; students continue to receive inadequate primary and secondary educations and confront high costs of college tuitions, burdensome student loans and dim job prospects; the prickly issue of immigration remains unresolved; jails remain crowded with casualties of the puritanical war on drugs; the social safety net remains vulnerable to attack from Republicans in Congress bent on gutting "entitlements."

With the nation still gripped by the thrall of neo-conservatism, Obama notwithstanding, the U.S. risks catastrophes that can only be averted or ameliorated by a radical change of direction toward American liberalism – a subject I plan to fully address in " The Egyptian Solution."

The argument for centrism

Let me hasten to add that I do not regard radical American liberalism as a panacea. As I stated in my "Why I Write" introduction to the *Cassandra Chronicles*:

> I do not believe any political philosophy has a corner on the truth, nor is any political approach optimal for all occasions. Consequently, I am inclined to support objectively whatever works at the time to further the universal aspirations for peace, prosperity, order, human rights, and the survival of the human species.

What will work presently, given the adverse consequences of the excesses of the right, is a radical shift in direction toward American liberalism, in my opinion (and hopefully yours by now). *However, should such a radical shift occur, if carried to extremes on the left, you will find me pulling with equal vigor and passion toward the right.* In a volatile world, we alternate between Keynes and Hayek.

For a while, Winston Churchill exemplified this sort of political adaptability entering politics as a Conservative, then switching to the Liberal Party at age 29, returning to the Conservatives at age 49. However, his failure to again adapt to the post-war British liberal *zeitgeist* led to his fall from power after World War II. Where the British people wanted peace, tranquility and security of a social welfare state, Churchill offered empire.

The appropriate overriding mindset, I submit, is analogous to gravity acting upon the political pendulum, tending toward that elusive state of equilibrium at the bottom of the pendulum's swing between left and right – in a word, *balance*. We must acknowledge the virtue in what the right says about the incentives for prosperity offered by freedom, within reason, to pursue self-interest and retain the fruits of one's labor and investment derived in free-markets. Defining "within reason" is the tricky part. Consequently, we must acknowledge the virtue in what the left says about the need to regulate the excesses of unbridled capitalism and achieve an equitable distribution of the tax burden and the fruits of economic growth. The left seeks a rising tide lifting all boats and not just the yachts of the rich, presently leaving the dinghies of the poor sunk and sloops of the middle class swamped in their wake.

As seen in Perón's and now the Kirchners' Argentina, Stalin's Soviet Union and Castro's Cuba on the left, and G.W. Bush's Reaganite, evangelical America on the right, there exists vice at the extremes of left and right resulting in economic, financial and social instability, economic entropy and violence. The trick is to achieve a state of equilibrium between the two extremes, preserving growth incentives while serving justice and achieving sustainability and socially stabilizing equity in the distribution of the fruits of prosperity, and ensuring liberty while providing security.

Before any meaningful change can occur, however, it will be necessary for reform-minded, American liberals/progressives to devise a completely new political model. Attempting to attain the requisite political power by employing today's mainstream Big Money, media-dependent political model is doomed to fail.

Need for new political model:

Today's electoral process is dominated by an unholy cabal of the superrich who pick political candidates and fund their campaigns; the lobbyists and political action committee executives who dispense campaign contributions; the candidates who accept such financial support and who are, therefore, obligated to support policies favoring their benefactors and the media and their hangers-on, who are the recipients of campaign funds in the form of paid advertising needed to garner votes. Therefore, money, "the mother's milk of politics," equals votes in today's elections, given the present structure of today's TV-dependent political process.

Liberals/progressives must recognize the impossibility of competing successfully against the moneyed interests by engaging in a political process where money equals votes. The 1 Percent controlling two-fifths of the nation's wealth will always be able to outspend the rest of the population, especially after *Citizens United vs. Federal Election Commission* gave the rich access to corporate treasuries to fund political action committees. As long as money equals votes, Big Money will prevail through the vehicles of the present two-party system, each party representing opposite wings of the same bird. I will describe in Chapter 10 what I have concluded is the left's surest way to meaningful political power through a new political model bypassing Big Money and television ads.

To Aristotle belongs the last word:

> Those who have too much of the goods of fortune, strength, wealth, friends, and the like, are neither willing nor able to submit to authority. . . . On the other hand, the very poor, who are in the opposite extreme, are too degraded. . . Thus arises a city, not of freemen, but of masters and slaves, the one despising, the other envying; and nothing can be more fatal to friendship and good fellowship in states than this: for good fellowship springs from friendship; when men are at enmity with one another, they would rather not even share the same path. But a city ought to be composed, as far as possible, of equals and similars; and these are generally the middle classes.
>
> Thus it is manifest that the best political community is formed by citizens of the middle class, and that those states are likely to be well-administered in which the middle class is large, and stronger if possible than both the other classes, or at any rate than either singly; for the addition of the middle class turns the scale, and prevents either of the extremes from being dominant. Great then is the good fortune of a state in which the citizens have a moderate and sufficient property; for where some possess much, and the others nothing, there may arise an extreme democracy, or a pure oligarchy; or a tyranny may grow out of either extreme — either out of the most rampant democracy, or out of an oligarchy; but it is not so likely to arise out of the middle constitutions and those akin to them.

Chapter 9: The Predicament. Why does the Republican middle class vote against its own interests? A tale of two moralities.

Having reviewed the interaction of economics, finance and politics to arrive at an understanding of how we journeyed from the relatively balanced, prosperous, fiscally cooperative and sane (if internationally unbalanced) Eisenhower 1950s to the polarized, economically and financially unstable, politically insane present, it is now time to examine the full extent of The Predicament today:

Domestically:

- Massive poverty and hunger amidst incalculable wealth making the rich stupendously richer, the poor desperately poorer and the middle class mark time or fall behind, producing the greatest inequality of wealth among advanced nations
- Mountains of personal debt incurred during the housing bubble pumped up in the 1990s and 2000s followed by massive foreclosures when the housing bubble burst in 2007 and by the Panic of 2008 and Great Recession with corresponding high unemployment, inhibiting recovery while debtors "deleverage"
- Mountains of government debt, jeopardizing the government's solvency, risking hyperinflation if the debt is monetized, depression and default if not, with attendant risk of political instability due to an inadequate safety net in the face of economic stress
- Rampant corporate corruption in an under-regulated economy and financial markets peppered with moral hazards
- Predatory lenders – credit cards, payroll lenders – charging interest rates that would make a loan shark blush
- Expensive energy coupled with dangerous dependence on often-hostile foreign oil suppliers
- Persistence of polluted air, unclean water and climate change with potentially catastrophic environmental consequences
- Substandard K-12 public education undermining future national competitiveness and youth opportunity
- Prohibitively expensive college educations with diminished availability of financial aid, leaving many graduates with a crushing burden of debt in the face of dismal job prospects upon graduation
- Unhealthy food leading to an epidemic of obesity and related diseases, like diabetes
- Expensive and contentious health care insurance, unevenly available producing thousands of unnecessary deaths a year

- Repressive anti-drug laws accompanied by rampant drug-related crime and excessive incarceration leading to crowded prisons and high rates of recidivism
- A hopelessly tangled, time-consuming and expensive legal system with draconian minimum- sentencing guidelines
- A politicized judiciary
- A dangerously polarized electorate
- A democratic process hijacked by moneyed interests at the expense of "the rest"
- A general lack of accountability among the ruling elite
- Curtailed constitutional rights, as in Patriot Act, Defense Authorization Act of 2012 and the Income Tax
- A gridlocked legislative system incapable of adequately addressing these problems

Globally:

- Yet another round of religious wars between historic enemies compounded by polarization of economic interests (i.e., oil)
- The mounting worldwide threat of nuclear and biological terrorism
- A warmer global climate and accompanying rise in sea levels and hazardous weather
- Unprecedented foreign indebtedness leading to a loss of financial sovereignty and the prospect of a devalued dollar and diminished standards of living for future generations with the potential for future runaway inflation and/or destabilizing default

A tale of two moralities

You might well ask why middle-class Americans on the right insist on supporting neo-conservative policies articulated by Reagan and later seconded by the younger Bush, in view of their demonstrably disastrous results for the middle class. Why do they vote against their own best interests?

On January 13, 2011 Paul Krugman wrote a profound N.Y. Times Op-Ed piece titled "A Tale of Two Moralities" in which he pinpointed the critical difference between the morality of conservatives and liberals. His piece gets to the heart of the quandary, revealing the two moral conceptions driving American politics today:

> "One side of American politics considers the modern welfare state — a private-enterprise economy, but one in which society's winners are taxed to pay for a social safety net — morally superior to the capitalism red in tooth and claw we had

> before the New Deal. It's only right, this side believes, for the affluent to help the less fortunate. The other side believes that people have a right to keep what they earn, and that taxing them to support others, no matter how needy, amounts to theft. That's what lies behind the modern right's fondness for violent rhetoric: many activists on the right really do see taxes and regulation as tyrannical impositions on their liberty."

I have often thought in similar terms of the "morality divide" between today's liberals and tribal conservatives.

Conservative morality:

The right's morality is wedded to the *rules* — a moralizing, ideological Master Narrative propounding (at least in theory) unfettered capitalism; free markets; low taxes; minimum government; strong military; willingness to use military force, if perceived to be necessary to support American ideals; and "representative democracy" equating money to free speech. Today's "conservatives" approve of whatever outcome the rules produce. In the conservative mind, the rules are morally justified, paramount and, therefore, unchangeable and unassailable. Accordingly, with simple, if flawed, logic today's "conservatives" believe the results their "moral" rules produce must necessarily be moral. To justify this conclusion in the face of ample evidence to the contrary, they twist logic and manufacture their own separate reality, safely cocooned within the airtight news bubble promulgated by right-wing talk radio and Rupert Murdoch's Fox News and *Wall Street Journal*.

Over the past three decades, conservative rules have produced results favoring the rich, undermining the poor and causing the middle class to stagnate economically. If the rich get richer, the theory goes, it is because they are worthy (hard-working, filled with initiative, persevering, intelligent, etc.); and if the poor get poorer, it is because they are not (i.e. they are slothful, indolent, uneducated, "make bad choices," etc). Thus, for the "unworthy," poverty is a fitting result, in the conservative mindset – never mind that poverty results mainly from the failure of the ruling elite to organize society so that all may prosper.

Overarching reverence for the rules explains why on the subject of healthcare, conservatives are unmoved by statistics showing that their rules produce 50 million uninsured, millions of bankruptcies, thousands of avoidable deaths. That same rule-reverence also explains why on the subject of abortion, conservatives are unmoved by evidence of thousands of "deaths by coat hanger" when abortion is outlawed, and on the subject of narcotics, conservatives give little, if any, weight to the violence, corruption and prison overcrowding stemming from continued criminalization of drugs. Likewise, conservatives tend to rationalize as regrettable but necessary the "collateral damage" inflicted by the American military upon populations it is ostensibly protecting and/or liberating to enjoy the benefits of democracy.

It also helps that these rules, particularly lower taxes, provide right-leaning middle-class Americans with more spendable income at a time when they are feeling the pinch of recession. They willingly overlook the disproportionate tax savings for the wealthy as long as they, the middle-class, get some relief. The argument for smaller government – notably, reduced "entitlements" comprising the social safety net – also becomes compelling to members of a middle-class who do not expect to need the safety net, and are, therefore, quite willing to dispense with it altogether for the poor whom they regard as undeserving.

Jonathan Cohn, a senior editor at *The New Republic* made the following pithy observation in the October 25, 2012 issue of the magazine under the headline "*E Pluribus Duo*":

> Advocates for the red-state ["conservative"] approach to government invoke lofty principles: By resisting federal programs and defying federal laws, they say, they are standing up for liberty. These were the same arguments that the original red-staters made in the 1800s, before the Civil War, and in the 1900s, before the Civil Rights movement. Now, as then, the liberty the red states seek is the liberty to let a whole class of citizens suffer. That's not something the rest of us should tolerate. This country has room for different approaches to policy. It doesn't have room for different standards of human decency.

To which I would add: not only do red states "seek the liberty to let a whole class of citizens suffer," but also the liberty to let a class of privileged citizens prosper to the detriment of a suffering middle class and the poor without concern for those who suffer.

The "liberty" argument plays well with the red-state middle class because they are financially squeezed between flat real incomes and rising consumption aspirations. They see tax cuts as a means of satisfying those aspirations and eagerly embrace the "moochers and makers" argument as a salve to their consciences for turning their backs on the poor. The reality they don't see, however, is that the rich elite who set policy back in the Reagan days, cut income tax rates for the rich proportionately by twice as much as for the middle class (and raised them for the poor!), and shifted the burden of paying for the government toward the middle class and the poor by raising Social Security tax rates, which as a proportion of income, fall most heavily on them, given the cap on Social Security contributions for the very rich. Moreover, in the second wave of tax cutting mania under the Bush 43 administration, the main thrust was to reduce tax rates on capital gains and dividends, which by that time had become the primary source of income for those whom Reaganomics had made rich beyond reason. During the 2012 election Romney proposed to eliminate all taxes on capital gains and dividends, so that instead of paying 14 percent of his income to the federal government, he would then pay nothing, while benefitting mightily from the protection of his property and maintenance of the infrastructure afforded by the government without which he wouldn't make a dime.

Elizabeth Warren, campaigning successfully to become Senator from Massachusetts, put it succinctly: "You built a factory out there?" she said. "You moved your goods to market on the roads the rest of us paid for; you hired workers the rest of us paid to educate; you were safe in your factory because of police forces and fire forces that the rest of us paid for. You didn't have to worry that marauding bands would come and seize everything at your factory, and hire someone to protect against this, because of the work the rest of us did."

Liberal morality:

Liberals, on the other hand, focus on the *results* produced by the prevailing rules, and if the results are morally or practically objectionable, liberals believe in changing the rules to produce a more morally and practically desirable result (the political equivalent of "managing by results"). Therefore, liberals tend to be unmoved by conservative arguments based primarily on the morality of their rules.

Unlike the conservatives, united by a common, unchanging creed, liberals tend to squabble a lot about just how the rules ought to be changed, simply because of the myriad combinations and permutations of possible results and socio-economic conditions their rule changes must address. Consequently, the lack of a pat Master Narrative tends to weaken cohesiveness within the liberal ranks. (Someone once asked me why the liberals seem to have such difficulty uniting behind a common platform, to which I replied: "Because they *think*, or more accurately, *continually rethink their positions* to adapt the rules to constantly evolving conditions and results, unlike conservatives who, having accepted the conservative rules, unite behind a pat, unchanging, conservative Master Narrative, be it Reaganomics or the Bible.")

That said, in the U.S., the closest thing to a liberal Master Narrative includes counterweights to the conservative platform: *progressive taxes* high enough to cover essential government expenses and thereby balance the budget, *sensible regulation*[14] of both capitalism and markets to curb unwanted consequences of corporate misbehavior, *balanced military spending* accompanied by *greater reluctance to wage war while seeking diplomatic solutions to international tensions,* and *greater control by the government* of the safety net purse strings, particularly as relates to Social Security and health insurance and care, to provide at least minimum necessary sustenance and medical care for all, preferably, as I will argue in my forthcoming *The Egyptian Solution*, with government-assured temporary employment. Liberals also favor *righting the disequilibrium of wealth and income,* which might otherwise lead to civil unrest and war.

Notably, operating within the aegis of the Democratic Party, the American left is essentially the opposite wing of the same bird and a far cry from what Europeans regard as the "left." Consequently, both sides agree on certain core principles: capitalism and the market mechanism for the allocation of scarce resources, the need for a standing army for defense, and democracy for obtaining the consent of the governed. Where they differ is the extent of the government's involvement in the implementation of these principles. Regrettably, Democrats, like Republicans, depend on Big Money for funding, thereby inhibiting the Washington-establishment left's ability to legislate against the interests of the moneyed class in favor of We the People, and to rescind the infringements on civil liberties imposed by the Bush 43 administration to wage its War on Terrorism. I will propose a solution to this quandary in Chapter 10.

Bottom line: Both conservatives and liberals, then, are driven by morality — conservatives by the morality of the *rules*, liberals by the morality of the *results*.

Somewhat paradoxically, right and both distrust and rely on government to implement their agendas in opposite ways. Following the moral imperatives of their rules, the right distrusts the social welfare side of government as wasteful, unfairly redistributionist and detrimental to initiative, innovation and the protestant work ethic. However, the right relies on the national security/law enforcement side of government to wage profitable Long Wars, presumably in defense of "freedom" and the extension of democracy, and to and enforce their puritanical moral code of conduct in such matters as abortion, illegal narcotics, sexual behavior and certain civil rights.

On the other hand, true to the moral imperatives of their desired results, the left distrusts the national security/law enforcement side of

---

[14] In implementing "sensible regulation" liberals would do well to follow the advice of fencing masters teaching students how to hold the foil: "Hold it as you would a bird, firm enough to keep it from flying away, but not so firm as to crush it."

government as warmongering and destructive, and sees the government as intrusive and repressive in the very areas of human rights favored by the right for government intervention. The left supports active government intervention to achieve desired results in the areas of social justice and the social safety net.

Whenever morality is engaged, both sides tend to become intransigent. Debates between conservatives and liberals, therefore, tend to be unavailing because neither side is willing to abandon what are to them moral principles nor are they willing to give weight to the other's arguments.

That is why it takes a calamity, like the Great Depression, to prompt a radical change of the rules. Only when the results of the existing rules are so unquestionably bad, unjust, dysfunctional, will the swing vote in the center re-prioritize, clearly raising up the importance of results over rules, unite behind a more coherent left in agreeing to change the rules radically and give a reform-minded president the mandate necessary to effect such change, as Franklin Delano Roosevelt received in 1932.

The Panic of 2008 and Great Recession provided a similar wake-up call to the electorate, sufficient to arrest the rightward swing of the political pendulum, resulting in the election of the liberally inclined President Obama who offered "hope and change." Unlike FDR, who assumed power more than 3 years after the Crash of 1929 and the ensuing Great Depression (by which time the electorate clearly understood the crisis to have been caused by flaws of the Republicans' policies, giving Roosevelt overwhelming support in Congress), Obama had the misfortune of coming into power only 4 months after the 2008 crisis began. Consequently, voters soon became confused about which policies to blame for their lingering economic discomfort in 2009 and 2010. Republicans were quick to shift the blame away from the Bush administration to the Democrats, challenging Obama's manhood for "refusing to take responsibility" for the ongoing crisis by blaming the Bush administration for the unacceptably high unemployment. Given the length of time required for households to deleverage following the orgy of imprudent lending fostered by Bush's policies, the blame quite properly rested with his administration. Nevertheless, Republicans benefitted from the predictable voter knee-jerk reaction against incumbents during harsh economic conditions, allowing Republicans in the 2010 elections to seize control of the House and whittle away at the Democrat majority in the Senate. Things improved enough by the time the 2012 elections rolled round for the electorate to give Obama another chance, particularly since Republican ideologues alienated women, youth, Blacks and Hispanics.

It remains to be seen whether the election of Barack Obama in 2008 on a platform of "hope and change," confirmed by his re-election in 2012, will result in a meaningful reversal of the political pendulum toward serving justice, promoting sustainability and achieving socially stabilizing equity in the distribution of the fruits of prosperity while preserving growth incentives inherent in free markets.

Chapter 10: The American Liberal Revolution. A new political model: Occupy Theaters

"Telling the truth at times of universal deceit is a revolutionary act."
H. G. Wells

We must give credit where credit is due: American liberals owe an enduring debt of gratitude to the demonstrators who launched what we might call the American Liberal Revolution in 2011 by occupying the capitol in Madison, Wisconsin on behalf of public workers' unions, and later, the Occupiers who took to the streets and public parks in New York, Oakland and across the nation, to awaken America and the world to the inequities, injustices and abuses inflicted by the 1 Percent upon the 99 Percent and demand (unspecified) redress. They demonstrated the courage of their convictions, putting their bodies on the line in the tradition of those who stood against the British at Concord and Lexington and wintered at Valley Forge. In so doing, they gave voice at last to the discontents of the too-long-silent, powerless majority of Americans yearning for "hope and change" promised by Barack Obama but largely thwarted by intransigent demagogues on the right committed to regaining and retaining power on behalf of their rich and powerful benefactors, no matter the cost to the nation.

Liberals can take heart, however, insofar as the political equivalent of Newton's Law of Motion ("For every action there is an equal and opposite reaction.") applies in their favor at what appears to be the end of the domestic political pendulum's rightward displacement, just as the right became energized at the end of its leftward displacement during the Johnson administration.

To be clear: Wisconsin demonstrators and the Occupy Movement are nothing less than the vanguard of a revolution in progress, driven by resentments toward "repeated injuries and usurpations" inflicted by the 1 Percent, not unlike those grievances inspiring the revolution by which our republic was founded. Unlike the earlier revolution, however, the American Liberal Revolution ("the Movement") has the ability to achieve its ends through the ballot, rather than the bullet, thanks to the foresight of our revolutionary founding fathers in creating the democratic process enshrined in the U.S. Constitution -- "if we can keep it."

Therefore, embracing a *democratic* (small d) American Liberal Revolution need not raise fears of mobs storming the Congress or of guillotines lining the Washington Mall; instead the Movement seeks peaceful, democratic change achieved through peaceful mass mobilizations along the lines of the Gandhi, Martin Luther King, Jr. models. The word revolution, after all, comes from the Latin *revolutio*, meaning simply "a turn around," without any implied necessity of violence. In general aviation, the prudent course of action when heading toward a storm is to "hang a 180" and get the hell away from it. That's it.

Nor should we shy away from the description of the Movement as "radical," meaning advocacy of "far-reaching, thorough political or social reform" – which is, in a nutshell, what it's all about – electing representatives to serve the interests of the general population rather than the moneyed elite. Our problems have been created by a certain set of policies enacted at the behest and in the interests of the 1 Percent. Solving them will require a political 180-degree turn, radically reversing those policies to serve the interests of We The People – nothing less.

Like our founding revolution, the incipient American Liberal Revolution has progressed and continues progressing through a predictable series of steps on the road to achieving its objectives:

- Revolutions originate with "injuries and usurpations" inflicted by government, giving rise to discontent. In 1776, Americans -- fed up with "taxation without representation" and other "sent-hither-Swarms-of-Officers-to-harass-our-people" grievances not unlike those we experience today -- declared they were no longer obligated to obey the crown, but instead were independent and free. . . to assume among the Powers of the Earth, the Separate but Equal Station to which the laws of nature and of nature's God entitle them." Today, "taxation without representation" remains contentious, inasmuch as the people are taxed, but elected representatives don't serve their interests, but rather serve the interests of wealthy campaign contributors. This alienation of elected representatives from the interests of the people they are supposed to represent, in favor of anonymous campaign donors with agendas radically at odds with the local population, has become particularly egregious since the Supreme Court's *Citizens United* campaign financing decision. (See PBS Frontline report "Big Sky, Big Money" http://www.pbs.org/wgbh/pages/frontline/big-sky-big-money/ of October 30, 2012) We are also aggrieved by "Swarms of Officers sent to harass our people" by intrusive and occasionally abusive IRS agents and law enforcement officers overstepping boundaries while waging wars on tax evaders, drug dealers, terrorists and protesters.
- Next come the public manifestations of that discontent by means of demonstrations in the streets – think protests and boycotts in response to the Sugar Act, Stamp Act, the Declaratory Act and Townshend Acts before the Revolutionary War as the analog of last year's protests by the Tea Party on the right, and on the left, in

Madison, Wisconsin spreading across the country with the Occupy movement.

- These demonstrations are then met with forcible repression by the authorities – think Boston Massacre as the analog of today's forcible evictions, tear gassing, pepper spraying and rough arrests of Occupy demonstrators from Davis and Oakland to Zuccotti Park. Such repression serves to sound the alarm, alert and unite the citizenry to support the revolution.
- Then follow acts of civil disobedience further exemplifying the resolve of the revolutionaries to change the established order – think the Boston Tea Party as the analog to the shutting down of the Port of Oakland.
- Next comes the phase during which the revolutionaries organize, formulating the movement's principles and objectives, rallying support for the revolution, electing leaders to guide it and devising plans to implement it. The 18th century analog would be the Continental Congresses, the publication of *Common Sense* by Thomas Paine, the Declaration of Independence by Thomas Jefferson, the formation of the Continental Army with George Washington as Commander-in-Chief. This is the organizational stage now confronting the Movement, and is one of the main themes presented in this chapter. Stick around.
- Then follows the implementation phase of the revolution, where the organized revolutionaries overcome the opposition through purposeful, concerted action leading to the installation of government responsive to the needs of the population. Lacking the alternative of the democratic process, the founding fathers had to resort to the Revolutionary War to achieve their ends. The Constitution they subsequently wrote provides today's revolutionaries the peaceful, democratic process for marshalling an overwhelming electoral consensus in favor of the radical objectives of the Movement. The means and method for achieving this consensus – analogous to the Constitutional Convention in 1887 -- will be discussed at greater length below.
- And finally there is task of governing according to the principles and policies fundamental to the revolution – think of the formation of the U.S. Government under the presidency of George Washington as the analog of the task of legislative reform and governance tomorrow's liberals will face after achieving electoral victory.

Just as the troops at Valley Forge did not win the Revolutionary War by remaining encamped, neither can the Occupy Movement win its

Revolution by hunkering down indefinitely in primitive, leaderless encampments around the country. The Movement must revitalize its momentum and thereby avoid becoming ineffectual and irrelevant now that the novelty of camping in public parks has worn off. It is past time for the Occupy campers to come in from the cold and get organized for the Revolution. Merely protesting is not enough to bring about meaningful change. At some point the Movement must expand its base, produce leaders, devise platforms, win elections, enact and implement reforms.

While our democracy has taken a pasting at the hands of the 1 Percent over the past three decades, it still respects the majority of votes cast in elections – for the most part. Numbers still count, so it is the task of the Movement to marshal sufficient numbers to elect representatives who will pass laws and run the country according to the will and for the benefit of *We the People* as the framers of the Constitution intended.

The question is, how?

To answer the question, we must first discard how <u>not</u> to go about it.

As described in the previous chapter (and it bears repeating), today's electoral process is dominated by an unholy alliance of the superrich who pick political candidates and fund their campaigns; the lobbyists and political action committee (PAC) executives who dispense campaign contributions; the candidates who accept such financial support and who are, therefore, obligated to support policies favoring their benefactors; the media and their hangers-on, primarily television, who are the recipients of campaign funds in the form of paid advertising needed to garner votes from a sedentary electorate. Therefore, money, "the mother's milk of politics," equals votes in today's elections, given the structure of the present political process.

Liberals must recognize the impossibility of competing successfully against the moneyed interests by engaging in a political process where money equals votes. The 1 Percent controlling two-fifths of the nation's wealth will always be able to outspend the rest of the population, especially after *Citizens United vs. Federal Election Commission* gave the rich access to corporate treasuries to fund political action committees. As long as the dominant political process is one in which money equals votes, the 1 Percent will prevail, regardless of which party is in office.

What the Movement requires, therefore, if any reforms are to be accomplished, is <u>a new political process</u> capable of establishing a dominant political consensus, untethered from big money, PACs, lobbyists and television ads. Such a political process requires just three critical components: lots of people, multiplex movie theaters and the Internet -- not much money, no paid network or cable television.

Here's how it would work – let's call the process "Occupy Theaters."

OVERVIEW:

The ends include a) developing a dominant political consensus around a comprehensive range of interests shared by the majority of the electorate without resorting to the present political processes dependent on Big Money or television b) formulating a corresponding platform around which such a majority can coalesce through a participatory democratic process c) selecting, through that same process, representatives of the popular majority to speak for the Movement and, through the electoral process specified in the Constitution, to represent the majority in the corridors of power at all levels of government d) governing in accordance with the principles expressed in the platform.

The means to these ends include the use of multiplex movie theaters around the nation as political venues, linked audio-visually through the Internet so as to constitute networks capable of real-time Assemblies at varying levels of participation, starting with individual theaters and, in time, expanding to include city, county, regional, state and national levels. Such Assemblies will be tasked with contributing planks to the platform, nominating leaders/spokespersons and drawing up plans for political activities – demonstrations, petitions, recruitment events, etc. -- to further the objectives of the Movement. Funding for the Assemblies will come from the Assembly attendees themselves – through ticket sales at rates comparable to attending a movie – collected at the door through the normal theater ticket sale process, with the proceeds being divided between the theater owners and the Movement according to an agreed-upon formula.

The method involves holding periodic Assemblies organized through social media on the Internet, and taking place in participating theaters around the country networked through the Internet at times when the theaters are typically not open for business in the mornings, and, given the nocturnal habits of today's youth, late at night.

This is what it would look like, step by step:

1. ***Movement activists organize on the Internet via social media, to achieve a critical mass of money and spokespersons sufficient to negotiate with national and local movie chain owners, to hold political Assemblies on specified mornings and late evenings (weekends, most likely),*** a time when the theaters would otherwise

remain empty and non-revenue-producing. Preferably contracts are signed by Movement representatives with movie chains at the national level to achieve uniform terms (regionally or locally) whereby participants pay the usual price of admission, say $10, at the ticket counter, and the proceeds are divided between the theater owners and the movement in an agreed-upon split.

   a. Theater owners, eager to rent out their theater during the "off hours," already solicit such rentals, as for example: http://www.amctheatres.com/Business/TheatreRentals/
   b. Theaters are already organized to collect and disburse funds efficiently and accountably. Ten dollars for each attendee per event seems a small price to pay for good government.
   c. To be inclusive, some provision can be made for those unable to afford it, exchanging some form of service to the organization in exchange for admission to the Assembly.
   d. The notion of bringing in new prospective supporters should be imbued in the culture to produce an exponential expansion of membership in the Movement.

2. Each auditorium in the multiplex theaters will be dedicated to a specific policy topic, for example: agriculture, defense and foreign policy, economy, education, environment, financial reform, health care, homeland security, housing, immigration, justice, military and veterans, privacy, water, women's health and others, depending on local interest in Special Interest Groups (SIGs). This arrangement brings the multiplicity of liberal issues under one roof while preserving the Movement's ability to concentrate on each in depth.
3. Each auditorium will be equipped with audio-visual equipment – video camera, lighting, microphones hooked up to the auditorium's sound and projection system. And – here's the critical part – ***each auditorium will have the capacity to be networked not only to every other auditorium in each theater, but also, through the Internet, to every participating auditorium in theaters across the country.*** Such networking will permit the Assemblies to link up variously at the local, city, county, state and, ultimately, national level organizing to achieve the necessary dominant political consensus.
4. Participants at any given theater, therefore, will conduct Special Interest Group (SIG) Assemblies inside each auditorium where they will discuss problems and solutions pertaining to their specific area of interest for the first hour, say. Speakers will rise spontaneously to express their concerns, opinions, recommended solutions with a view to achieving the previously described ends of the Movement.

5. After the SIG Assemblies in the various auditoria have conducted their business, they will then join a theater-wide Assembly via electronic network and related audio-visual technology, including, as desired, multi-media presentations, displayed on each screen throughout the theater. This will require some technical skills and equipment, well within today's capabilities, provided in some combination by the theater and the Movement. Speakers nominated by acclamation in the SIG Assemblies in each auditorium will have the opportunity to present a summary of their Assembly's work to the theater-wide Assembly, with a view toward 1) achieving theater-wide consensus around agreed-upon objectives 2) nominating spokespersons for the group who will represent the theater-wide Assembly to the next level up in the network, say city-wide. Think of the process in terms of a political "America's Got Talent" or "American Idol" format, with local tryouts followed by bigger venues with voting conducted by cell phones and laptop computers to organize locally in support of the Movement, including developing plans of action for demonstrations and other political activities to further the Movement's objectives.
6. Eventually, the theater network can be expanded vertically to conduct networked Assemblies at the county, state and ultimately national level. Such expanded networking should take place vertically *within* Special Interest Groups endeavoring to find common ground on their particular area of interest and expertise, and later melded *across* areas of interest to devise a comprehensive platform, embodying the objectives the Movement, expressed in such a way as to awaken, inspire and motivate the members of the Movement to undertake effective political action; develop a leadership cadre to represent the Movement in elections at all levels of government; and organize overwhelming popular support for the Movement's objectives, translating ultimately into electoral victories.

This new method of political organization offers many advantages to the 99 Percent, in its quest to achieve electoral success.

It requires far less money than the present paid-media-intensive political process – no need to pay for expensive TV ads and media consultants, little need for renting expensive office space (much of the movement's business can be conducted as a virtual organization via the Internet).

Being funded by affordable individual contributions collected at theater ticket counters, it avoids becoming captive to the Big Money interests, enabling it to serve the interests of the 99 Percent. Money will no longer equal votes.

Theaters provide ideal venues for the new political system: they are available at times of the day when they are usually unused; they are also ubiquitous, and therefore accessible to all interested members of the 99 Percent; people know where they are, how to get to them; there is plenty of (usually) free parking available; they are comfortable, familiar, offer food and drink as well as rest-room facilities to participants and offer no provocation for the authorities to disrupt Assemblies with police action (unlike tent cities in public parks).

Multi-screen theaters are ideally suited to provide a multi-issue political Movement with venues to discuss individual policy themes in separate, focused Assemblies and later to consolidate such discussions in General Assemblies at the local, state and national levels. Importantly, theaters today already possess much of the multi-media, audio-visual, Internet and networking equipment necessary to organize networked Assemblies at the various levels of participation. (Theaters are already offering networked content, like the British National Theater and N.Y. Metropolitan Opera, through NCM Media Networks' Fathom Events (http://www.ncm.com/ncm-fathom))

Most importantly, Occupy Theaters puts the *polis* (the body of citizens, i.e., the people) actively back into politics, enabling the citizenry to come together – shoulder to shoulder, face-to-face – to fashion and implement their democracy with live human interaction, rather than sitting at home alone in their recliners being force-fed the 1 Percent's stale, lifeless, self-serving political propaganda through television. Like traditional town meetings, the Movement can provide a more effective, interesting, motivating, nurturing and enduring political process than the impersonal biannual ad-fest offered by traditional politics. People will experience the thrill of being part of something bigger than themselves, something historical and game changing. It's the difference between the warm medium of live, participatory theater, and the cool medium of television. Think of it as the next evolutionary step in high-tech politics, with a very human touch.

The Occupy Theaters political model dovetails nicely with a piece by Cognitive Policy Works founder and director, Joe Brewer: "It is No Mystery: The Real Reason Conservatives Keep Winning — Progressives won't win until we get a lot better at building binding communities of trust and shared identity." (Cognitive Policy Works, June 28, 2012)
Brewer states the problem:

> And what about Progressives? *We are divided into issue silos, unable to form lasting coalitions that bond us together under the same ideological flag*, and easily kept on the defensive through the age-old strategy of Divide and Conquer. We have difficulty trusting each other and *our*

> *funders are unable or unwilling to invest in talent for talent's sake* — they always need to monitor the outcomes of their giving and almost never fund the operational needs of our advocacy organizations. This is the real reason why we lose. It isn't that their ideas are better. The difference is entirely in the execution.

His prescription:

> Building trust across organizations requires a three-pronged approach. First, we have to *know our own values* so that we can articulate them with authenticity and authority. Second, we must *make these values explicit and engage in the practice of radical transparency* to leave no questions about where we stand and what we care about. And third, we've got to *seek out those who resonate with these values* at the core level of their personal identity. It is upon this foundation that we can engage in the vital work of building trust.

This Occupy Theaters proposal — to sever the dependency on Big Money and TV by activating a new political model based on Assemblies in a network of movie theaters linked together electronically — overcomes Brewer's stated problems, by uniting liberals/progressives in a common network where they can form lasting coalitions and bonds under the same ideological flag, and by self-funding by collecting entrance fees at the door (the price of a movie ticket) sufficient to fund the Assemblies.

The proposal also responds to Brewer's three-pronged prescription: Through local, city, state and national Assemblies taking place in the movie network, values can be debated and platforms agreed upon in a process of "radical transparency." Theaters — familiar venues to all — are the logical place where people can be invited to join the critical mass of liberal/progressives necessary to nominate representatives and build the necessary electoral momentum to elect these representatives to office.

Obstacles:

I foresee two significant, though not insurmountable, obstacles to the Occupy Theaters proposal: the danger of counterproductive populist demagoguery overtaking the consensus, and the problem of achieving a productive liberal consensus within a large and diverse group of people (what might be termed the "herding cats phenomenon").

I don't underestimate the dangers of populist demagoguery, having observed the enduring ill effects of Peronism in Argentina, continuing to the present under the misguided rule of Cristina Fernandez de Kirchner – one among many such examples. The Founding Fathers, mindful of this danger, wrote into the Constitution a system of "checks and balances" intended to counter potential demagogic tendencies leading to the downfall of democracy as articulated in the previously cited quote:

> A democracy cannot exist as a permanent form of government. It can only exist until the voters discover that they can vote themselves largesse from the public treasury. From that moment on, the majority always votes for the candidates promising the most benefits from the public treasury with the result that a democracy always collapses over loose fiscal policy, always followed by a dictatorship. The average age of the world's greatest civilizations has been 200 years.
>
> Great nations rise and fall. The people go from bondage to spiritual truth, to great courage, from courage to liberty, from liberty to abundance, from abundance to selfishness, from selfishness to complacency, from complacency to apathy, from apathy to dependence, from dependence back again to bondage.

We have seen how, through Reaganomics, this principle has been realized in favor of the moneyed interests, precisely the opposite outcome from that articulated by the author of the quote. Big Money, operating through the traditional channels of communication (notably television), has voted itself "largesse from the public treasury," resulting in the present "loose fiscal policy" menacing democracy with dictatorship. The U.S. presently seems to have reached the stage where the electorate is both apathetic and, to some extent dependent (mostly seniors who themselves largely underwrote that dependency with payroll taxes), while the moneyed interests are aggressively active and happily dependent on low taxes, lax regulation and Long Wars. Meanwhile, through the Patriot Acts and the National Defense Authorization Act of 2012, the stage has been set for dictatorship.

Occupy Theaters offers a populist check and balance to the present excesses of Big Money politics. However, through the First Amendment, expanded by the Supreme Court's *Citizens United vs. FEC* decision, Property will still have its say via the traditional media channels, in turn exercising its own counterbalancing check and balance restraining the tendency toward populist demagoguery inherent in the direct democracy of Occupy Theaters. It ultimately comes down to whether you believe in *Vox Populi* or not. I do, sharing Churchill's view that "Democracy is the worst form of government, except for all the others."

Assuming Occupy Theaters becomes operational, the "herding cats" problem, traditional in left-wing politics, will ultimately be resolved in one of several ways: a unified third party movement or a coalition of fragmented left-leaning parties along the lines of European democracy. Such political forces could be expected to either supplant the Democratic Party (much as the Republican Party did the Whigs in the mid-19th century) or to exercise its influence through the Democratic Party, much as the Tea Party has within the Republican Party recently. Frankly, I don't know which of these alternatives could be expected to prevail; so once again, we must rely on the will of the people expressed through Constitutional means to find a way to make democracy work.

These issues remain open to discussion and debate, for which purpose I offer a Facebook Page (American Liberal Revolution) and a website (www.the-predicament.com) as venues, and on Twitter, #AmLibRevolution and @AmLibRevolution.

It's a daunting task, and yet the history of the Republican Party suggests that it can be done. Consider: only six years elapsed from the founding of the Republican Party by a small group of discontented Whigs to the election of the Party's greatest President, Abraham Lincoln.

Without this radically new political model, (or some other workable alternative to the present model. independent of Big Money and TV) the Movement cannot hope to prevail inasmuch as they will be competing in the existing political model, run by Big Money and TV, a game the moneyed interests will always win.

Confronted with a government dominated by and serving the interest of the 1 Percent, the 99 Percent must mobilize to turn around the government to represent and serve the interests of We the People, by whose authority and for whose Life, Liberty and Pursuit of Happiness the Constitution was established. Occupy Theaters offers the best, and perhaps last chance to achieve these revolutionary ends peacefully.

Chapter 11: Seeking a peaceful international *modus vivendi*. The world: "community" or "cauldron"?

My Dartmouth classmate, psychoanalyst Ted Beal, and I recently exchanged the following e-mails within the Class of '62 "Great Issues Discussion Group." The thread was titled: "In war we all desecrate the enemy. . . really?" discussing the U.S. soldiers photographed urinating on dead Afghan "insurgents." Ted wrote:

> Jungar ["Restrepo" filmmaker] suggests we are all responsible for the context of the act and not the act. I think all citizens in our society share some responsibility for the creation of this larger societal context. There is no justification for the act of the soldiers, only explanation.
>
> It is not possible to engage in routine "legalized" wartime killing without dehumanizing the victim. To switch off your dehumanizing filter the moment your enemy ceases to breathe is difficult. I see soldiers who remain very effective at physically killing others but leave the service because they can no longer do it emotionally. Any war, not just counterinsurgency, requires a continuing self-discipline and sense of honor.
>
> The larger context is that we need to figure out how to relate more effectively with "our enemies" not just by killing them and having to deal with their surviving friends and family.
>
> If the world is not a "community" then is it just a cauldron?

I replied: Ted,

> As always, your depth of empathy, objective insight and humanity are an inspiration — surely a tribute to your professional training and experience. How pithy to ask, "If the world is not a 'community' then is it just a cauldron?"
>
> Your comment (". . . we need to figure out how to relate more effectively with "our enemies" not just by killing them or having to deal with their surviving friends and family.") goes straight to the heart of the matter, extending well beyond the confines of the incident giving rise to this thread.
>
> We are presently engaged in a shooting war between conflicting ideologies with a strong hostile religious undercurrent hearkening back to the Arab Empire, the Crusades and the Ottoman Empire. The interjection of religion into the conflict tends to make the antagonists more obdurate, ruthless and brutal, since protagonists on each side believes they are "doing God's work," paradoxically justifying in their minds barbaric behavior antithetical to the basic precepts of their religion ("Thou shall not murder"

"Love thine enemies." and "Turn the other cheek." For example, see the long, deadly Wars of Religion accompanying the Reformation.) I am reminded of Ambrose Bierce's trenchant poem, *Arma Virumque* ('Arms and the Man' – opening line of Vergil's "Aeneid") written during the U.S. Civil War:

> "OURS is a Christian army"; so he said
> A regiment of bangomen who led.
> "And ours a Christian navy," added he
> Who sailed a thunder-junk upon the sea.
> Better they know than men unwarlike do
> What is an army, and a navy too.
> Pray God there may be sent them by-and-by
> The knowledge what a Christian is, and why.
> For somewhat lamely the conception runs
> Of a brass-buttoned Jesus firing guns.

Millions within the Christian community in the United States believe the biblical book of *Revelation* literally, anticipating the prospect of "blood flowing out of the winepress [of God's wrath] rising as high as the horse's bridles for a distance of 1,600 stadia" in a coming battle of Armageddon predicted by John of Patmos. *The policy implications of such extremist convictions, if subscribed to at the highest levels of government, become truly frightening – particularly when matched by suicidal zeal within the extremes of Islam.* Apparently it has already occurred. If the report initially carried in the University of Lausanne's *Allez Savoir* and picked up by *Mother Jones, The Guardian*, and other mainstream press outlets, is to be believed, President Bush invoked biblical prophesy when trying to justify the war in Iraq to French President Jacques Chirac in 2003, saying "Gog and Magog are at work in the Middle East. . . . The biblical prophecies are being fulfilled. . . . This confrontation is willed by God, who wants to use this conflict to erase his people's enemies before a New Age begins." Bush's comments "stupefied and disturbed" Chirac, who "wondered how someone could be so superficial and fanatical in his beliefs." Chirac, once out of office, reportedly confirmed the story according to a book, published in France in March 2009, by journalist Jean Claude Maurice.

The great fear engendered by the present conflict is irreversible escalation to all-out war — a terminally apocalyptic outcome in an age of atomic, biological and chemical weapons.

In the 20th Century we witnessed two all-out, global wars, the first triggered by a relatively inconsequential act, the assassination in June 1914 of Archduke Ferdinand and his Duchess in Sarajevo. The second, basically a *revanche* of the first in Europe, was triggered by the short-sightedness of Clemenceau and Lloyd George in imposing a humiliating, punitive peace on Germany at Versailles, and in the Orient, triggered by U.S. imposition of a steel and oil embargo on Japan in July 1941, ultimately in response to Japanese atrocities in Manchuria. That is not to justify the behavior of the Axis powers before the wars, but rather, as you put it, to *explain* – in this instance, how repeated provocation and retaliation lead to uncontrollable, irreversible escalation. Each of these triggers engaged the mechanism of irreversible escalation, resulting in all-out wars in which all weapons and resources were thrown into the fray, including nuclear bombs.

Presently, the process of escalation ("provocation and retaliation") is clearly evident, arguably starting with the CIA's overthrow in 1953 and subsequent confinement of Muhammad Mossadegh in Iran, followed by the overthrow of the Shah, the Iranian Hostage Crisis in 1979, the bombing of the Marine Barracks in Lebanon, the first bombing of the World Trade Center, the first Gulf War, and various other acts, like the bombing of the embassies in Tanzania, and Nairobi, the U.S.S. Cole, culminating in 9/11 and retaliatory wars in Afghanistan and Iraq.

From the assassination of Archduke Ferdinand, we learned how at the time of the incident it is not known that the dogs of war have been unleashed. From the time of the assassination in June until the guns of August 1914 were fired, the question on everyone's lips was "Will there be war?" Yet anyone familiar with the German predicament -- flanked by the allied Russia to the east and France and England to the west -- should have realized the inevitability of war the moment Russia and France began to mobilize. (See: the Schlieffen Plan.) We further learned how the conflict stemming from a retaliatory act cannot be neatly confined to a limited theater of action, as Emperor Franz Joseph and Kaiser Wilhelm discovered after invading Serbia. Consequently, we should be careful about crossing lines beyond which lies irreversible escalation. For that matter, today who can say the line has not already been crossed?

All of which brings me back to your central point: ". . . we need to figure out how to relate more effectively with 'our enemies' not just by killing them and having to deal with their surviving friends and family."

Today, humanity is faced with a choice: continue to escalate and risk irreversible escalation to all-out war and annihilation, or DE-ESCALATE and seek a peaceful *modus vivendi. Consider the daunting challenge (given our history and the lethality of modern atomic weapons), requiring* ***an eternity*** *of no more all-out wars if humanity is to survive.* In short, we cannot afford *one* slip into the bloody waters of irreversible escalation, *ever*. The Russell-Einstein Manifesto put it succinctly in 1955: "Here, then, is the problem which we present to you, stark and dreadful and inescapable: Shall we put an end to the human race; or shall mankind renounce war?"

We are now on the cusp of yet another escalation with Iran, backing Iran into a corner with crippling sanctions (as we did Japan in July 1941). Israel is threatening air attacks on Iranian nuclear facilities to prevent the Iranians from acquiring nuclear weaponry[15]. The Iranians are threatening to close the Strait of Hormuz, the choke point for about a third of the world's current oil supply. Should these events come to pass, the consequences would be global, risking yet further escalation to the point where the world's two largest religions, both nuclear-armed [Pakistan already, Iran soon?], square off against each other.

During the Cold War, mutually assured destruction (MAD) served as a deterrent to war between rational adversaries, state actors committed to their own survival. Today, the prospect of mutually assured destruction may not stay the hands of religious zealots for whom martyrdom holds rewards in paradise and heaven, and posthumous honor on earth among peers.

To any rational, humane individual, the risks of all-out war today are sufficient incentive to embrace de-escalation and the quest for a *modus vivendi* with Islam as the only sane alternative. The logical first step in de-escalation is to remove all Western troops, mercenaries, drones, in short, all threat of violence from land regarded as "holy" by Muslims so as to deprive Jihadists of their primary recruiting tool. Such a gesture might reasonably be

---

[15] Since those words were written, Israel mobilized massively in September (2012) on its borders with Syria and Lebanon to the north in what would appear to be a defensive move securing its flanks in anticipation of Arab and Persian response to an Israeli attack on Iranian nuclear facilities. Israeli Prime Minister Netanyahu and Iranian President Ahmadinejad ramped up the confrontation at the U.N. in September. Netanyahu warned that Iran's progress toward a nuclear bomb would be irreversible by next spring or summer. He demanded that world powers draw a "red line" to trigger military action if Tehran refuses to stop before then. Faced with U.S. opposition to drawing such a line, Netanyahu has since indicated greater acceptance of diplomacy, for now.

expected to open the channels of communication between the West and moderate Islam in much the same way as *détente* and *rapprochement* succeeded in ending the Cold War peaceably. Leave it then to moderate Islam to talk radical Islam down off its perch. Perhaps then we may realize the world is a community and not a cauldron.

Best regards, David

Not long ago, I watched the final episode of Season 1 of Aaron Sorkin's "The Newsroom" (airing the day before the 2012 Republican National Convention in Tampa). In this episode, titled "The Greater Fool," Sorkin pulls back the curtain on the Tea Party religious fundamentalists now exercising overpowering sway within the Republican Party.

He begins by debunking the Party's claim that America was founded as a Christian nation, quoting such seminal figures as John Adams, Thomas Jefferson, and the Constitution itself (1st Amendment) to which he could have added James Madison and George Washington. He chides otherwise mainstream Republicans for pandering to religious fundamentalists in the Tea Party, showing a clip of then-presidential-candidate John McCain stammering though the assertion that "The Constitution established the United States of America as a Christian nation." Sorkin then underscores the hypocrisy of the Tea Party religious fundamentalists, observing that "the biggest enemy of the phony Republicans is Jesus Christ, who said "heal the sick, feed the hungry, care for the weakest among us and always pray in private." However, Sorkin saves his most withering fire for the climax at the end of the show, in which he cites the damning attributes of the Tea Party religious fundamentalists:

- Ideological purity
- Compromise as weakness
- A fundamentalist belief in scriptural literalism
- Denying science
- Unmoved by facts
- Undeterred by new information
- A hostile fear of progress
- A demonization of education
- A need to control women's bodies
- Severe xenophobia
- Tribal mentality
- Intolerance of dissent
- Pathological hatred of U.S. Government

He concludes: "They can call themselves the Tea Party, they can call themselves conservatives, they can even call themselves Republicans (although Republicans certainly shouldn't). But we should call them what they really are: The American Taliban. And the American Taliban cannot survive if Dorothy Cooper is allowed to vote." (Dorothy Cooper is a 75-year-old Black woman who lacks government-issued ID qualifying her to vote according to newly enacted voter identification requirements in Republican-controlled states.)

My personal view is that if the American Taliban succeed in "taking this country back" by disenfranchising those who are most ill-served by right-wing principles (embodied socially by religious fundamentalism, economically by Reaganomics and militarily by "Long War" policies), the disconnect between what the majority of American people want and what the ruling elite deliver could eventually become so great as to provoke a cataclysmic counter-reaction. If, in their zeal to preserve power at all costs, the American Taliban and their allies among the rich and powerful elite, continue to frustrate the will of a majority of Americans at the ballot box, the repressed majority might resort to violent revolution and/or civil war to which an American Taliban-controlled government would likely respond by instigating a war of religion abroad as a means of remaining in power by unifying the country against a common enemy: the matching polar opposite, Muslim extremism, the definition of which would soon be blurred to include all Muslims.

> "When fascism comes to America, it will come wrapped in a flag and carrying a cross." (Attributed to C.S. Lewis)

I wonder how the Class of 2012 will fare in today's nuclear-armed world balanced, as Jim Hale put it half a century ago, between "despairing, fatalistic" pessimism and "realistic" optimism about the prospects of nuclear holocaust. Will their America embrace "a long-range and calm perspective of the rivalry and struggle" between Islam and the West? Will they "learn to live with a standing threat to our culture" and to "reduce the proportions of the [Radical Islamist] menace" as a means of making "our competition and rivalry less dangerous for the future of mankind," in the spirit of Ambassador Dean's counsel in 1962? *Can the U.S. survive and thrive without an antagonist?*

To put it bluntly, I have argued in the foregoing chapters, that continuation along the apocalyptic path of right-wing extremism – favoring polarizing and destabilizing inequality of wealth, unbalanced fiscal policy, unrestrained corporate power and Long Wars between religions – risks irreversible escalation to all-out war and annihilation.

If, indeed, every action is met with an equal and opposite reaction, such a catastrophe might unleash a violent counter-reaction by economically distressed multitudes along the lines of the French Revolution – a particularly dangerous prospect in a country with more guns than people.

The possibility of another Great Depression unleashing violent revolution at home coupled with an apocalyptic war between religions abroad represents the full, horrifying potential extent of The Predicament.

Accordingly, given the horrific end results of our present course, it is imperative to reverse course now, through principles of American liberalism calculated to restore suitable balance in the distribution of wealth and the burden of taxation, as well as between defense and social spending, and economic progress and environmental sustainability; rein in the excesses of the corporate plutocracy; support the education and wellbeing of the population, and de-escalate the present expanding conflict between extremist Muslims and Christians so as to arrive at a sustainable *modus vivendi*. Only by such a radical reversal can we hope to realize the universal aspirations for peace, prosperity, order, human rights, and the survival of the human species.

Don't expect our current leaders, Muslim or Western, to reverse the present course to calamity. There exists a dedicated, determined constituency for war among leaders on both sides of the divide who, if given their head, will make war a self-fulfilling prophesy and then denigrate pacifists as having been on the wrong side of history.

If de-escalation and a *modus vivendi* is to be achieved, it will be up to a critical mass of "the people" on both sides, mindful of the dangers of irreversible escalation and sharing the universal aspirations for peace, shared prosperity, and the survival of the human species. Avoiding apocalypse will be the job of ordinary individuals, conscious of our common humanity, who, like Muhammad Ali, refusing to be drafted because he "had not quarrel with them Viet Congs," recognize that the farmer in Kankakee, Illinois has no quarrel with the shopkeeper in Tehran and vice versa. Wars are the result of misguided leadership seeking to further the interests of the ruling elite and not those of the people. It is up to the people – an informed electorate, as Eisenhower said – to insist their interests be served.

By now you probably feel: 1) overwhelmed by the sheer explosive power of the ticking time-bomb comprising The Predicament 2) disheartened by the failure of senior generations to acknowledge it, let alone take positive steps to defuse it and 3) despairing of the Millennials' ability to do so. Such doubt may also prompt you to believe your future is hopeless and my exhortations to action, and those of other like-minded liberals, as naively quixotic. Perhaps it is and perhaps they are – if you allow it.

On the other hand look at how far Americans have come in the realm of civil rights – from the cruelty of slavery, later Jim Crow oppression and, in the 1950s, shameful discrimination against Blacks depicted in *The Help*, to the repudiation of "separate but equal," the integration all government service, equal opportunity of employment and housing, of recognition and even idolization of Black athletes and actors, and the election of our first Black President.

Look how far America has come in the realm of rights of the disabled and gay rights – albeit imperfectly realized so far, but exhibiting significant progress nonetheless.

Look at how far America has come in the realm of women's rights – from women as disenfranchised, lightly-educated chattel in the 19th century; later in the 1950s career-limited as schoolteachers, secretaries, nurses or housewife as depicted in *The Mona Lisa Smile* and *Mad Men*; to full participation in the corridors of power and to unlimited career opportunities in business, the professions and military service, thanks to "Devils who wore Prada." (See Chapter 15 and "Sympathy for the Devil Who Wears Prada" in my *Cassandra Chronicles* back issues.) With more women than men now graduating from college, we have reason to hope women may succeed in reversing the traditional ratio of men to women in positions of power, thereby quenching the testosterone-fueled fires of perpetual war with a much-needed tidal wave of estrogen. Sarah Palin, Michelle Bachmann and Ann Coulter notwithstanding, I have long agreed with Dr. Daniel Amen's premise that if the world is to be saved, it will be up to women do it, bringing to bear their qualities of empathy, intuition, cooperation, nurturing in a world now dominated by fear, greed and aggression. We're trending in the right direction. But will women make it in time?

None of these social transformations was achieved from the top down, but rather from the bottom up, at the insistence of *We the People* expressing ourselves through political action.

Not only *can* we do better, we *have* done better when *We the People* recognized the power of ideas whose times have come and acted to make real such ideas – quixotic at the time and resisted by the establishment. "Too much sanity may be madness. And maddest of all, to see life as it is, and not as it should be," said Miguel de Cervantes Saavedra in *Don Quijote*

Hopefully within Islam, there are Muslims reading these words who share the conciliatory, pacifist sentiments expressed in this book – Muslims who will express, in effect, these same sentiments from a Muslim perspective, urging their coreligionists to "embrace de-escalation, and the quest for a *modus vivendi* with the West as the only sane alternative." *Inshallah*, such a message will produce a new political process within Islam's present fluid, evolving political structure, creating an overwhelming consensus to elevate new, like-minded Islamic leaders embodying the highest principles of their religion to achieve reconciliation and peace.

> Enough, if something from our hands have power
> To live, and act, and serve the future hour.
>
> William Wordsworth

Chapter 12: *E pluribus unum*

Approaching July 4, 2012, my sister, Missy, and I attended a concert at St. John The Divine Catholic Church in Sun City Center, Florida, a retirement community. The program, performed by amateur musicians drawn from the community under the aegis of the South Shore Symphony Orchestra, celebrated American composers in an Independence Day tribute. They included Copeland, Bernstein, Ellington, Gould, Rogers and Hammerstein. And, of course, the program would end with a rousing Sousa march.

As the program got underway, I experienced a lump in my throat and struggled to keep it together, moved by gratitude for and pride in not only the unique contributions of these quintessentially American composers, but also in the earnest determination of the musicians and conductor to do them justice. The orchestra seemed a microcosm of American society – ordinary, talented, dedicated men and women of varied ages and ethnic backgrounds, good middle-class people united in a common purpose, the very embodiment of *E pluribus unum* – from the many, one.

As a seasoned symphony patron, I could readily discern the difference between what I was hearing and the pitch-perfect, seamlessly blended, flawlessly timed offerings of the many world-class symphony orchestras I have had the good fortune of hearing over the years. Even as they wrestled gamely with the intricate syncopations of Copeland's *Hoe-Down* and struggled with the unusual intervals and tricky, accented rhythms of Bernstein's *West Side Story* overture, even as the trumpets disagreed about the pitch of a particular high note, and as the violinists' lips moved counting the beats during rests between phrases, the musicians resolutely conveyed the unquenchable spirit of artists everywhere who love the universal, unifying, uplifting language of music. In every gesture, every facial expression encouraging and exhorting the orchestra, the conductor, Dr. Susan Bailey Robinson, a vivacious, middle-aged woman, expressed her love of and joy in the music she and her ensemble were creating for us. As the last strains of Sousa's *Liberty Bell March* faded, I turned to Missy and whispered hoarsely, "This is what America is all about."

President Kennedy once said: "Our problems are man-made, therefore they may be solved by man...No problem of human destiny is beyond human beings." If we Americans find the will and the way to express in our institutions of government, education and commerce the same harmonizing, uplifting, unquenchable spirit of *E pluribus unum* conveyed by the musicians of the South Shore Symphony Orchestra, we surely will solve our problems and secure our destiny and that of succeeding generations of Americans. Spread the word. We *will* do better. It's part of our DNA.

Epilog

My account of the South Shore Symphony Orchestra's musical tribute to the American soul was written in Florida as the nation prepared to celebrate the 236th anniversary of its Declaration of Independence. Nearly five months later, twenty days after the United States re-elected Barack Obama as its 44th President, I attended another concert with my cousin, Michael, this time under the auspices of the Buenos Aires International Jazz Festival at the Centro Cultural in the tony Recoleta district of the city. On this occasion, the Jorge Anders Jazz Orchestra presented a free concert featuring the music of Duke Ellington and other American jazz greats, plus several of Anders' own compositions in the American "big band" tradition.

In the course of his long and distinguished career, the Argentine composer and band leader had arranged music for several American jazz legends, including Duke Ellington's son, Mercer, and The Duke Ellington Orchestra. Having had the good fortune, many years earlier, to hear Duke Ellington and his orchestra play in San Diego, I can attest to the fidelity of Anders compositions and the renderings of his orchestra to the spirit of the immortal Duke.

The names of the young Argentine musicians in Anders' orchestra had a distinctive Northern Mediterranean ring to them – Tallarita, Bernadelli, Terán, Francisco, Canosa, Pesci, Botti, Carrasco, Cámara, a talented pianist of Polish extraction, Alejandro Kalinoski, and a bespectacled, balding, rotund alto saxophonist in his eighties, Hugo Pierre, a legendary fixture on the Argentine jazz scene. About halfway through the concert, Pierre delivered a rendition of Ellington's 1938 classic, "Prelude to a Kiss," that, quite frankly, tore my heart out, lovingly recreating those slow, sliding, soulful phrases the Duke so bounteously bequeathed the world.

Once again, I reveled in the company of talented artists who love the universal, unifying, uplifting language of music. However, unlike the players of the South Shore Symphony Orchestra, these were Argentine musicians with European roots, faithfully expressing their love of the American soul, deeply, passionately. Here was "community" in the purest, most profound sense of the word – a kinship transcending the barriers of time, space, language, race, politics and culture.

Having engaged earlier in several discussions with Argentine friends who were justifiably critical of American politics, I was comforted by the warm applause expressing the audience's understanding, appreciation and love of the essence of American character revealed in music. "They like us. They really like us," I mused, borrowing a line from Sally Fields. Here was confirmation of a phenomenon I've observed throughout my travels: people everywhere, especially young people, appreciate the essence of

American character most visibly expressed in music, fashion, consumer goods, movies and television.

Notably, earlier in the month, KISS and then Lady Gaga had rocked River Plate stadium in Buenos Aires. On Avenida Corrientes, glitzy tango shows coexist side by side with offerings from Broadway like "Chicago" and "Victor Victoria." Uruguayan television broadcasts "White Collar," "Glee," "The Big Bang," "Modern Family." The Punta Carretas mall in Montevideo featured "Skyfall," the latest James Bond movie, and stores selling Johnson & Johnson baby items, Apple electronics, Blockbuster videos, Budget Rent-a-Car, Samsonite luggage. Traveling in the Balkans the month before, I had admired the tall, slender, very beautiful Slovenian and Croatian women indistinguishable from New York models, dressed fashionably in Calvin Klein jeans and Liz Claiborne, Donna Karan and Kenneth Cole tops and accessories. Slovenian kids sported "I ♥ New York" sweatshirts and Chicago Bulls jerseys. A billboard in Ljubljana featured Missy Peregrym from "Rookie Blue." Kids in Cuba had pleaded with me to give them my S.F. Giants ball cap. In Egypt, a Nile Valley farmer proudly displayed on his wall a photograph of Barack Obama, beneath which a woman in Islamic dress knelt in prayer.

In short, people around the world love and admire the free spirit, individuality and innovation inherent in the American pop culture and want to be a part of it. "They like us. They really like us."

This cross-cultural admiration and affection works both ways. American audiences adore the music and dance of "Tango Argentino," and form tango clubs around the country. Classical music from Europe fills American concert halls, played by Asian superstars like Lang Lang, Midori and Yuja Wang. Dance troupes from Russia, Asia and South America develop loyal American followings. Brazilian bossa nova and samba infuse American jazz. Dave Brubeck established himself on the world jazz scene with "Rondo a la Turk" in 5/4 time. We recently mourned the passing of sitar player Ravi Shankar. European and Asian designers set standards of fashion for American women and men. Art movie house audiences from San Francisco to New York, Chicago to Houston admire the works of legendary directors like Kurosawa, Fellini, Bergman, Truffaut, Fassbinder, de Sica, Ray, Bunuel, Renoir, Godard, Cocteau, Wertmuller, Bertolucci, Ang Lee and performances by contemporary actresses like Penelope Cruz, Salma Hayek, Marion Cotillard, Maribel Verdú, Audrey Tautou, Lena Olin, Juliette Binoche, Mila Kunis, Archie Panjabi, and actors like Javier Baradem, Antonio Banderas, Roberto Benigni, Christoph Waltz, Jackie Chan, Chow Yun Fat; immortals like Brigitte Bardot, Carmen Miranda, Marcelo Mastroiani, Sofia Loren, Gina Lolobrigida, Alain Delon, Catherine Deneuve, Jean Luis Trintignant, Toshiro Mifune, not to mention the many Aussie, Irish, Welsh, Scottish and English actors we almost think of as our own.

The world also shares its common humanity through literature, painting, sculpture, printmaking, photography, calligraphy; but it is through the performing arts, and, more specifically through music, an expression of the soul or human essence requiring no translation, explanation or training to appreciate, that communion between disparate people is most readily and profoundly achieved. It is little wonder that when opening communication between alienated civilizations, cultural exchanges with music at the fore lead the way toward reconciliation, understanding, cooperation and peace.

Dad used to say, "If left to their own devices, 99.9 percent of the people in the world can get along with each other just fine. It's the leaders who screw things up."

As I listened to Duke Ellington being played that evening in Buenos Aires, I wondered how much better a conversation between Barack Obama and Cristina Fernandez de Kirchner would proceed if, before they spoke, they listened to Hugo Pierre and the Jorge Anders Jazz Orchestra playing "Prelude to a Kiss" followed by American violinist, Sarah Chang, playing a tango by Carlos Gardel with the Orquesta Tipica Andariega. Or better yet, if Barack and Cristina simply left matters to Hugo and Sarah.

I've often thought if there's a reason for saving the world it's so musicians can play. Maybe they can return the favor.

Chapter 13: Addendum. Personal narrative. The journey from Republican conservative to liberal begins: Questioning conservative foreign policy. U.S. Navy – Cuban missile crisis, Hill 327 in Vietnam (1962-1966)

Returning to graduation day on the Dartmouth Green, June 10, 1962, little did I suspect at the time that the Cold War confrontation alluded to in the Commencement speeches by Ambassador Dean, Commander Shepard and my classmate, Jim Hale, would place me at sea on a destroyer patrolling the perimeter of the Cuban Quarantine within four months of graduation. In mid-October, 1962, aboard the U.S.S. Hank (DD-702), we were all exhausted after riding out a hurricane at sea while escorting the carrier Saratoga (CV-60) in the Atlantic. The Hank had been detached and ordered back to Norfolk, Virginia, and we were looking forward to some well-deserved rest in port. However, shortly after we turned west, the Saratoga signaled "Follow me," and we lit off all boilers, scrambling to keep up in the wake of the Saratoga steaming south at flank speed. As we headed for the Mayaguana Straits, I had noticed uncommonly high activity in the cryptography shack, but we junior officers had no clue about the reason for the flap until we watched President Kennedy's speech on the wardroom TV on October 22. Instantly the wardroom erupted into excited cheers and chatter. With no frame of reference but World War II movies, normally easygoing junior officers hurried about wild-eyed, anachronistically shouting: "Let's kill the slant-eyed bastards!"

While consisting mostly of dull steaming as an escort for a replenishment group, the U.S.S. Hank's participation in the Cuban Missile Crisis had its moments for us. During one of these, we escorted an oiler into Guantanamo Bay for repairs. General Quarters having been sounded as we neared Santiago on the southern coast of Cuba, I was at my battle station high up in the main battery director. We could see a tall plume of smoke rising from the city. Suddenly we spotted two unidentified, propeller-driven aircraft heading out from the city straight for us.

"Air action port," I shouted into the voice-powered intercom. Immediately the two forward twin 5-inch 38 mounts swung into action, one turning to port, the other to starboard.

"No, no," I shouted into the intercom, "To port, the other way." Both mounts dutifully reversed directions, crisscrossing like demented windshield-wipers, pointing in opposite directions. By this time the aircraft had zoomed across our bow waggling their wings -- two A1-Skyraider-drivers from the brown-shoe Navy having a good laugh at the black-shoe Navy's expense. Had they been bogeys, we would have been dead ducks. Later in the wardroom, ensign O'Brian, a good Catholic boy who had been on the bridge as the warplanes approached, confessed to having promised

God he would go to mass every day if he lived through what he thought was a Cuban attack. Not the Tin-Can Navy's finest hour.

We steamed into Guantanamo Bay unscathed, giving the off-duty watch a few hours to survey the base where the Marines were locked and loaded, deadly serious and ready to defend the perimeter. As it turned out, the Cubans had no intention of attacking, and instead satisfied national pride by turning off the water supply, to which the Navy responded by activating a freshwater still of its own. Three years later I would return as a member of the Marine defense detachment, to find the base returned to its normal, relaxed country-club existence, with officers' dependents comfortably housed and schooled, the O-Club and the bowling alley back in operation, and Cuban workers trekking daily through the gates.

At sea on the perimeter of the blockade, we had little sense of the existential peril inherent in the situation. We saw nothing of the alarm back home, knew nothing of the preparations for invasion. We simply went about our jobs, feeling we had the upper hand at sea and never doubting the Soviets would turn around. Indeed, we did confront a Soviet cargo ship with tarpaulins covering missiles on deck, which did reverse course. I remember target practice off the fantail with Thompson submachine guns in preparation for a boarding party, never called away.

Two-and-a-half years after the Cuban Missile Crisis, after a Med cruise; transit through the Suez Canal; six-weeks in the Red Sea (including visits to Jedda, Djibouti and Aden); Naval Gunfire Liaison Officers' training in Coronado, California; a brief stint with the 12th Marines on Okinawa and six months crammed into a troop ship waiting for President Johnson to make up his mind, I landed in Danang, Vietnam with the 9th Marine Expeditionary Brigade. I later learned the landing in Danang (OPLAN 32) had been planned in 1959 during the Eisenhower administration! Apparently the military-industrial complex plans its antagonists far in advance.

I disembarked on March 12, four days after the initial landing on March 8, leading a Naval Gunfire forward observer team. So much for "safe at last in the wide, wide world." Alan Shepard's remark, "we must have an antagonist," abruptly took on very personal significance, as I climbed aboard my radio jeep, feeling very John Wayne with a Colt .45 strapped to my waist. Leading my small convoy toward our or position on Hill 327, just below the Hawk Missile Battalion on the perimeter of the airbase, I remained persuaded – doubtlessly conditioned by countless heroic World War II movies – that we Americans were the good guys, our cause was just, our wars necessary, and their "collateral damage" regrettable but unavoidable.

However, my views about the purity of American motives for the war changed one day as I gathered my spotting team around our observation post atop the hill, overlooking the lush green rice paddies extending for many miles to the south.

"Look at those peasants down there," I said. "Do you suppose they care one way or the other whether there's a democratic or communist government in Saigon?"

We fell silent for a moment, gazing at the tiny figures stooped over the fields in the distance, and then one by one, the men shook their heads or answered: "No, they probably don't." "Then why are we here?" I asked.

Somehow the official line, "to defend the freedom-loving South Vietnamese people from communism," felt uncomfortably hollow, as did those places in my chest and gut where *esprit de corps* and pride of service resided. We talked a bit more, resigning ourselves to the general conclusion that we were there because there was profit in it for arms suppliers, while at the same time conceding that maybe there was something to the "domino theory." We never discussed it again. "Ours not to reason why. . ."

Privately, however, my thoughts returned to Hanover, and a panel in the Orozco mural showing a bandoliered peasant holding a rifle, about to be stabbed in the back by a bemedaled general; while to the side, a gold-epauletted admiral reached over the shoulder of a dark-suited, fedora-topped old man, both grasping at a huge bag overstuffed with gold coins. (Reproduced with permission of the Trustees of Dartmouth College.)

On May 6, 1965, I was ordered to take a helicopter with my team to Chu Lai, 57 miles southeast of Danang. We were sent to provide naval gunfire support, if needed, for the landing to take place the next day – the largest since Inchon, we were told. The area previously swept by the South Vietnamese army (ARVN), posed little danger of a Viet Cong attack. The landing would be unopposed and naval gunfire support would not be needed. The U.S. Army advisors to the ARVN jerked the Marines' chain, setting up a sign welcoming them: "Ahoy, Marines. Welcome aboard. Area secured courtesy Ly Tim District Army Advisors."

The evening before the landing we hung out with the Army guys in the ARVN base camp, skinny-dipped in the South China Sea, cooked our C-rations over a bonfire and settled in for the night in the tall grass a few yards beyond the high-water mark, after setting up a sentry watch rotation. The next morning we awoke before dawn, established radio contact with the destroyers offshore, cooked a C-rations breakfast and sat back to watch the landing, sipping hot cocoa. I started chronicling the landing with my camera, doubtlessly the most complete photographic record of the landing in existence (locked away in a trunk in the attic somewhere).

It all went by the book. Dawn breaks. The amphibious ships form a line two miles offshore. The order comes: "Land the landing force." The Marines clamber down nets to the papa boats, which then circle, waiting for the order to cross the line of departure. The loaded AmTracs slide into the water. H-hour at 8 am, the first wave of AmTracs and papa boats head for the beach with helicopters flying overhead. The helos land on the beach, disgorging . . . Wha. . . ? Press photographers! The photographers fan out across the beach as the AmTracs clank ashore, disgorging Marines charging up the beach at high port, yelling. The yells die out as they are greeted not only by photographers but also garland-bearing flower girls and top brass. Not your father's amphibious landing. A platoon of Marines runs up to our position, locked and loaded, breathless, eyes darting, startled to see us lounging casually, drinking hot cocoa.

"Where are the gooks?" they demand to know. (I suppose by then our generation had moved on to movies about Korea.)

"There aren't any. The ARVN already swept the beach," I reply.

"We were told there were 3,000 gooks waiting for us," the platoon leader insists.

"How about some cocoa?"

It was that kind of war – at least in the beginning.

Fortunately, my tour in country ended in June '65 before the war turned really nasty. (Early stages of wars often seem deceptively benign, like "the Phony War" early in World War II, the first Battle of Bull Run in the Civil War or the initial phase of the War in Afghanistan and the quick early victory in Iraq prompting Bush 43 to prematurely declare "Mission Accomplished.")

I returned stateside, took a month's leave back in Argentina before reporting for duty at Camp Lejeune, N.C. in the Second Air-Naval Gunfire Liaison Company (2d ANGLICO – one of five such companies). In late October 1965, four months after leaving Vietnam, I happened to tune in to a televised national news report of a Viet Cong sapper attack on the Hawk Missile Battalion a few yards above my observation post on the south side of Hill 327. The sappers had managed to infiltrate the battalion's defensive perimeter and toss some satchel charges among the missiles. The only way they could have gotten there was to move past my observation post. While the report made no mention of casualties, I couldn't help but wonder about the fate of my team and the officer who replaced me, thinking "There but for the grace of God. . ."

The five Marine ANGLICO units enjoy the distinction of being the only outfits in the Department of Defense trained to support both the Marine Corps and the Army with firepower from the air, the sea as well as artillery from the ground if necessary. An odd hybrid, they are led by Marine aviators and Naval officers, both out of their element alongside troops on the ground. Since some units of the Army and Marines the 2nd ANGLICO supported were airborne, we had to be too, so they shipped me off to Ft. Benning, Georgia, where, after three weeks of intense parachute training by barking-mad Army drill instructors, I earned a small bump in pay for "hazardous duty," and jump wings entitling me to exit a perfectly sound airplane at 1,200 ft. with a few pounds of silk strapped to my back and midriff.

For the remaining year of my 4-year active-duty commitment I languished in the boonies of North Carolina, except for a short trip to the Naval Gunfire Range at the island of Vieques, Puerto Rico, and a three-month side-trip back to Guantanamo Bay, where I did a 2-week barking-mad stint as leader of the junior-jump school, preparing my troops for Ft. Benning. Later, back stateside, Corporal Farber, a muscular Marine who assisted me, learning of my intention to return to civilian life, urged me to reconsider, saying: "Y'know, sir, I had my doubts about you leading the junior jump school, you being Navy and all; but after watching you in action, I just can't see you sitting behind a desk." I don't recall ever receiving a nicer compliment during my time with the Marines. In August 1966, two days before my 26th birthday, I mustered out of the regular Navy as a full lieutenant.

Despite my ambivalence about American motives for U.S. military engagement in Vietnam, I left the Navy a card-carrying member of the establishment, glad for the experience, with enduring regard for the men I served with, honored to have served alongside them.

Chapter 14: Disenchantment with Long-War foreign policy. Introduction to real-world economics, finance. Civilian life in San Francisco and Stanford GSB (1966-1969)

In August 1966, I ventured across the country to San Francisco, where I landed my first civilian job in Wells Fargo's sleepy Trust Department in the corporate headquarters at the corner of Montgomery and California streets, the heart of the West Coast's financial district. Still conservative, it took me a couple of months to switch from my black Navy tie to more audacious colored neckwear – about the same time I decided I could no longer stand the boredom of the Trust Department and switched to the livelier Investment Department, run by Jim Vertin, where I valued privately held stocks held by the bank on behalf of Trust Department clients. Nothing depended on my analysis other than the setting of the bank's fees for trust services. The real action, I soon discovered, resided in the Securities Analysis section where analysts, in what became known as "the Temple of Beta," plugged into world events through chattering ticker-tape and telex machines, and pitted their analytical skills against a faceless, unforgiving, yet potentially rewarding marketplace for publicly traded securities. Realizing I'd have to get an MBA to play in that particular sandbox, I applied to and was accepted at Stanford, less than an hour's drive down highway 101 in Palo Alto, matriculating in the fall of 1967. Meanwhile, I watched, with eerie detachment on the nightly news, the emergence of the hippy movement in Haight-Ashbury, the "Human Be-In" in Golden Gate Park and the "Summer of Love" in the City. Not my scene.

My two years at the Stanford Graduate School of Business (GSB) in Palo Alto spanned the time when public opinion shifted decidedly toward large-scale, loud and active opposition to the war in Vietnam.

In 1967, 700,000 people marched down Fifth Avenue in New York in support of the troops in Vietnam. Only 50,000 (some say 100,000) demonstrated against the war in Washington, DC. Later in the year Martin Luther King, Jr. led an anti-Vietnam war march in New York; another protest march took place in San Francisco. In Houston, early in the year, they indicted Muhammad Ali, born Cassius Clay, for refusing induction into the U.S. armed forces. He courageously refused to step forward with simple, yet penetrating eloquence: "I ain't got no quarrel with them Viet Congs." Boxing authorities stripped him of his title and exiled him from boxing for 43 months. His five-year sentence for draft evasion was set aside on appeal. The anti-draft movement gained momentum, with protesters burning draft cards or returning them to the authorities, and seeking sanctuary in Canada.

The tide of public opinion turned decisively against the war after the Tet Offensive on January 30, 1968, exposing the mendacity of earlier rosy assessments by the military about progress in the war. Until then I had remained ambivalent about the war, reluctant to deprecate my service and that of my comrades-in-arms, while at the same time questioning the motivation for the war. The Tet Offensive exposed the war's futility, again bringing to mind the question I had posed on Hill 327: "Why are we here?"

Press reports from Vietnam after the Tet Offensive, including accounts of atrocities filtering out into the press later in the year, exposed not only the war's wastefulness and slim chances of success, but also its immorality. Reluctantly, I was forced to admit we were no longer the good guys, our cause was not just, our war unnecessary, and its "collateral damage" inexcusable. (See *Kill Anything That Moves: The Real American War In Vietnam* by John Turse.) To this list of criticisms, I added "insane" when correspondent Peter Arnett quoted an Air Force major saying, "We had to destroy the town in order to save it," following the destruction of Ben Tre in February, 1968.

During my time at Stanford the country appeared to be coming apart at the seams – all covered live on nationwide TV. In March 1968 troops were called in to restore order in Memphis after a riot erupted during a protest march in support of striking sanitation workers led by Martin Luther King, Jr.. Shortly afterward, King's assassination in Memphis sparked race riots around the country. President Johnson, challenged from within his own party by Eugene McCarthy and Bobby Kennedy, stunned us by announcing he would not run for re-election. I watched in horror the TV live coverage of Bobby Kennedy's assassination minutes after his victory speech upon winning the California primary. In August 1968, protesters during the Democratic National Convention in Chicago were beaten in what was described as a "police riot." Revisionists claim it wasn't, but I know what I saw. Watching the brutal mayhem on TV by cops who removed their identifying badges, prompted me to send a telegram to the head of the California delegation (San Francisco Mayor Joseph Alioto?) pleading for action to be taken to stop it. Johnson's Vice President, former Minnesota Senator Hubert Humphrey, won the Democratic presidential nomination, defeating McCarthy and latecomer, Sen. George McGovern, on the first ballot, only to lose to Richard Nixon in November 1968.

The Stanford campus between 1967 and 1969 embodied the swing in public sentiment against the war. In November 1967 Stanford students protested CIA recruiting on campus followed later in the month by a peace vigil at Memorial Church attended by 2,000 students. I wasn't among them. Ambiguity toward the war could be seen in the reaction on campus to the suspension of seven students who participated in the CIA protest. Two hundred to 300 students occupied the Old Union to protest the suspension while at the same time a reported 1,500 students gathered outside the building deciding in a close vote to reject the sit-in tactics of their fellow students. Similar ambiguity existed within the faculty, which, in a tumultuous session, narrowly voted in favor of amnesty for the suspended students, overturning President Sterling's recommendation. Protests on campus turned increasingly nasty, with the Navy ROTC building set ablaze in suspected arson. Some time later Sterling's office was torched. Similar student occupations took place on other campuses, notably at Columbia, Harvard and, on the Dartmouth campus, even our own Dean Seymour was carried out of his office feet first (although to hear him tell it today, it was a good-natured romp). As for most of the country, the events of 1968 – particularly General Westmoreland's tone-deaf request for 209,000 more troops within six weeks of the disastrous Tet Offensive (he was relieved 2 weeks later) -- turned the campus decisively against the war.

By 1969 anti-war sentiment became virtually unanimous. On May 1, 1969 the occupation of Encina Hall prompted President Lyman to call the police, raising the specter of a potentially bloody confrontation, averted when the students decided to beat a prudent retreat. As I walked around the campus in those days, the signs of protest could be seen in the conspicuous long-hair, headbands, tie-died clothing, bell-bottom jeans and peace and Black-Power emblems sported by students; the occasional whiff of patchouli incense and marijuana; the ubiquitous posters calling for participation in anti-war rallies and organizational meetings; and the taped cracks in the windows of the main library and many other campus buildings. Popular music – rock 'n roll, folk, R&B, pop – infused the campus with anti-war sentiment. (I doubt there has ever been a more convincing demonstration of the power of music to unify and drive overwhelming public opinion in the country, and indeed the world, in common cause for peace, than in the Sixties and Seventies.) I added my small statement, affixing a large "flower-power" daisy to the doors of my olive-green 1964 Mustang fastback in a wry emulation of the stars stenciled on the doors of olive-drab military vehicles I had ridden in Vietnam.

While my sentiments at the time coincided with those of the anti-war protesters, I didn't approve of their law-breaking tactics; nor did I actively join in the protests – partly because I was immersed in my studies, and partly because of conditioned revulsion toward frightening mob scenes I'd seen staged by Perón's *descamisados* and corresponding awareness of the damaging consequences of mob rule. Upon reflection, in time I concluded the protesters were right to resort to mass demonstrations and, within limits, civil disobedience, since those seemed to be the only means of getting the establishment's attention. Attending Gene McCarthy's speech at Memorial Auditorium further reinforced my sympathy for the anti-war movement, touched as I was by the candidate's heartfelt sadness and despair expressed about the tragic events unfolding in Vietnam and at home.

As expected, the business curriculum at the Stanford GSB represented a radical change from the more ethereal liberal arts I had learned at Dartmouth. Given my economics degree and my year in the Trust and Investment Departments, I gravitated toward economics and finance, although we were required to meet distributive requirements pretty much across the spectrum of business skills: marketing, accounting, operations-and-systems analysis, production, organizational behavior, money and banking, statistics (again) and economics (again, but different this time).

Four years in the Service and the year at Wells Fargo served me well, providing some real-world seasoning, maturity and motivation, and helping me to graduate sixth in a class of 150 students (of which only 4 were women). Real-world experience also injected an element of cut-to-the-bottom-line impatience in my class participation, as occurred one day in a business strategy class.

The professor, whose name I forget, was encouraging the class to formulate business strategies for a case study we'd been assigned. My classmates were getting into the spirit of the occasion with far-fetched, grandiose schemes. The professor was uncritically accepting them all as if they were planting the seeds of the next Hewlett-Packard. Seated off to the side of the U-shaped, tiered classroom, I eventually grew impatient with the exercise, leaned back, put my feet up on the desk and insolently began reading the campus newspaper, holding it up so as to shield myself from the proceedings. As the class wound down, I slammed the paper shut and exclaimed: "What about the numbers?"

"What?" said the professor, startled.

"What about the goddamn numbers?" I insisted. "People are waving their hands, creating captive insurance subsidiaries here, transportation hubs there, factories here and there without the slightest idea of where the money's coming from to finance them, what they'd cost, how long they'd take to build, whether there's a market for what they make and whether they'd be profitable. It's all mental masturbation. Where do we find the numbers to back up these strategies?"

Holding an awkward silence for a few seconds, the professor replied weakly: "The library . . ." Dead silence.

I didn't bother to reply; nor, I think, did I ace the course. Mercifully, the bell rang ending the class, giving fresh meaning to the phrase, "saved by the bell."

Three courses did, however, satisfy my thirst for real-world numbers, and would prove to be seminal to my eventual 25-year career as an economics/investment newsletter writer and public speaker.

The course in money and banking, taught by a former Federal Reserve official, clued me in to the workings of the Fed, the fractional-reserve banking system, the tools at the Fed's disposal to fulfill its dual mandate of price stability and full employment, the mechanics of counter-cyclical monetary policies achieved through manipulation of the money supply with corresponding effects on short-term interest rates, and basically how the Fed creates billions of dollars out of thin air by a few keystrokes at "The Desk's" computer terminal at the New York Fed. Here, at last, there were real-world, real-time numbers on the graphs! During the course I discovered my ability to construct a coherent narrative by linking a series of interrelated graphs demonstrating economic and financial cause-and-effect. I began embedding graphs alongside text in my assignments and even draw them freehand in the margins of my exams, a format I would later adopt during a quarter century of writing newsletters and making presentations, and, indeed, this book.

Jack McDonald's course on investing introduced us to Graham, Dodd and Cottle (the cookbook for securities analysis); Monte-Carlo simulation; Bayesian inference; Miller-Modigliani theorem; modern portfolio theory, diversification and covariance; discounted cash flow calculation of return on investment; linear regression and other elevated concepts I've long since forgotten. It was all very heady stuff, which like calculus and other advanced mathematical and statistical concepts learned at Dartmouth, I rarely, if ever used, even when writing newsletters on the economy and financial markets for 24 years.

McDonald's investment course included a contest in which teams competed to produce the highest return on a hypothetical $100,000 stake, paper-trading stocks in real time for the duration of the course. As leader of the winning team, I was called on to present our strategy, duly performed in a "gunslinger's" outfit, complete with boots, jeans, calico shirt, fleece-lined jacket and my holstered Ruger six-shooter, lowered from beneath my jacket as I took the stage – to the accompaniment of a chorus of groans from my classmates.

A course in long- and short-term economic forecasting taught by Wayne Huizenga provided equally rewarding contact with the real world. His instructions – to forecast key economic variables one year out and five years out – were relatively simple. "I'm not so much interested in *what* you forecast as I am on *how* you get there, avoiding inconsistencies in key economic interrelationships, like for example, predicting accelerating GDP growth and slowing consumer spending." He pointed us to certain government sources of data, like "Business Cycle Indicators" and the Fed's "U.S. Financial Data." Here at last were source documents plugging me in to the economy – more blessed graphs with real-word, real-time numbers! I dove into the assignment with gusto, wallowing in data like a pig in, well. . .

The forecasting exercise so excited me I was moved to write M.O. Clement, then head of the Economics Department at Dartmouth (and, if memory serves, instructor for my final course in economics my senior year), extolling Huizenga's forecasting course and recommending the incorporation of a comparable course into the Dartmouth economics curriculum. In praising the course, I used what was then a loaded word. "This was the most *relevant* course of my entire academic career," I gushed. I knew the word was loaded, because rebellious students in the late 1960s were howling about the irrelevance of the liberal arts curriculum and the faculty, still trapped in Ivory Towers, bristled at the criticism. But I used it anyway, because, to use the catchphrase of the day, I was "telling it like it is."

Needless to say, Clement replied, dripping with condescension: "As you surely know, Mr. Smith, relevance is not the purpose of a liberal arts education," he sniffed. He went on to say that such a course would be a waste of time for pre-meds and pre-laws and graduates going on to other pursuits, and so would not be taught at Dartmouth. Outraged, I wanted to shout: *What about the hapless economics majors you send out into the world wanting to ply their trade but can't because they lack any practical understanding of how the economy works*? Clement's lame excuse made me fully realize that they didn't teach real-world economics because, clueless, they lacked any connection to the world beyond their Ivory Towers. One of my great regrets in life is that I seethed but didn't reply to M.O. Clements saying: "Relevance may not be *the* purpose of a liberal arts education, but neither is willful, studied *irrelevance*!" So this vent will have to do. It may also serve a reminder not to piss off a writer. There, I feel much better.

As mentioned previously, I rarely, if ever used advanced theory and mathematical concepts learned at the B-School during my subsequent career as a security analyst, mergers and acquisitions analyst, financial planner, market strategist and economist. For me it was enough to eyeball a series of graphs, looking for trends, anomalies, perturbations and co-variations, which, combined with an understanding of basic economic and financial principles, and leavened with a contrarian mindset, would reveal cause and effect, proper weighting of variables, likely trend extensions or changes in trends, enabling me to construct coherent narratives, forecasts and profitable strategies once I settled down to my life's work and began writing newsletters and giving paid lectures at the age of 44, in the mid-1980s.

The main advantage, I discovered, in studying esoteric concepts, and, indeed, in getting the MBA itself (aside from opening doors), lay in freeing me from intimidation by smartass hotshots slinging jargon when I got out into the real world. Once they learned I had a Stanford MBA, they knew that I knew, and they didn't dare bullshit me.

Chapter 15: Introduction to Darwinian corporate capitalism. Bangor Punta and Piper aircraft M&A on the East Coast (1969-1972)

Awarded my MBA with distinction in the summer of 1969, I held my ticket to the corridors of power in Corporate America and was determined to join the action at the highest possible level. Leaving the Stanford campus distanced me from the tumult of the anti-war protests and caused me to focus my full attention on the pursuit of a corporate career.

In my final term at Stanford I sampled the offerings of corporate recruiters on campus in the spring – Wall Street, management consulting, and manufacturing were among the most popular. But through the intercession of a distant relative, I obtained an interview with Nicolas M. ("Nick") Salgo, the charismatic Board Chairman of the Bangor Punta Corporation, then headquartered on Madison Avenue in New York, soon to be relocated to one of those big, black glass buildings by the railroad station in Greenwich, Connecticut.

Salgo, a Hungarian immigrant with both an LL.D. and Ph.D. awarded in Budapest, worked there and in Geneva before coming to the U.S. in 1948, becoming in the early 1950s a top aide to William Zeckendorf, the legendary real estate developer. Salgo struck out on his own in 1959 developing properties, including the Watergate complex, becoming prominent as one of the "top ten financial geniuses" according to *Fortune* Magazine. He spoke fluent French and German, in addition to his native Hungarian and fluent, if accented, English. We hit it off, and he invited me to join his mergers and acquisitions staff at Bangor Punta.

Bangor Punta was Salgo's brainchild, a Fortune 500 conglomerate, formed in 1964 by merging the Bangor and Aroostook Railroad – a cash cow – with the Cuban Punta Alegre Sugar Company -- a huge tax-loss carryforward created when Castro expropriated it. Nick saw the obvious potential of the merger, wanting to use the tax-sheltered cash to form a conglomerate (Wall Street darlings in those days). However, before he could start buying companies, he had to overcome the legal constraint forbidding railroads from buying unrelated businesses. He solved the problem by being the first to come up with the idea of having a company create its own parent holding company, which was free from the constraint on unrelated acquisitions – an idea later adopted by major banks. Free to buy non-railroad-related businesses through the holding company, Salgo and Bangor Punta President, Dave Wallace, went on an acquisitions binge.

Wallace is a tall, former Army infantry officer during World War II. A Yale engineer and Harvard lawyer, Wallace came to Bangor from the white-shoe, New York law firm of White and Case, to run the day-to-day. Very sharp. Very New York ("Howaya?"). Very open and approachable, yet commanding.

Bangor acquired an assortment of companies in unrelated industries, like the small-arms manufacturer, Smith & Wesson and several other public security companies; boat companies (Luhrs, Ulrichsen, Jensen/Cal, O'Day, Starcraft); Waukesha Motors, Producer's Cotton Oil Company, emblematic jewelry companies and more.

According to Wall Street common wisdom at the time, such unrelated acquisitions reduced risk through diversification and boosted earnings growth through operating synergies. Wall Street rewarded these qualities with reasonably high price-earnings (P/E) multiples for conglomerates' stock. In reality, while the diversification was real, operating synergies were largely illusory but the Street awarded conglomerates high P/E multiples based on a simple financial strategy diligently practiced by Salgo.

Salgo would buy (usually privately held) companies with solid earnings at lower P/E multiples than Bangor carried – say, 10X and 15X respectively. He'd issue new Bangor stock valued at 15X earnings to buy the target company for 10X earnings. The stream of earnings thus acquired for 10X would be re-valued upward by the Street at Bangor's 15X multiple, producing an instant pop in Bangor's stock price. The higher stock price, in turn, enabled Salgo to buy additional lower-valued companies with yet more high-valued Bangor stock, and so on.

Coincidentally, I had written a term paper at Stanford on the conglomerate phenomenon, concluding that the acquisitions process driving the appreciation in conglomerate stock prices could continue as long as the market continued to value conglomerate stocks with high price/earnings (P/E) multiples. But a bear market would create a double whammy by lowering conglomerate stock prices, undermining the their ability to continue acquiring companies, thereby short-circuiting acquisition-based earnings growth, causing a potentially fatal downward revision of the conglomerate's P/E multiple. Such downward revaluations would further undermine the acquisitions process making it hard for the stricken conglomerate to get up off the mat.

"Interesting," was Salgo's only comment when he read it.

Shortly after I joined the company, Bangor locked into an epic proxy fight with archrival Chris Craft over Piper Aircraft. Chris Craft's Chairman, Herb Siegel, had made a hostile takeover bid, and the Pipers asked First Boston to come up with a "white knight" to save them from Siegel's clutches. The Piper family was willing to offer their minority Piper shareholdings to Bangor if we'd go after enough stock to achieve a controlling interest in the company. We did and they did, and Bangor entered the general aviation business.

Since Piper was Bangor's largest-ever acquisition, Salgo and Wallace wanted someone to keep a close eye on it, acting as liaison between the two companies. In addition they needed a point man to explore prospective acquisitions in aviation business. They picked me for the job, thanks in part to the fact that I had held a pilot's license since the age of 19, and my family had been the Beechcraft distributor in Argentina since the 1930s.

The job provided a marvelous vantage to observe and participate in the corporate corridors of power at the highest level, just as I had hoped. In addition, Piper furnished me with my own Piper Arrow and later a hot Comanche single-engine airplane to shuttle back and forth between Westchester, N.Y. and Lock Haven, Pa., with additional side trips to Piper's factories in Lakeland and Vero Beach, Fl., and the headquarters of various other potential aviation acquisitions, like Bellanca, Mooney, Swearingen and Grumman's American Aviation. I was also named Assistant V.P. in charge of Piper's foreign assembly program, involving trips to Brazil and Argentina.

The Brazilians decided not to partner with us, and instead went on to develop Embraer, later to become a hugely successful manufacturer of commuter aircraft. Piper's Argentine distributor did proceed with an assembly plant in the province of San Juan, for a time ending the importation into Argentina of competitive single-engine aircraft, including Beechcraft's Bonanza distributed by our family business, much to my uncle Bob's consternation (although it didn't affect sales of his bread-and-butter twin aircraft).

Accompanying Salgo to Europe, I looked in on Beagle in the U.K, Socata and Aerospatiale's Corvette jet in France as potential acquisitions or marketing joint ventures. Nothing ever came of these forays, but they provided yet more insight into business conducted at pretty high levels and an opportunity to fly all manner of general aviation airplanes. My logbook totaled over 800 hours. Literally, I was flying high.

Piper, not so much. Piper's earnings came under pressure in the months following the acquisition, in part because the Susquehanna flooded the Lock Haven plant during a hurricane, and in part because AIG, perhaps sensing deep pockets in the new parent company, abruptly doubled Piper's product liability insurance premiums. Product liability insurance proved to be Piper's and, more broadly, general aviation's Achilles heel, precisely because general aviation manufacturers built sturdy, long-lived airplanes – most still flying after 50 years.

With liability for damages caused by accidents (stemming from alleged design and/or manufacturing defects) extending over the long lives of their airplanes, manufacturers were caught in a perfect storm: The pool of airplanes covered by product liability insurance expanded every year with the addition of newly produced planes without offsetting reductions in the fleet of aging, long-lived planes. The liability pool also expanded as trial lawyers became increasingly adept at blaming the manufacturers for accidents, invariably producing large damage awards due to their often-fatal consequences for high-income-earning owner-pilots and their passengers. Compounding the problem, trial lawyers would seize on any aircraft improvements and modifications as evidence of design defects in the earlier models, making manufacturers wary of improving the safety of their product (like the introduction of counter-rotating propellers in twins, improving engine-out performance) – a totally counterproductive dynamic. Product liability premiums were paid from the proceeds from new airplane sales. Consequently, potential liabilities covered by insurance outstripped the growth of new airplane sales from which premiums were paid, imposing an ever-increasing insurance burden on each new aircraft sold, increasing prices, dampening sales and cutting into profits. The General Aviation Manufacturers Association (GAMA) eventually persuaded Congress to pass laws placing time limits on manufacturers' product liability, but not before manufacturers suffered sometimes-terminal financial hardship from the cost of insuring their products.

In an early meeting in Lock Haven with Bill and Pug Piper, president and S.V.P. of new aircraft development, respectively, Bill asked me, now that the proxy fight was over, whether Bangor would simply withdraw to Greenwich and let Piper go about its business as before. I gave a non-committal reply with as much reassurance as I could muster in good conscience, not really knowing what Bangor had in mind, but suspecting that Wallace would hardly keep his hands off his largest acquisition. Within a year, everyone at Piper from the vice presidential level up, including Bill Piper had been replaced with Bangor appointees. I was beginning to see the dark, Darwinian side of Corporate America.

Epilog:

I'm not very familiar with the Bangor/Piper story after I left in 1972, though Wikipedia offers a pretty convoluted account, with Bangor being bought and sold several times, as was Piper, which also underwent reorganization in bankruptcy.

Chris Craft proved to be a tenacious sore loser, continuing to battle Bangor and Piper in the courts for damages arising from alleged violations of securities laws during the proxy fight. Piper countersued in a suit ultimately settled in Piper and Bangor's favor by the U.S. Supreme Court in 1977.

The Piper family suffered severe financial reverses after the merger in which they swapped their stock for Bangor stock. Old Man Piper, the company's founder, died in 1970, shortly after the merger, triggering a sizeable estate tax calculated on the value of his Bangor stock within a year of his death. The high price of Bangor stock at the time created a commensurately high tax liability. Unwisely, the Pipers held on to their Bangor stock, which, by the time the tax came due, had declined significantly, forcing them to sell much of their fortune to satisfy the taxman.

Nick Salgo sold his interest in Bangor in 1974, "amid internal dissent," according to his son. I'm not surprised, inasmuch as Salgo's irrepressible penchant for deal making tended to outrun the company's financial resources and Dave Wallace's patience. The sharp stock market decline in 1974 depressed the value of Bangor stock, doubtlessly further curbing Salgo's ability to do deals within Bangor, just as I had predicted in my term paper.

Interesting.

Salgo went on to great success in finance, philanthropy, art-collecting and public service. A major contributor to the Republican Party, Salgo realized his longstanding ambition to return to his native Hungary as U.S. ambassador during the Reagan administration. With the rank of ambassador he also served both President Reagan and President G.H.W. Bush as a special negotiator on properties, including the disposition of the infamous U.S. embassy in Moscow bugged by the Soviets. For his work he was awarded the National Intelligence Distinguished Service Medal in 1992. Nick died in 2005 at the age of 90 in Florida.

Dave Wallace retired comfortably in Greenwich, Connecticut, and not long ago made headlines with a seven-figure bequest to Yale.

I learned some valuable lessons about the workings of Corporate America and the capitalist system, as well as about myself during my interlude at Bangor and Piper.

The sad fate of the Piper family, who for decades had quietly gone about their business unmolested, tucked away in a remote corner of Pennsylvania, revealed just how brutal the capitalist system can be for the unwary. By going public, the Pipers essentially abandoned the relative tranquility and safety of a lake for the shark-infested ocean of the stock market. They came to rue the day their ambition for growth and personal enrichment led them to seek capital in the stock market, in the process surrendering control over their company and their fate to the vagaries of the marketplace. Be careful what you wish for. (Mark Zuckerberg take note.)

The fate of both Piper and Bangor Punta (or Xerox and Kodak, for that matter) illustrate the unpredictable and ephemeral condition of U.S. corporations operating in the wild-and wooly West of modern global capitalism. Captains of industry often pay a heavy price for their shot at fame and fortune in Corporate America. They can never rest on their laurels and assume past successes will carry them forward to similar reward in the future. "You are only as good as your last deal," and "Things change" are immutable laws of capitalism. They force successful managers to focus on the near term and constantly look over their shoulders, to the sides and ahead, alert to danger and opportunity, both within and outside the corporation – like Pony Express riders galloping through Indian Country, ready to change direction at the first sign of smoke signals. Constant attention to the marketplace must be paid, and changes responded to with profitable strategies, mindful of "the numbers." Failure to do so can be fatal to both the company and its employees. Prudent CEOs fortify themselves against such *contretemps* with generous salaries, bonuses, stock options, perks and golden parachutes often having little or no correlation with the corporation's success. Clubby boards of directors, whose allegiance to management appointing them supersedes that owed by law to the shareholders, approve this *largesse*.

The price to be paid to play the game goes beyond corporate success or failure duly recorded in annual reports and in the stock price. There's the psychological and personal toll as well. We may think "business is business" but it's also personal. I used to watch Dave Wallace, staring out a window after receiving a piece of bad news, jaw set, face reddening, fists clenched and body trembling with contained rage as he processed the information. There's the emotional roller coaster, as I witnessed in the Bangor executive suite during the knuckleduster with Chris Craft: the elation accompanying a winning move, and the sickening feeling in the pit of the stomach, when realizing you've been outsmarted or outplayed. There are suicides, like Randy Johnson, Piper's V.P. of Domestic sales, who put a bullet in his skull for unexplained reasons after the merger. There are marriages torn apart, for want of attention. The screaming matches between spouses depicted in the movies – "You're never here for us!" "I'm doing this for you and the kids!" – are clichés. But clichés are clichés for a reason.

Years later, I would be reminded of such personal tolls when watching *The Devil Wears Prada*. (I will have to assume you've seen the movie.) Miranda paid the price of success in her failed marriage, but more importantly, in acquiring her isolated, ruthless, hard-bitten persona, giving rise to her characterization as "the Devil." What twenty-something Lauren Weisberger, the author, was too young to know is that success within the "old boys club" in the 1950s and 1960s, *required* women of Miranda's generation not only to become demonstrably more capable than the men against whom they competed, but also to become tougher, harder and more ruthless. *So for them,* diabolical ruthlessness was a prerequisite for success beyond the traditional careers open to women at the time: nurse, secretary, teacher and housewife. Forced to become tough and ruthless, these women also paid a heavy spiritual toll, sublimating their intrinsic nurturing and cooperative natures to the demands of a bitch-eat-dog competitive world. Consequently, today's women graduates take for granted their unfettered opportunities, readily available without requiring them to become "diabolical." Therefore, they might think twice before cheering Weisberger's pat ending, in which Andy chucks the metaphorical cell phone in the fountain and takes an idealist's job as a muckraking journalist. "The Devil" paid the price for her salvation.

Bottom line: young graduates need to think long and hard about whether they have the stomach and drive for the rough-and-tumble of corporate life at the top before placing a foot on the bottom rung of the ladder. I realized I didn't when it came to making the next move in my career.

By 1972, with Bangor appointees filling all key positions at Piper, I felt little need to continue my role as liaison between the two companies, a conclusion I discussed with Dave Wallace. He agreed, and offered me my choice of a suitable job with any of Bangor's subsidiaries. However, the idea of being buried away in some subsidiary didn't appeal to me after having observed and participated in the corporate decision-making processes at the highest level with direct access to both the chairman of the board and the president. I had an innate need, inherited from my father, to see things from the "big-picture" perspective -- rather like an observer at a chess match, looking down on a chessboard, following the movement of the pieces, knowing their location and capabilities, figuring out the underlying strategies of the players and then predicting the likely outcome of the game. Taking Wallace's offer would have basically limited me to being a piece on the board.

So my thoughts returned to securities analysis, the type of work that had prompted me to go to business school in the first place. Securities analysis offered the closest approximation to the big-picture perspective I sought. At this stage, I knew I'd have to go in as a junior analyst, limited to analyzing individual stocks, or perhaps an industry. But the career path in securities analysis typically leads to a broader perspective eventually as head of a research department, or as chief market strategist, where I would be required to take into account the broader influences of the overall market, the domestic and global economies, the effects government policies and world events.

So I got back in touch with Rich Kingsley, who had been my boss as the head of Securities Research at Wells Fargo, and who by then had moved on to head up the research department at a boutique New York Stock Exchange Member firm, Shuman Agnew, a couple of blocks up California Street from where I began my investment career at Wells. Rich, who had been something of a mentor to me at Wells, promptly offered me a job in his small department, consisting of 3 other analysts.

Chapter 16: Enlightenment, breaking with the past. Securities analyst, the *est* training, financial planner back in San Francisco (1972-1979)

Securities Analyst:

My stint as a securities analyst for Shuman Agnew in San Francisco proved to be unexpectedly brief. Within a year of my arrival, Morgan Stanley bought the company resulting in redundancies within the Research Department. Being the last to arrive, I was the first to go, sometime around my 33d birthday in 1973. I felt bad for Rich, who seemed to have a harder time letting me go than I did in leaving. Nevertheless, the shock of being fired for the first time took its toll on my self-confidence and self-esteem. This wasn't supposed to happen to Ivy-Leaguers with Stanford MBAs. The uncertainties and dark side of life in Corporate America suddenly became very personal. Within a few months, Rich and his entire research department would be gone.

The *est* Training:

Interestingly, (and, some would argue, by no coincidence) months before I was fired, I had acquired the tools to deal with such issues after taking Werner Erhard's *est* training in May 1973. These were the early, heady days of the "human potential movement" flowering in wacky, wonderful San Francisco in the seventies. There had been precursors to *est*, other disciplines ranging from purely secular (Dale Carnegie, Silva Mind Control, Freudian and Jungian psychology) to semi-religious (various types of meditation, Scientology, The Salvation Army, Alcoholics Anonymous), to the traditionally religious, like Christianity, Buddhism, Hare Krishna, one could argue, most, if not all, religions. (Werner also credits tutoring by Richard Feynman, Michel Foucault, Humberto Maturana, Sir Karl Popper, and Hilary Putnam, though whether that took place before or after he created *est* in 1971, I don't know.) However, borrowing bits and pieces from some of these ("whatever works"), adding his own insights and methodology, and, after a legendary moment of clarity on the Golden Gate Bridge, this remarkable, self-taught former encyclopedia salesman combined it all into an astounding "enlightenment-in-two-weekends" package. With *est,* Werner thrust the human potential movement into the national, and even global consciousness. (You know it's a worldwide phenomenon when Woody Allen pokes fun at it in his movies.)

In those days, Werner and the other seminal trainers of *est* – Stewart Emery, Randy McNamara, Landon Carter, divvied up the load in presenting the training, and I enjoyed the privilege of experiencing them all, starting off the weekend with Stewart, then Randy and Landon, and ending up memorably with Werner.

Rather than attempting to explain the training, I offer the following analogy: Imagine a marble rock 17 feet high. Now imagine smashing the rock with a mighty sledgehammer, causing the rock to crack and crumble, shedding fragments so as to miraculously leave only Michelangelo's David standing naked in the sunlight. Then imagine David, freed from the shards of rock previously encasing him, touched by a magic wand, bringing him to life and self-awareness of his perfect body, enabling him to move through life removing obstacles to experiencing love, health, happiness and full self-expression in the process of life itself. Then imagine you are David. Werner and his trainers wielded the hammer and waved the wand in training in turn crushing, disorienting, scary, emotional, intriguing, funny, sublime, inspirational, enlightening and ultimately liberating and euphoric.

At the end of the training (but before the final "graduation exercise") Werner led us through an exercise to make sure everyone had "gotten" the ultimate message of the training. He asked for a show of hands from those who had "gotten it." Of the 300 or so participants, nearly all hands went up. Applause. Then he asked for a show of hands from those who definitely knew they hadn't "gotten it." Most of the few remaining hands went up. Mine remained by my side. Werner then went to the nearest raised hand, and the conversation went something like this:

"I don't get it," says the trainee.

"Good," Werner replies. "There's nothing to get, so you got it."

"I get it," the trainee would say, with a spreading smile. "So 'getting it' is whatever you get."

"If that's what you got."

Applause.

The remaining hands began dropping one by one, and, with repetitions of similar exchanges, the last hand came down.

"Is there anyone who doesn't know or isn't sure if he got it?" Werner asked, addressing the one remaining logical possibility.

My hand went up. Werner came over.

"You're not sure you if got it?" he asked.

"Yes," I reply. "Because if I definitely knew I hadn't 'gotten it,' I'd have to know what 'it' is, in which case, I would have 'gotten it.'"

"OK," said Werner, waiting for the other shoe to drop.

"So you get what you get and that's 'it'?" I continued, frustrated. "So what?"

"Perfect," Werner replied, pleased. "Because the other side of 'What's so,' is 'So what?'"

Stripped of all expectation, I got it.

And have been "getting it" for the most part ever since. And when I'm in deep shit and don't "get it," I remind myself of Werner saying "The other side of "What's so" is "So what?" which translates into one of *est's* guiding precepts: "What is, is, and what ain't, ain't" and I "get it" all over again. Enlightenment is not a permanent state for most of us.

"What is, is; and what ain't, ain't" strikes most people who haven't taken the training as tautological. But that is a mental conclusion and not an experiential reality, a state of being. Experiencing that there is nothing (no-thing) to "get" frees one to experience everything in life as it is in the moment, without freighting it with one's expectations, accumulated baggage, belief systems, judgments, assumptions, positions and other filters to run the experience through, coloring and warping it. "My position is that I have no position," Werner said on the last day of the training. (You cannot imagine how powerful that makes you in a debate.)

Individuals exhibiting this un-freighted, clear, transcendent state of awareness are memorably described by Robert Heilbroner as a "Fair Witnesses" in "Stranger in a Strange Land."

> Fair Witnesses are *prohibited* from drawing conclusions about what they observe. As a demonstration, Harshaw asks Anne to describe the color of a house in the distance. She responds, "It's white on this side"; whereupon Harshaw explains that she would not assume knowledge of the color of the other sides of the house without being able to see them. Furthermore, after observing another side of the house would not then assume that any previously seen side was still the same color as last reported, even if only minutes before. (Wikipedia)

What is, is, what ain't, ain't. That's it. Mind-boggling simple yet profound.

Any response to an experience beyond the neutral, objective "So what?" contains something added by the person experiencing it— judgment, assumption, belief system, position, etc. That's OK. It's what we do. However, the enlightened "experiencer" recognizes the addition and either makes a conscious choice to keep it, replace it with some other addition, or discard the addition, adding nothing at all.

When, on occasion, they remain "stuck" in their negative response, unable to transcend it, graduates are trained to resort to a meditative "truth process." During the truth process they mentally regress to earlier, similar events, looking for similar bodily sensations, thoughts and emotions, and then examine the decisions made then provoking the response, answer the question "What's the payoff?" from the decision. They then choose either to keep the payoff and remain stuck with the decision and the response, or let it, and the negative response, go – "experience it out," in *est* jargon. "Who you are is the chooser," Werner would say. *Est* graduates tended to either choose no addition, remaining with the neutral "So what?" detachment, or consciously chose to add something positive to their experience, like love; joy; some liberating, transcendent realization or point of view. When people experience laughter through tears, or two people suddenly break into laughter in the middle of an angry quarrel, that's what they are doing.

Get it?

Invariably, most *est* graduates emerged from the training in a state of euphoria, bonded by the common harrowing and sublime experience of the training, feeling liberated from their "baggage," able to see the familiar transcendentally as if for the first time, overflowing with new "realizations," imbued with a newfound sense of responsibility for and control over their lives, trusting in "the universe" as somehow aligned with their purpose, free to communicate openly and to hear and tell "the(ir) truth" unvarnished, without judgment or "making others wrong." They tended to share their excitement about their experience of the training, and what they "got out of it," with any and all who would lend an ear, and urge them to take the training, in much the same way as Christians who have been "born again." While there was no religious component to *est,* the two experiences doubtlessly share the same essential joyful reality of "becoming centered," getting in touch with one's inner core – one's "David" or the "little light" of the Christian song – the one experience occurring with presumed divine intervention, the other not, maybe. Many *est* graduates went cheerily about telling everyone "the truth" (or more properly, "their truth") sending marriages either spinning out of control or becoming genuine, loving and fulfilling, and the same with friendships, jobs, etc. Often careers took radical turns, as did mine, as I'll explain in a minute.

For much of the seventies, San Francisco was abuzz with talk of *est* and alive with *est* events at hotels around the Bay Area. Graduates were given the opportunity to take further courses – "Sex and Money" and "What's So" were popular. Graduates also volunteered to assist at *est* events and work in the *est* office. Some of us joined the Guest Seminar Leaders' Program (GSLP) designed to train individuals to lead seminars tasked with enrolling visitors in the training.

My participation in the first GSLP proved to be highly rewarding, introducing me to what years later would become a profession: public speaking. I led four guest seminars, with an average enrollment ratio of 25 percent, which was pretty good in those days. We trained to confront and overcome fears of public speaking, and to "be ourselves" when speaking before an audience, but were given no script about the training to present at guest seminars. "Just share your experience of the training," we were told. It wasn't easy, since for us, the training was like Zen, an experience of oneself with "no dependence on words or letters." We could talk about what went on the training, and the benefits we derived from it, but couldn't coherently explain what it was, how it worked or why. Nor were we supposed to. Mostly people signed up because they wanted a piece of what they saw onstage: the experience of "being ourselves."

Inevitably a reaction against *est* sprang up mostly among those who had not taken the training and occasionally from journalists who took the training with the express intention of "debunking" it. Negative articles (http://www.rickross.com/reference/est/est38.html) began appearing in the press, typically *ad hominem* attacks on Werner, with titles like "The Führer Over *est*" by Jesse Kornbluth Many in psychology-related professions attacked it as an infringement of their territory – incredulous that people could get better after two weekends without their professional help. Some friends, relatives and acquaintances angrily dismissed *est* as a "cult," and *est* graduates as "*est*-holes," turned off by the startling frankness of *est* graduates, or their use of *est* jargon – the maddening "got it,"(i.e., "I understand") in particular – or by rejection from graduates who found their relationship irreparably dysfunctional. That was OK with us. We knew what we had gotten and valued *it*. End of story.

Epilog: Amidst controversy over taxes, Werner eventually left the U.S. for years, continuing his many good works overseas, a story best told in the video, "Transformation, The Life and Legacy of Werner Erhard" (http://www.wernererhard.com/film.html) and on the following web sites: www.wernererhard.com, and www.wernererhard.net. Google "Werner Erhard est" and you will get 372,000 results, typical: http://www.rickross.com/reference/est/estpt1.html Werner sold the rights to the *est* training to his brother, Harry Rosenberg, in the mid-1980s. Harry ran it as The Forum and, as near as I can gather, passed it on to the employees in 1991, continuing to the present day under the aegis of Landmark Education, LLC, headquartered in San Francisco under employee ownership. (www.landmarkeducation.com*)* I'm delighted to see two of the "originals"— Randy McNamara and *est's* second president, Laurel Sheaf – still featured as Landmark Forum Leaders. Having previously noted the ephemeral fortunes of Corporate America, it's reassuring to discover an island of continuity in a sea of uncertainty.

It would be interesting to compile a dossier on the subsequent careers of the hundreds of thousands of *est* graduates, most of whom, I suspect, applied what they learned at *est* to "make a difference" in the world. Two examples close to home:

In 1975, Stewart Emery spun off from *est,* and, with Carol Augustus, another seminal *est* staff member, founded Actualizations, an international learning and development organization sponsoring human-potential seminars, several of which I attended. In the late 70's Stewart was selected by the national media as one of the ten most influential people in the Human Potential Movement. He then went on to write several books (notably "Success Built to Last" and "Actualizations: You Don't Have to Rehearse to Be Yourself" – just the sort of thing the GSLP prepared us to do). With several associates, Stewart remains active as a speaker and high-level executive coach in the Bay Area.[16]

Cherie Carter-Scott, a fellow *est* guest seminar leader and her sister, Lynn Stewart, formed the Motivational Management Services Institute in 1974 (I helped design their first brochure), a human development and training firm (http://themms.com/). Cherie has since acquired a doctorate, and, like Stewart Emery, through seminars, books and personal coaching goes about the business of assisting others to live fulfilled, successful lives. (http://www.drcherie.com/)

My own post-*est* career, as will be revealed below, has been ultimately driven by the same desire to contribute to a positive outcome for individuals and society by sharing whatever knowledge and insight I have gained along my way, through speaking and writing in the public forum. (www.davidlsmith.com.) (Must be something in the water at *est.*) Moreover, the *est* training, contributed enormously to my career as an economic/financial analyst, forecaster and market strategist by enabling me to consistently see things objectively as they are, without preconceived agendas or expectations or need to conform to the conventional wisdom, readily willing to revise my analysis and projections in light of constantly changing circumstances – the very attitude at the core of this book. (Werner's admonition – "My position is that I have no position," – offered a productive point of departure for each newsletter.)

The accuracy of my forecasts (described by one of my corporate clients as "uncanny") provided reassuring confirmation that, indeed, I understood how the economy and financial markets worked. As a forecaster and market strategist I quickly developed a healthy contrarian mindset essential to success in investing, causing me to swing between bullish and bearish expectations in a timely fashion as circumstances warranted. There was one notable exception after the first Gulf War, a "teachable moment," during which I thought, briefly, I was smarter than the market, and advised subscribers to remain on the sidelines as the market rose for another two years. In life you either succeed or learn from failure. It was an expensive lesson in learning to "ride the horse in the direction it's going," as Werner used to say. During the late 1980s, this objective mindset, grounded in the economic and financial realities of the day, would become instrumental to the evolution of my thinking from conservative to liberal on economic and

[16] (http://www.successbuilttolast.com/index.html)

fiscal matters. (The resolution of this seeming paradox – advocating a liberal position now while not being wedded to a position – was previously explained.)

Elizabeth, my wife of 11 years, took The Landmark Forum training in San Francisco not long ago, and "got it," I'm pleased to say. I attended her Wednesday post-training event open to invitees of the recent graduates. At one point, Larry, the trainer, invited guests to comment on their experience of the graduates since the training. I got up and shared a bit about my experience of taking the training in 1973 with Werner, Stewart, Randy and Landon (a few surprised gasps), and concluded by saying: "I wasn't sure if after all these years, whether the training works as it did back then. But in talking to Elizabeth and observing you all tonight, brings tears to my eyes to see the magic is still here."

Financial Planner:

As I intimated earlier, *est* "opened up the space" (to use the *est* jargon – it's coming back to me now) for a radical career change. Whereas my earlier ambitions had been toward "big-picture," sheltered staff positions, I accepted a line position in one of the toughest, most exposed occupations out there: commission sales. To be specific: retail sales of securities and insurance products and services, a fiercely competitive market requiring tons of cold calling to get started.

Casting aside the security of a predictable paycheck, frankly, scared the hell out of me. (For all but one year thereafter, I haven't had a predictable paycheck since.) I was now a pawn on a chessboard – totally out of my comfort zone, the very state *est* prepared me to surmount. I would need every tool in the *est* toolkit to survive the next few years through the economic turbulence of the seventies, punctuated by two oil shocks – one in 1973, the other in 1979, producing soaring inflation, crashing stock markets and two hallacious recessions as bookends. The term "stagflation" became popular in the seventies.

The company was Capital Analysts, a branch of the Fidelity Mutual Life Insurance Company (now non-existent, surprise!), a couple of floors below my previous employer at 650 California St. I loved that building for it's floor-to-ceiling windows with unobstructed, glorious views of the Bay, bridge to bridge. If you're going to live and work in San Francisco, you gotta have a view. For someone dedicated to the Olympian Big Picture perspective, the location was perfect.

To gain an edge over the competition, Capital Analysts blended its product sales into a comprehensive financial service – total financial planning – commonplace today, but fairly novel in 1973. Total financial planning encompassed estate and business succession planning as the means of selling life and disability insurance, and income tax, investment and retirement planning as the means of selling "tax-advantaged" limited partnerships in real estate, oil and gas, leasing, cattle and agriculture. These were in vogue, given the prevailing high tax rates, and the oil shocks, recessions and inflation knocking corporate stocks and bonds into a cocked hat throughout the 1970s and early 1980s.

Financial planning's arduous, multi-step sales process involved cold calling for an initial appointment, typically at the client's place of business, at which I'd deliver a variant of the Connecticut General "funnel talk" to gain the client's confidence, demonstrate the benefits of our service, and obtain agreement for a second appointment, usually at the client's home, to gather data about the client's financial situation: assets, liabilities, businesses, insurance, wills, family situation, etc. and ascertain the client's goals and objectives. I'd then bring back the data for analysis as the basis for designing a plan to achieve them by, for example, recommending re-drafting wills, re-titling properties, the formulation of business succession plans, setting up retirement plans, corporations, etc., and ultimately through the acquisition of financial products. The client and spouse were then invited into our conference room for a formal flip-chart presentation, attended, if necessary, by our supporting staff members. At the conclusion of the presentation, I'd close the sale, collect signed apps and checks, and thus earn a commission and a modest fee. The implementation of the various plans had to be coordinated with the client's attorney, and often the client's accountant. The entire process required time, patience, persistence and sales skills acquired the hard way, through experience, trial and error. (One example: nervous client's wife asks "Is this investment safe?" I answer, "*I* think so" (emphasis on "I" indicating confidence) She hears "I *think* so." which she interprets as uncertainty, killing the sale.) Wheels could come off the wagon in many places along the way and often did, to my intense frustration, duly "processed out" with techniques learned at *est.*

Not surprisingly, I tended to be long on analysis and short on people skills, not being at heart the amiable, expressive, gregarious type, with a "smile and a shoeshine," who tend to be most successful at retail sales. Consequently, I achieved only moderate success at it – the universe's way of telling me it "wasn't my bag" nor was I willing to adapt to make it so. Therefore, I supplemented my income by assuming part-time duties of equity coordinator, analyzing and selecting limited partnerships for the office to sell, and briefing my colleagues on their merits. For me, the seventies provided a needed dose of maturity, street smarts, occasional hard-knocks, seasoning, and sales education. I liken my experience in the seventies to a course in microeconomics, a necessary prerequisite before moving on to macroeconomics in the eighties and beyond.

Chapter 17: Developing a worldview. Becoming a public speaker – securities wholesaler in San Francisco (1979-1986)

One day in early 1979, opportunity knocked on my door in the corpulent form of Bucky Brock, head of Brock Oil in New Orleans, one of our oil-and-gas limited partnership sponsors. Bucky plopped himself down on the couch in my office and asked if I knew any good wholesalers. I suddenly found my hand shooting up.

Wholesalers of oil and gas, and real estate partnerships in those days were the fair-haired boys of the retail securities industry. Stocks, bonds and mutual funds, as I mentioned, were in the tanks, because of the recessions and inflation caused by the oil shocks of 1973 and 1979, respectively. During the interval between 1965 and 1982 we witnessed the worst bear market in history with the Dow steadily losing 75 percent of its value in real terms (after adjusting for the rampant inflation at the time), over a period of 17 years. These headwinds for stocks and bonds became tailwinds for oil, gas and real estate, so limited partnerships for these types of assets filled in the void left by the more traditional corporate securities. In addition, limited partnerships offered tax advantages the corporate securities couldn't, as previously mentioned. Consequently, successful wholesalers representing the sponsors of these limited partnerships earned six-figure commissions by traveling around their territories, making presentations to securities brokerage houses, financial planning firms and financial industry trade associations.

I didn't get the job at Brock Oil because one of the big brokerage houses in his selling group wanted Bucky to hire one of their people they wanted to ease out gracefully – an offer Bucky couldn't refuse.

However, Bucky had given me the idea, so I interviewed for a wholesaling position with Jim Latham, president of Transcontinental Oil whom I had met previously during one of my trips to his offices in Shreveport in my capacity as equities coordinator for Capital Analysts. Jim was a Louisiana "good ol' boy," belonging to that unique breed of risk-taking, oil-patch entrepreneurs who stick straws in the ground hoping to suck out oil and gas. Jim was smart, ambitious, personable in that courtly southern sort of way, and a graduate of the Naval Academy, who had taken the Air Force option upon graduation – so we had the Navy in common. I began wholesaling on the West Coast for Jim at Transcontinental early in 1979, and when Jim struck out on his own in 1980, I became his national sales manager, as president of a wholly-owned subsidiary, a member firm of the National Association of Securities Dealers, employing 5 regional wholesalers under me.

Wholesaling for Transcontinental, and later Latham Exploration, (Lexco), beginning in 1979, required me to make frequent product presentations before audiences, large and small, comprised of financial professionals and, sometimes, their clients. Consequently, quite by happenstance, I had stumbled upon what would become one of my two ultimate professions: public speaking -- all thanks to Bucky Brock plopping himself down on my couch that day. In wholesaling in the early eighties I finally hit my stride, with huge success in raising money for Lexco at a time when investors were clamoring for oil and gas limited partnerships.

My *est* GSLP training on how to "be yourself" onstage proved invaluable, and I developed an easygoing, yet engaging, conversational delivery for my wholesaling presentations that would later carry through to my 25-year career as a public speaker beginning in the mid-1980s. Pieces of the career puzzle began fitting together nicely.

Not content with simply presenting my product as a wholesaler, I engaged my penchant for thinking in terms of "the big picture" by devising a presentation on the global oil market to provide a context for oil and gas as a timely, profitable investment. Diving into "the numbers" I came across the work of M. King Hubbert and his successors, Buz Ivanhoe and Colin Campbell at the M. King Hubbert Center for Petroleum Supply Studies. King Hubbert, a Shell geoscientist, who famously (and controversially) predicted in the 1950s that U.S. oil production would peak in 1971 and then decline irreversibly, introduced what would eventually become a movement under the rubric of "Peak Oil."

The proponents of Peak Oil, notably Ivanhoe and Campbell, predicted a peak in global oil output would occur sometime around 2010. This outlook portended continuing increases in oil prices, with oil prices reaching a "permanently high plateau" after oil production peaked in the face of relentless increases in energy demand. High oil prices, in turn, would provide the capitalist free-market incentive for development of alternate fuels to fill in the energy void left by declining production of the finite, diminishing supplies of oil -- economics 101. Widely disseminated today (even "The West Wing" did an episode on it), Peak Oil theory remained virtually unknown back in the early 1980s. Consequently, my presentations became popular within the community of financial professionals, resulting in frequent invitations to speak.

I enjoyed remarkable success as a wholesaler for three years, raising about $60 million for Lexco for oil and gas exploration and development. Then in 1983 things began to unravel. Jim had obtained large lines of credit from various banks. Putting up Lexco's equity in drilling rigs as collateral, and combining the proceeds of his loans with equity raised through the Lexco private placements, he began drilling a series of expensive, deep wells. Soon afterward, the demand for drilling rigs tapered off, impairing the collateral value of the rigs, causing the banks to cut their lines of credit, leaving Jim with insufficient funds to complete wells already in progress.

Bottom line: Lexco folded in October 1983. The Lexco partnerships were taken over by another operator, and I was out of a job again.

I shifted gears and continued to wholesale real estate limited partnership tax shelters as an independent contractor for several more years, headquartered on the top floor of what was then the Wells Fargo Building at 44 Montgomery St. overlooking the Bay – again satisfying my penchant for an Olympian perspective far above the fray.

In the government's view, tax shelters were fine as long as they were confined to the very wealthy, effectively sheltering income in a 70 percent top income tax bracket using "private placements" requiring very substantial investment of capital. However, when the middle class had the audacity to avail themselves of similar tax-reducing techniques massively through publicly registered limited partnerships requiring minimum investments as small as $5,000, the Reagan administration put its foot down with the Tax Reform Act of 1986 putting virtually the entire tax-shelter industry out of business and bringing my wholesaling career to an abrupt end.

Fortunately, even as I became an independent contract wholesaler between 1983 and 1986, I concurrently began building an independent national presence as a public speaker with a radical change of message from my prior career as an oil and gas partnership wholesaler. As a public speaker and, soon thereafter, a writer, I found the means to quit my position as a pawn on the chessboard, and assume the Olympian perspective I craved, looking down on a chessboard, following the movement of the pieces, knowing their location and capabilities, figuring out the underlying strategies of the players and then predicting the likely outcome of the game.

Chapter 18: Moving to the left in economic policy. Becoming a writer about economics, finance and politics. Public speaker and newsletter writer (1984 – 2008). Blogger and author (2008-2012). Four school mottos.

During my wholesaling years in the first half of the 1980s, I complemented my presentation on "Peak Oil" with another proprietary presentation titled "How Investments Respond to Economic Cycles," revealing the interrelationship between economic and investment cycles. These two presentations would become the stepping-stones for my eventual career as a newsletter writer and public speaker addressing economic and financial issues of the day while studiously avoiding political commentary, at least until 2003 (about which more later).

Two basic premises undergirded the latter presentation: 1) Economic cycles unfolded in repeating patterns of expansion and contraction, marked by 3 phases encompassing 7 waypoints I identified using a proprietary selection of readily available economic and financial indicators and 2) Various asset classes (stocks, bonds, precious metals, oil/gas) each responded to the various stages of the economic cycle with repeating (and, therefore predictable) cycles of their own. Consequently, profitable asset allocation and intermediate-term market timing became largely a matter of identifying where we were in the economic cycle with reference to the aforementioned indicators and positioning one's portfolio according to prior cyclical patterns.

Over the past two decades, this cyclical dynamic has become better, though by no means, universally, understood. Back in the early 1980s, however, these concepts were quite novel. Consequently, the two slide presentations – "Peak Oil" and "How Investments Respond to Economic Cycles" – became wildly popular among investment professionals and their clients, so that by 1984 I had developed a thriving, national and even international speaking career within the investment community as an investment professional's professional. In time, during the late 1980s through the 2000s, as an economist, futurist and market strategist, I would become a sought-after keynote speaker at diverse industry trade conferences, corporate-sponsored events and educational institutions extending well beyond the investment community's ambit. (See: www.smithspeaker.com)

By early 1984, I had spotted the fatal flaw in the generally accepted predictions in the 1970s and into the early 1980s of continually rising oil prices. Such expectations rested on the widely accepted assumption of what economists call "inelasticity of demand" for oil, i.e., that oil demand would continue to rise no matter how high prices went. Given the modern economy's heavy dependence on oil, the assumption seemed reasonable on the surface. However, that assumption underestimated consumer propensity to conserve expensive energy (e.g., carpooling, turning down thermostats, driving smaller cars, etc.) and, more importantly, the determination of the Federal Reserve and other central banks around the world to quash the inflation caused by rising oil prices, even though it meant crushing the economy, sacrificing the second of the Fed's "dual mandates," namely full employment, in favor of its primary mandate, price stability.

Responding to oil's inflationary threat meant reducing the money supply in real terms (after adjusting for inflation), starving the economy for credit and driving up interest rates. Called "tight money," this policy had the effect of crushing economic activity, and with it, the demand for oil. Fed Chairman Paul Volker embodied this dogged determination to choke off inflation whatever the cost, pushing up short-term interest rates to unprecedented heights above 20 percent in the early 1980s, producing a double-dip recession with nearly 12 percent unemployment at the trough in December 1982. The recession caused a slump in the demand for oil, to which the OPEC cartel responded by curbing supply with quotas to sustain high oil prices – classic oligopolistic behavior. The high price of oil, in turn, encouraged a worldwide flurry of oil exploration and development, boosting deliverable oil supplies. The combination of declining demand and rising supply created a global glut of oil – a classic precondition for a collapse in oil prices – an eventuality, I reasoned, that OPEC's production restraint could postpone, but not avoid.

My analysis of the global oil market over the course of the first two oil shocks (beginning in 1973 and 1979 respectively) had revealed a repeating, two-way interactive pattern of behavior between oil prices and economic activity, an interdependent relationship amplified by central bank intervention in the credit markets. This interaction did not manifest itself until after the first oil shock in 1973; so we were dealing with a relatively recent economic phenomenon.

To summarize: High oil prices generated by OPEC oil production restraint created inflation, countered by "tight money" and high interest rates from the Fed, producing economic contraction. A recession, in turn, curbed the demand for oil, while high oil prices spurred the development of new oil supply, resulting in an oil glut and an eventual reduction in oil prices. Low oil prices, in turn, dampened inflation, prompting "easy money" and low interest rates from the Fed, stimulating economic expansion. In short, everything revolved around the price and availability of oil. I called this interactive pattern "The Petrocycle."

The popularity of my two presentations among financial professionals, coupled with the insight into the Petrocycle by early 1984, prompted me to complement my burgeoning speaking career with a newsletter, initially titled *Cyclical Investing Quarterly Report,* (www.cyclical-investing.com). I wrote my first issue on my personal "Independence Day," July 4, 1984. Not surprisingly, given my development of the Petrocycle thesis, the opening line of the first issue stated: "The economic outcome over the foreseeable future will be determined, as it has been during the past decade, by the contest between the interests of oil and industrial capital over the price and availability of oil."

This is the point where I executed a life-altering career shift and change of message: Whereas between 1979 and early 1983 I marketed oil and gas limited partnerships by adopting the conventional wisdom, based on the assumption of a continuing uptrend in oil prices, by early1984, I had re-evaluated this central assumption and figured out that the preconditions existed for an oil price collapse, as previously described. Consequently, between mid-1984 and late 1985 I went around the country predicting an imminent collapse in oil prices (which until then had remained near their record levels in the $30-$34/barrel range). As corollaries, I also predicted the oil price collapse would be followed by a thriving economy and a once-in-a-century booming stock market – predictions radically at odds with the prevailing expectations at a time.

Mainstream observers remained wary of the economic recovery after the deep, double-dip recession in 1980-1982, and of the stock market in the wake of the 17-year bear market ending in August 1982. This widespread pessimism reflected the all-too-human tendency to project the recent past into the indefinite future, a phenomenon one might term "demon extrapolation." My 1984 contrarian predictions materialized in spades, beginning with an oil price collapse from around $30/barrel to $10 between December 1985 and March 1986, followed by a booming economy and soaring stock prices lasting, with only minor hiccups, until January 2000.

In effect, by July 4, 1984, nearing my 44th birthday, I had re-invented myself as a "contrarian" writer and speaker, an economic and financial radical, profoundly skeptical of the conventional wisdom, and especially critical of the propensity of mainstream pundits to engage in "demon extrapolation." (See: www.cassandra-chronicles.com/The Contrarian Mindset Report.pdf) My contrarian mindset would provide handsome rewards for my audiences and subscribers over the next 24 years.

As I sat down to write the first *Cyclical Investing* newsletter, I placed before me John Maynard Keynes' tribute to his mentor, economist Alfred Marshall, titled "The Master Economist."

> The master-economist must possess a rare combination of gifts. He must be mathematician, historian, statesman, philosopher – in some degree. He must understand symbols and speak in words. He must contemplate the particular in terms of the general, and touch abstract and concrete in the

> same flight of thought. He must study the present in the light of the past for the purposes of the future. No part of man's nature or his institutions must lie entirely outside his regard. He must be purposeful and disinterested in a simultaneous mood; as aloof and incorruptible as an artist, yet sometimes as near the earth as a politician.

"The Master Economist" has been my lodestar ever since.

Strangely, despite five years of newsletter writing, I did not come to regard myself as a writer until the summers of 1989 and 1990, when I attended the Bennington Writing Workshops at Bennington College in Vermont. For a month during the summer Bennington transforms into a magical, very feminine, retreat from the world. Aspiring writers – young, old, and middle-aged (as I was at the time) with varying degrees of experience and competence – gather in another of Robert Frost's "lovely, dark and deep" New England woods (not far from his grave) to plumb the wellsprings of their souls, pouring their contents onto blank pages which are then shared in classrooms and impromptu groups gathered in the dorm lounges and on the tranquil college green. Seasoned professionals, mostly academics, with a wide range of literary accomplishment and fame, guided us in our creative endeavors. For a solid month, we wrote, and wrote and then wrote some more – poetry, fiction, non-fiction, according to our individual predilections. Little pieces became tangible "works," which we would refer to by title as one might speak of "The Old Man and the Sea," or "The Awakening" (without invidious comparison, of course). "How's your 'Prohibition's Hangover' coming along?" someone might ask. Sometime during my first workshop, I discovered my soul as an artist, much to my surprise, and acknowledged to myself that indeed I am a writer. Henceforth when asked, "What do you do?" I would respond, "I think, write and speak, hopefully in that order."

The *Cyclical Investing Quarterly Report* eventually morphed into a monthly publication, re-titled simply *Cyclical Investing.* (See: www.cyclical-investing.com) establishing a remarkable track record of fulfilled contrarian predictions, including:

- The 1986 oil price crash and subsequent booming economy and financial markets
- The 1987 stock market crash. Exit signal given October 16, 1987, 3 days before crash.
- Rebounding economy and stock market following the crash; re-entry signal for stocks on October 31, 1987.
- The 1990-91 Gulf War, oil-price spike, stock market slump and recession

- The sluggish stock market in 1994
- The resumption of the bull market in 1995
- The peak in the stock market in 2000. Exit signal given January 4, 2000
- The recession of 2001
- The bull market in gold immediately following 9/11/01, buy signal around $300/oz.
- The devaluation of the dollar beginning in 2002
- The Third Oil Shock beginning in 2003 and ensuing inflation
- The economic and stock market rebound in 2003. Re-entry signals April-June 2003
- The 'Stagflation' of 2008 followed by the Great Recession

At the time I began writing *Cyclical Investing* on July 4, 1984, I was well on my path toward radicalization – by which I simply mean sharp disagreement with the prevailing conventional wisdom, and, therefore, advocacy of policies, perceptions and prognostications 180 degrees out from mainstream thinking. My epiphany in April 1965 on Hill 327 in Danang, coupled with my proximity to protests on the Stanford campus after the Tet offensive in early 1968 put me on the path, setting me against conservative dogma blindly supporting a militaristic foreign policy resulting in Long Wars. My financial contrarian mindset developed in early 1984, culminating in the creation of the *Cyclical Investing Quarterly Report* on July 4th of that year, stood in stark contrast to the conventional financial and economic wisdom. Having acquired an objective, contrarian financial mindset, I began to waver on conservative domestic economic and fiscal policies then embodied by President Ronald Reagan.

As of the time of Reagan's election in 1980, I still retained my conservative convictions regarding the efficacy and fairness of unfettered free-market capitalism and faith in the responsiveness of the U.S. democratic process to the will of the people. I must confess, to my subsequent embarrassment and, indeed shame, to have voted for Reagan in 1980, inexcusably seduced by his supply-side siren song.

By the 1984 election, however, after witnessing the emergence of the early Reagan dual deficits (fiscal and international balance of payments) and deepening my own understanding of the domestic and global economies and financial markets in connection with my budding speaking and writing career, I began to waver in my opinion of his allegedly "conservative" fiscal and domestic economic policies. So I sat out the 1984 election, refraining from voting for either Reagan or Walter Mondale. I also sat out the 1988 election between George Herbert Walker Bush and Michael Dukakis, although I did attend the 1992 Republican National Convention in Houston as a translator for Spanish-speaking guests from Central and South America – out of curiosity rather than conviction.

By 1992, however, I had moved sufficiently toward the left to vote for William Jefferson Clinton and to part ways intellectually from my conservative idol, William F. Buckley, Jr. While respecting then, as I do now, the man's towering intellect, wry wit, high moral principles and integrity, the economic principles he championed were producing undesirable results, a fact I acknowledged and he didn't. Perhaps the subject of another book someday. (Buckley died in February 2008 at age 82, before he could witness the *Götterdämmerung* of conservatism run amok.)

My leftward momentum would continue as I voted for Ralph Nader in 2000, John Kerry in 2004 and Barak Obama in 2008 – not that they represented a liberal panacea, but they were, nonetheless far better than the Republican alternatives.

As a public speaker and newsletter writer, I became a close observer of the economic and financial scene from 1984 until I ceased publishing *Cyclical Investing* 24 years later on the 4th of July 2008 (a second personal declaration of independence). Along the way my firm conservative convictions eroded regarding the efficacy and fairness of unfettered free-market capitalism and faith in the responsiveness of the U.S. democratic process to the will of the people, based on my observations of the counterproductive consequences of Reaganomics, the corrosive introduction of religion into the political discourse and the corrupting influence of money on the political process.

For most of those years I avoided introducing politics into my writing and speaking. In the early 2000s, however, observing George W. Bush's reprise of Reaganomics (which by then I realized contained the seeds of economic and financial disaster) and military folly in the Middle East following 9/11, I found it impossible to resist inserting political commentary into *Cyclical Investing* and occasionally into my speaking engagements.

Notable in the latter category was a speech I gave in San Antonio a few days after 9/11 in which I warned against responding to the attack with blunt military force, and instead advocated the use of Special Forces, black ops, intelligence-gathering services and both domestic and international law enforcement, forensic financial tracking and interdiction, rather than full-scale military invasions and long occupations wasting precious blood and treasure on both sides. The audience responded enthusiastically to my presentation, urging me to somehow communicate the message to Congress. Unfortunately, I had no clue about how to go about it, and limited the dissemination of my message to my frequent speaking engagements around the country – predictably to no avail.

Interesting to note, in late November 2012, Jeh Johnson, Defense Department General Counsel, speaking at Oxford University in Britain, articulated this same message after posing the question: "How will this conflict end?" He continued: "It is an unconventional conflict against an unconventional enemy and will not end in conventional terms. We cannot and should not expect Al-Qaida and its associated forces to all surrender, all lay down their weapons in an open field or to sign a peace treaty with us. They are terrorist organizations. Nor can we capture or kill every last terrorist who claims an affiliation with Al-Qaida. Nor can I offer any prediction about when this conflict will end. . . or whether we are, as Winston Churchill once described it, 'Near the beginning of the end.' I do believe that on the present course, there will come a tipping point at which so many of the leaders and operatives of Al-Qaida and its affiliates have been killed or captured, and the group is no longer able to attempt or launch a strategic attack against the United States such that Al-Qaida as we know it, the organization that our Congress authorized the military to pursue in 2001, has been effectively destroyed. At that point we must be able to say to ourselves that our efforts should no longer be considered 'an armed conflict' against Al-Qaida and its associated forces, rather a counter-terrorism effort against individuals, who are the scattered remnants of Al-Qaida, or are parts of groups unaffiliated with Al-Qaida for which the law enforcement and intelligence resources of our government are principally responsible."

The truth of the matter is that the degradation of Al-Qaida, as illustrated by the killing of its leader, Osama bin Laden, and the killing and/or capturing of other Al-Qaida leaders and foiling of various terrorist plots after 9/11 resulted from the application of Special Forces, black ops, intelligence-gathering services and both domestic and international law enforcement, forensic financial tracking and interdiction, rather than the full-scale military invasions of Afghanistan and Iraq. The application of blunt force in Afghanistan simply drove al-Qaida into neighboring Pakistan, Iraq, Yemen and elsewhere, to be dealt with by Special Forces, black ops, drones and similar small-scale resources. The invasion of Iraq energized the formation of Al-Qaida in Iraq where previously there had been no such presence, and therefore, proved to be counter-productive. Consequently, I believe the verdict of history will reveal the invasions of Afghanistan and Iraq to have been colossal, wasteful and unnecessary blunders undertaken with little purpose or effect other than to enrich and empower the military-industrial-technological-political complex. We have reason to hope for the downsizing of the War on Terror to a "counter-terrorism effort by law enforcement and intelligence resources" (as it should have been from the outset), given Mr. Johnson's remarks at Oxford in the wake of the withdrawal from Iraq in 2011 and the proposed withdrawal from Afghanistan in 2014 (or sooner, if the recent "sense of the Senate" resolution urging an acceleration of the timetable is followed).

As the disastrous consequences of the Bush 43 presidency became increasingly apparent to me, I felt compelled to dive into the political fray. (I had the opportunity to observe the ascendancy of G.W. Bush from inconsequential governor of Texas to toxic president of the U.S. up close from the vantage point of a Houston resident between 1990 and 2008 – even to the point of attending his second gubernatorial inauguration in Austin – again, out of curiosity rather than conviction.) In April 2003, as the invasion of Iraq got underway, I shunted my political views into a new newsletter: *David L. Smith's Cassandra Chronicles* (www.cassandra-chronicles.com). I launched the publication – essentially a freewheeling compilation of essays and research papers on topics of current moment – starting with "Why We Fight: The real reason Messrs. Bush and Cheney invaded Iraq," The benefits I sought to provide included the following:

- To deepen readers' understanding of the effect of government policy, geopolitics, military developments, political philosophy and the grand sweep of history on current and future events. My hope was to stimulate thought "outside the box" that would give them the satisfaction of contributing to a positive outcome.
- To present likely "overview" scenarios from the U.S. and global perspectives that take into account valuable "lessons of history," on the theory that if we do remember the past we will not be condemned to repeat it, to rephrase Santayana.
- To help readers avoid surprises and anticipate crises.

I included the tag line below the masthead with part of Keynes' quote from "The Master Economist": "Study the present in the light of the past for the purposes of the future."

I continued to write the *Cassandra Chronicles* for six years, (5 of these years overlapping with the publication of monthly *Cyclical Investing* reports) publishing 19 separate essays the titles of which are reproduced below:

- "Why I write" Statement of editorial purpose and principles. (April 2003)
- "Why We Fight: The real reasons Messrs. Bush and Cheney invaded Iraq" (April, 2003) (Includes "Why I Write.")
- "The Trifecta That Wasn't: Flawed monetary and fiscal policy, danger from overseas lenders." (June 2003)
- "Eye on the Prize / The Perfect Storm: Possible scenarios in the Middle East (November, 2003)
- "The Clash of Civilizations: Christianity vs. Islam Redux" (April, 2004) plus "Update" (April 15, 2004)
- "Dust to Dust in the Garden of Eden: Lessons from the British Mesopotamia Campaign (1914-1919) and Occupation of Iraq 1920-1932)" (September, 2004) (Condensed version)

- “Oedipus Wrecks – What a difference an 'H' makes: G.H.W. Bush and G.W. Bush” (November, 2004)
- “Prohibition’s Hangover: The Income Tax -- Why a Graduated National Sales Tax is Better” (March, 2005)
- “God, Government and Mammon – The Reformation Redux: Church and State in America” (June, 2005)
- “Point and Counterpoint – Letters to the Editor” (December 2005)
- “The Asian Caper – Profit and Peril from Across the Pacific” (January 2006, updated to June 2008) Companion piece: "The Prudent Gambler: How to avoid loss and capture gains when Asia takes home all the marbles" (January 2006)
- “The Third Oil Shock – How to Avoid Loss and Capture Gains from the Developing Oil Crisis” (April 2006) and "Update June 2008"
- "Point and Counterpoint: Sympathy for The Devil Who Wears Prada and Laffer's Little Curve Debunked" (September 2006)
- “Iraq: Vietnam Deja Vu” (March 2007)
- "Fearless and Tyrannical: Why the Bush administration gets away with it" (September 2008)
- "The Panic of 2008: Everything you wanted to know but were afraid to ask" (October 2008)
- "Wall Street 2009: Pulling back from the abyss" (February 2009)
- "The Asian Caper, Part II, The Golden Trap" (April 2009)
- "Point and Counterpoint III: The Surest Road to Recovery" (July 2009)

Interested readers can download these back issues by going to www.cassandra-chronicles.com/back_issues_page.html.

Some of these essays were essentially research papers to be included in the book I had been writing, off and on, since the early 1990s I recently titled *The Egyptian Solution – And Other Lessons Of History To Get Us Out Of This Mess.* (www.the-egyptian-solution.com) The book begins with:

> **Mission Statement**: *The Egyptian Solution* reveals Lessons of History useful in resolving our present predicament, mindful of George Santayana’s warning: “Those who cannot remember the past are condemned to repeat it.” This task will occupy the first half of the book. The second half will explore ways in which these Lessons could be applied presently to support universal aspirations for peace, prosperity, order, harmony, human rights, sustainability, and the survival of the human species.
>
> If history teaches us anything, it is this: Humanity suffers episodes of collective madness from time to time -- arguably much, if not most of the time.
>
> Despite the deceptive appearance of normalcy in the corridors of power and in society at large, a strong

undercurrent of insanity governs human affairs in a crazy minuet between governments and the governed, leaders and followers. The results of such madness are policies and actions ultimately detrimental to the polities enacting them – essentially scoring on own goal.

Generations recently come of age should be aware of this uncomfortable truth and always question whether the world in which they live has fallen down a rabbit hole and we are all now gathered around the table sipping tea with the Mad Hatter.

This realization must come early in life or in time young generations will gradually be drawn into the collective mindset, conditioned to regard the current flow of human events as "normal," and become unable to grasp the sheer folly of it all until it's too late.

It is for this reason I write to members of today's younger generations, the Millennial generation in particular, applying the same logic prompting youngsters of my generation in the Nineteen Sixties to say "Never trust anyone over 30." I'm hoping today's younger generations will make an exception in my case, despite my having surpassed three score and ten.

As of this writing *The Egyptian Solution* remains a work in progress, hopefully to be released not long after publication of the book you are now reading. Whereas *The Predicament* introduces the Millennial Generation to the sources of their present predicament, *The Egyptian Solution* offers a blueprint for what I believe to be the most promising road for younger generations and conscience-driven allies within senior generations to extricate themselves from the mess bequeathed to them by generations extending back to what Tom Brokaw has labeled "The Greatest Generation," and beyond . . . "the sins of the fathers," etc.

In addition to the foregoing endeavors, I have been actively blogging, sharing pithy observations about the foibles of American society since July 2008. (www.cassandra-chronicles.blogspot.com).

And so I finished the first edition of *The Predicament* on July 4, 2012, another personal Independence Day, six decades from my jejune awakening as a conservative in Perón's Argentina in the early 1950s.

The journey from conservative to radical liberal began with my intellectual initiation between 1958 and 1962 at Dartmouth during which a cloistered economics department reinforced my conservative leanings with economic theory devoid of input from the real world.

Concerning U.S. foreign policy, I remained a card-carrying, conservative Cold Warrior through my early days of military service as a junior officer on board a destroyer on station off Cuba during the 1962 Missile Crisis. However, doubts about the legitimacy of U.S. militarism crept in while observing peasants at work in their rice paddies during my stint on Hill 327 in Danang, Vietnam in 1965, prompting me to ask, "Why are we here?" Such doubts evolved into full-fledged opposition to the war while at Stanford during the aftermath of the Tet Offensive in 1968.

My revulsion toward militaristic foreign policies surged unexpectedly in 1984, when one of my speaking engagements took me to Japan, where I added a 2-week vacation touring the country. It did not take long for me to become enamored of the Japanese people and their culture, known for its haiku poetry; the world's first novel; artful dancing and music; contemplative Zen Buddhism; sublime Noh and Kabuki theater; inspired art and calligraphy; delicate bonsai horticulture and skillful flower arranging; exquisite silk textiles; elaborate and elegant styles of dress and grooming; meticulous personal hygiene; unflagging courtesy and good manners; excellent conversation; honorable traditional values and an overriding quest for harmony – *wa* – with self, neighbors and nature.

To the credit of their parents and grandparents, Japanese schoolchildren have been raised with no hint of resentment toward their erstwhile American conquerors. Kids in little blue sailors' uniforms came up to us excitedly as if we were rock stars, eager to practice their English, exchange coins and offer candy. Shopkeepers, waitstaff, vendors, the families we visited, welcomed us with convivial good humor and delicate manners bred within a society exquisitely adapted to overcrowding unimaginable to most Americans.

Everything the Japanese did conveyed a sense of art: the preparation of food, the arrangement of flowers, the feng shui design of the ryokans we stayed in, the tea ceremony and wedding reception we witnessed, the design of public parks and their stone gardens. This sense of art infusing all they do extended even to the groundskeeper at the Imperial Palace slowly sweeping leaves with Tai-Chi-like grace. The great bronze Buddha, 45-feet tall, seated at Nara beckoned crowds with one raised hand commanding our attention and the other, palm outstretched in a gesture of giving, as if to say, "If you would know me, come, know my people."

After a hectic two weeks of tightly-scheduled events, conducted with precise military timing by our affable, samurai-descended guide, Yoshino-san, the tour ended at the Hiroshima Peace Memorial Park, where for the first time we were cut loose for the rest of the afternoon, free to walk back to our hotel whenever we liked.

I felt thunderstruck as I entered the Museum, immediately confronted by a scale model of Hiroshima, blasted into rubble by the atomic bomb, symbolized by a small bulb hanging overhead. In an instant the full horror of the events of August 6, 1945 struck me in the chest; I could hardly breathe. As I wandered through the exhibits, the sight of burnt, twisted household artifacts; charred clothes and photographs of pitiful survivors, burnt, dazed, maimed and mutilated, of the shadows of vaporized people etched on sidewalks, made me recoil in horror of what we had done to a people I had come to know, appreciate and care for. For the first time in my life I felt shame for my country, shame for the military in which my father and I had served, shame for being an American, for being a human being.

To this day I cannot recall the scene without losing it, as I did when I fled down the steps to the broad expanse of the park below the Museum. Seeing a couple approaching in the opposite direction along the gravel walkway to the Memorial Cenotaph, I struggled to put on my dark glasses to conceal my tears. The couple drew near – a tall, erect man with close-cropped, grey hair, elegantly dressed in a western business suit, and on his arm, a petite older woman, wearing a traditional kimono, perfect symbols of the generation which had endured the war and its aftermath. I turned my face away, attempting unsuccessfully to conceal my distress and hide my shame. Out of the corner of my eye, I could see the couple briefly glancing my way and then doing what Japanese do, slowly walking on, giving no sign of having noticed.

The grim skeleton dome of the iconic Industrial Promotion Hall loomed in the distance as I approached the Cenotaph where a group of about 30 schoolchildren were gathered taking their group photo. This time I hid behind my camera, and began shooting pictures with a telephoto lens. One girl, around 12 years old, noticed me, smiled and waved. I waved back and kept shooting as the group moved on to the next monument, the 1,000 Paper Cranes for Peace. She'd look back from time to time, just to make sure I was following and, seeing that I was, would wave again, and I'd wave back and shoot another picture without ever catching her in the act of waving. The group moved on before I captured a farewell wave, much to my disappointment. I stood by the 1,000 Paper Cranes hoping the group would return so I could snap her final wave. Some minutes later blue sailor suits approached from the direction they had gone and I readied my camera for the missing shot. Looking through the telephoto lens I could see no trace of my newfound friend, and then suddenly a goofy kid jumped out of line, made a face and waved just as I snapped the shutter. I laughed, lowered my camera and waved back. I had the shot I came for – and, in the friendly, clowning gesture of an innocent Hiroshima boy, some kind of redemption.

Reflecting on the day later in the hotel room, Dad's comment came back to me – about 99.9 percent of the world getting along, particularly if they take time to become acquainted, as long as leaders don't screw it up. The day's experience made clear how indeed most of us *do* get along, even after unpardonable atrocities inflicted upon each other. This ability to forgive and forget nourishes the will of former enemies to reconcile and carry on as partners. Yet this same forgetfulness can condemn us to repeat the mistakes of the past, acquiescing when misguided, hubristic leaders on both sides, entrusted with lethal powers wildly beyond their ability to intelligently manage, decide to resolve differences through war.

My views on militaristic U.S. foreign policy devolved into outright cynicism after George W. Bush perpetrated pointless, un-winnable, criminal Long Wars in Afghanistan and Iraq in the first decade of the new millennium. Three Long Wars of choice during four and a half decades left no doubt in my mind regarding the intentions of the military-industrial complex to embrace the very model Ambassador Dean in his 1962 Dartmouth commencement address ascribed to the Soviets, believing "the existence of international tensions is a normal – indeed a desirable – state of affairs . . .[sustained by] belief in subversion, infiltration and so-called wars of liberation, while never ceasing to proclaim that it is peace-loving." By any objective standard, in the first decade of the new millennium President Eisenhower's misgivings about the military-industrial complex and the scientific-technological elite as well as Orwell's grim depiction of a Big-Brother society had become fully realized. Reluctantly, I was forced to admit we were no longer the good guys, our cause was not just, our wars unnecessary, their "collateral damage" inexcusable, and continuation of Long War policies counterproductive to our national interests and the wellbeing of our people. Therefore, I came to fully embrace the liberal revulsion toward arrogant, immoral U.S. militarism and its self-serving corollary, wartime profiteering. Major General Smedley Butler, USMC, twice awarded the Medal of Honor, said it all back in the 1930s: "War is a racket."

Along the way, I acquired the necessary tools to analyze and understand "how the world works" economically, financially and politically. Stanford Graduate School of Business in the late 1960s plugged me into the real world of economics and finance with courses in money and banking, investing and macro-economic forecasting. My three years at Bangor Punta and Piper, ending in 1972, provided a front-row seat to the workings of corporate finance and operations at the highest levels, imbuing me with a healthy regard for the fickle fortunes of Darwinian capitalism. Werner Erhard's *est* training in 1973 elevated my perspective to that of "fair witness," and equipped me to make the career mid-course corrections into the rough-and-tumble arenas of retail sales and later wholesaling financial products. My natural inclination, acquired from my father, to understand and explain "the way the world works," organized in an Olympian, coherent, historical world view blossomed as a wholesaler, as did my public speaking skills, leading in July 1984 to the ultimate reinvention of myself as a speaker and newsletter writer. Two summer writing workshops at Bennington confirmed in my own mind my status as a writer and commitment to the craft as my life's work.

A quarter century of remarkably accurate economic and financial forecasting reassured me of the validity of my worldview, leading me to abandon the conservatism of my youth and embrace radical liberalism as a rational counterweight to the excesses of the Reagan Revolution and its reprise under George W. Bush. As a close observer and commentator in the economic, financial and political realms, I documented the means and methods by which today's military-industrial-technological-political complex have served the interests of the rich at the expense of the rest of us, and especially the younger generations, producing a shameful list of undesirable consequences – The Predicament – stemming largely from the three pillars of Reaganomics: tax cuts for the rich and tax increases for the rest, lax regulation and Long Wars.

Epilog: I did not plan my career path, but rather lived life forward, making sense of it only in retrospect. My life, I discovered, seemed to play out like the jazz improvisations I practiced on the piano – a discipline, like the love of music, instilled in me by my Mother. Unexpected perturbations or changes viewed as problems, or obstacles or crises at the time, when appropriately responded to, could be transformed into opportunities, so that in retrospect, the entire event made sense. Charlie Parker used to say that he never hit a wrong note because he could follow any "sour note" with a riff making it seem like the note was intended. Guitarist Joe Pass echoed the idea with "If you hit a wrong note, make it right by what you play afterwards" – "resolution" in music parlance. Miles Davis put it succinctly: "There are no wrong notes." Indeed, "blue notes" in jazz – departing from the "safe notes" of the scale, are what make the blues and jazz interesting – think Chick Corea. You hear J. S. Bach doing the same thing. His melodies chug along in accepted baroque form and suddenly he hits some wildly unexpected note, and follows it with musical filigree making the composition sublime. Likewise, discordant, even sour harmonies can be turned sweet – think of Thelonious Monk. On a personal scale, this dynamic dovetails with the notion that we only achieve growth by stepping out of our "comfort zone" and then adapting. Werner discovered the same thing, sharing his "new realization" in a theater one day: "When you encounter an obstacle," he said, "expand your purpose to include it." We find variations on this theme in the Chinese hanji symbols for "crisis," the combination of symbols for "danger" and "opportunity." Maybe Dr. Pangloss was right: "all is for the best in the best of possible worlds" if you simply resolve to make it so. Werner called it "riding the horse in the direction it's going."

With my various personal re-inventions along the way came many lessons, some quite basic, yet nonetheless essential in today's world:

Change is the only constant, so don't succumb to demon extrapolation and follow the crowd. Anticipate change, including several changes of careers along the way, some not of your choosing. Adversity contains the seed of opportunity, if you will only recognize and seize it. Be aware, alert, ready, adaptable, and, as Houston Pastor A. Louis Patterson would say, "Specialize until you're special." Take the time and make the effort to "Know thyself" as the instrument to know others and the world around you. And if what you do doesn't occasionally put a lump in your throat and move you to tears of gratitude for the opportunity to fully experience your unique, innate talents and to fulfill your ideals, aim higher.

With the active assistance of the Millennial Generation for which I now write, I hope *The Predicament* and *The Egyptian Solution* will reach a broad audience prepared to act. However, perhaps my fate and that of these publications resides in the mottos of the various schools I have attended, all of which make sense in retrospect:

- ***Sic Itur ad Astra***: "Thus one goes to the stars" denoting ambitions for "the way to immortality" Grammar school at St. Andrew's Scots School, Buenos Aires, Argentina
- ***Fiat Lux*** "Let there be light" denoting enlightenment. High school at the American Community School, Buenos Aires, Argentina
- ***Vox Clamantis in Deserto*** "A voice crying in the wilderness" which could be interpreted either way: an expression of hope of deliverance – as in John the Baptist – or of the futility of being ignored. Dartmouth College, Hanover, N.H.
- ***Die Luft der Freiheit Weht***: "The wind of freedom blows," an outcome to which all can aspire. Stanford University, Palo Alto, CA.

Whether we face deliverance from our present Predicament with the wind of freedom at our back, or oblivion will be largely for you, young members of the Millennial Generation, to determine.

The supreme challenge for your generation will be to bring sanity to the discourse, perhaps long before it is your turn to formally wield power in office.

Go in thy native innocence, rely
On what thou hast of virtue, summon all,
For God towards thee hath done his part, do thine.
John Milton: "Paradise Lost"

Enough, if something from our hands have power
To live, and act, and serve the future hour. . .
William Wordsworth

C

D

E

F

G

H

I

J

K

L

M

N

O

P

R

S

T

U

V

W

Y

Z